11-30-76

Woman's Day
HOMEOWNER'S HANDBOOK

by HUBBARD H. COBB

SIMON AND SCHUSTER : NEW YORK

Designed by Irving Perkins
Manufactured in the United States of America
By The Maple Press, York, Pa.

1 2 3 4 5 6 7 8 9 10

Library of Congress Cataloging in Publication Data
Cobb, Hubbard H   1917–
  Woman's day homeowner's handbook.

  Includes index.
  1. Dwellings. 2. Home economics. I. Woman's day.
II. Title. III. Title: Homeowner's handbook
TX301.C54   643   76-28969
ISBN O–671–22395–X

ACKNOWLEDGMENTS

As much of this material first appeared in *Woman's Day*, I'd like to thank the editor, Geraldine Rhoads, for giving her permission for its reproduction in this book. I would also like to thank members of the editorial staff of *Woman's Day* for their valuable assistance in the preparation of the material. Special thanks to Evelyn Grant, Carolyn Storm, Cynthia Kellogg and John DeSantis for their suggestions as to content, and to Marcia Bliss Marks who edited much of the original material and to Louise Pastore for verifying countless facts and figures.

Hubbard H. Cobb

Old Lyme,
Connecticut

CONTENTS

INTRODUCTION

THOSE OF US who own our own homes have many things in common.

First, we certainly want a safe and secure house—a haven, not a place full of anxieties and worries.

Second, we want a comfortable house with enough space, equipment and conveniences for our family's needs. We want a house to *run* right.

Third, we don't want a house to become such a financial burden that we are robbed of much of the pleasure of homeownership. This third point has become increasingly important in the past few years because of inflationary pressures which, alas, show no signs of abating as the cost of energy and services continues to spiral. Many of us are already finding the financial load almost impossible to carry and are looking for ways to lighten it.

It is the intent of this book to provide as many practical ways as possible to satisfy these desires.

Part One deals with what you can do to make your home a safe and secure one. You'll find a chapter on home safety—how to prevent home accidents. There is a chapter on fire in the home—how to plan in advance so every member of the family can get out in case of fire, what types of fire extinguishers you need to fight various kinds of fire, how to fight a fire and other safety tips.

There is a chapter on burglary—how to prevent your house from being broken into, what you should do if you find that it has been broken into and what you can do to help get back stolen articles.

Another chapter in this section deals with lightning—how it can damage expensive electrical equipment in your house, even if it strikes some distance away, and how you can prevent it from doing any harm.

Part Two includes chapters on ways to make your place more comfortable—home improvements. There is a chapter here on how to spend your improvements dollars wisely—which improvements will add value to your house and which will add little or no value regardless of how much they cost. We tell you how much the more common home improvements cost, how to reduce costs of those you do make and how to add space to your house. There are also chapters on inside and outside painting and on control of noise in the home.

Part Three is devoted to ways and means of lightening some of the financial burden of present-day home ownership. You'll find a chapter on how to reduce the cost of home repairs and services, another chapter on simple repairs you can do yourself. Monthly utility bills take a big bite out of the family budget, so there is an entire chapter on what you can do to reduce the cost of electricity, gas and water.

In Part Three there is a big chapter on how to reduce the cost of heating your house—a major expense these days. Here you'll find helpful tips on how to get the most out of your fireplace and how to add a fireplace or stove if you don't have one. The subject of solar heat is also covered, because there are many families who have already cut their heating costs by 50 percent or more by using free heat from the sun. Solar heat is something you should know about because it may well be something you'll be able to take advantage of in the not too distant future.

For many, cooling the house at low cost is almost as important as heat in the winter, so there's a chapter on how to cool your house with less energy.

Part Four of this book is a buyer's guide to houses and land. A chapter on house specialists can help you get the most for your money when you buy. Another chapter tells you what you should know and what to look for when you inspect a used or older house. An entire chapter is devoted to a new house that is affordable for many—the so-called "no-frills" house.

Condominiums are also covered—an attractive way to live if you know what to look for and how to read the fine print before you sign the sales contract. Information on manufactured houses is also included, as are some things you should know before you buy country property or other land for a vacation house, a primary house, or just to hold on to as an investment in your future.

This is hardly the sort of book that you can just curl up with some rainy evening and read through from cover to cover. It has no plot, no characters, no sex and no violence. But we do hope that after you have read the particular chapter that pertains to your immediate problem you will take time to examine the rest of the book thoroughly so that you will know just how much helpful information it contains. Once you have done this you can then use it as a reference book when you need it. One of these days, for example, you may decide to make some substantial improvements in your house, and that will be the time to really study the chapters on improvements. Or perhaps tomorrow's mail will bring a whopping bill from your friendly electric utility firm and you'll decide the time has come to start conserving energy and money. This book will tell you how to do it.

Part One

HAVE A SAFE AND SERENE HOME

The law says your home is your castle but leaves it up to you to make it a safe and serene one and not a castle filled with hazards and anxieties.

The chapters in this section can help you to have the kind of castle most of us want—the safe and serene one. It begins with a tour of a typical house, describing its basic parts and functions in the simplest possible terms. You'll find helpful information here on how you can prevent many of the more common kinds of home accidents from ever occurring, how to protect your house and possessions from burglary, how to be sure that the family will be protected in case of fire, when you should worry about lightning and when you can just sit back and enjoy the fireworks.

1
GET TO KNOW YOUR HOUSE

THE MORE you know about your house, the more money—and worry—you'll save each year. By efficient use and upkeep of the various systems, you can prevent troubles before they happen, or at least keep them small. And you'll get more help from this book if you understand how your house is put together and how the various systems in it—plumbing, electric, heating, etc.—operate and what has to be done to keep them happy.

While most houses are built pretty much in the same basic fashion, each house differs somewhat from every other—even from one that appears to be an identical twin. You can learn a great deal about your particular house just by taking a tour from basement to attic, but you may have to go to outside sources for some specific information. If it is a new house, the builder or developer should be able to answer all your specific questions— the type of paint used on the outside walls, the exact location of the septic system, the capacity of the electric service, the thickness of the insulation in the roof and walls and so forth. If it is a used house, the former owner or the real estate broker who sold you the house should be able to answer many of your questions or tell you who can answer them.

It will help you understand more about your house if you have a set of the plans that were used to build it along with a survey of your lot. You'll certainly need these if you plan to make major improvements or additions. Plans and survey maps are generally on file at the local building department.

Other sources of helpful information about your house are local utility companies—electric, gas and water—and the men or firms who either installed or have been servicing specialized systems— the plumber, electrician, heating contractor, etc.

Now let's take a tour of a typical house. We'll explain the functions of the key elements, point out which ones are apt to cause trouble, and describe how you can avoid or correct the trouble before it gets out of hand.

FOUNDATIONS

Foundations are generally made of poured concrete or masonry block and support the entire house. They are pretty rugged, so even if you do find a crack here and there you don't have to worry about the house falling down. But cracks in the foundation walls do make a handy place for termites to enter the house, and if the house has a basement, they allow water to get in. Small hairline cracks can be filled with caulking compound. Those over ¼ inch in width can be filled with cement mortar. If you want a waterproof joint, use a waterproof masonry compound.

BASEMENTS, CRAWL SPACES AND SLABS

If your house has a basement, your main concern is with water getting into it at certain times of the year and damaging the expensive equipment generally located here. Trying to waterproof the walls of an existing basement can be an expensive and not always successful undertaking. Most people with wet basements install a sump pump that automatically pumps out any water that flows in.

Basement windows can be a problem because they are so close to the ground. Keep earth, dead leaves, plants and shrubs away from these windows. And keep both metal and wood frames and sashes painted to prevent decay or rust.

Many houses don't have a basement but only a crawl space between the earth and the first floor. Crawl space is just what you'd expect it to be—enough space to crawl around in but not enough to stand upright.

Crawl spaces are usually unheated, so the underside of the floors above should be insulated. Crawl spaces can also become damp unless the earth is covered with plastic sheeting and there are openings in the foundation wall to allow air to circulate. There should be at least four such openings no smaller than 8 by 16 inches, and they should be screened to keep insects and rodents from moving in.

Slab houses have neither basement nor crawl space. A concrete slab is poured right over the ground and it serves as the first floor of the house.

SILLS

Sills are heavy wood planks fastened to the top of the foundation wall. They serve as a nailing base for other wood elements of the house. Check the sills from the basement or crawl space, and if you see a wide crack between the top of the foundation wall and the sill, fill it with caulking compound or stick strips of insulation in to seal it up. If you don't, the crack can allow cold air and even moisture to get into the house.

FLOOR JOISTS AND GIRDERS

Floor joists are the wood planks that support the floor. They also serve as a base for the ceiling of the room below, so they could be called "ceiling joists." The ends of the first-floor joists rest on the sills. Rough flooring of either boards or plywood goes over the joists and serves as a base for the finish floor—hardwood, tile, carpeting, etc.

A heavy wood or steel girder is often used to provide the joists with additional support if they are very long. And sometimes the girder will be given additional support by wood or metal posts.

The main problem you run into with joists, girders and posts is that wood shrinks, creates clearances, and the joists don't get the support they need. This can make the floor vibrate when you walk across it. It's generally easy enough to fix this state of affairs by driving thin wood wedges—strips of wood shingles are ideal—into any crack between the top of the post and girder, between the top of the girder and the joists or even between the top of the joists and the rough flooring.

WALL FRAMING

The framework of the outside walls of a wood-frame house is made of 2-by-4-inch lumber. The vertical members are called "studs" or "studding" and are set 16 inches "from center to center"—that is, from the middle of one stud's thickness to the middle of the next stud's thickness. The siding goes on one side of the studding and the interior wall material on the other. The space between is generally filled with insulation. (This space is about 3½ inches deep—not 4 inches as you might think. Lumber dimensions are tricky. A 2-by-4 is really around 1½ by 3½ after it has been dried and finished to construction standards.)

SIDING

Siding is the exterior covering of the house and may be wood, aluminum, vinyl, asbestos shingles, brick veneer or stucco. You want to keep an eye on siding because any problem here could allow moisture to get into the outside wall, and that means a lot of trouble.

Wood is the most familar type of siding, and it comes in many forms—shingles, clapboard, board-and-batten, sheets of plywood and so forth. Wood siding requires some sort of protective finish. Paint is the most popular of these; you can figure that you'll have to repaint every six to eight years.

Wood siding is subject to decay, so you want to prevent it from becoming damp. Don't allow the siding to come into direct contact with the ground, and keep plants and shrubs at least 18 inches away from the siding. Be sure that the seams where wood siding joins any kind of masonry—the chimney, stone or stucco, etc.—are filled with caulking compound.

Aluminum, vinyl and asbestos shingles will last almost indefinitely if properly applied. They do not need to be painted unless for decorative reasons. And they all take paint well as long as you use the proper kind of paint.

If aluminum or vinyl siding is not properly installed, the siding can buckle, and this takes a pro to correct. Asbestos shingles are very brittle; if you give one a hard crack it is very apt to break and must be replaced.

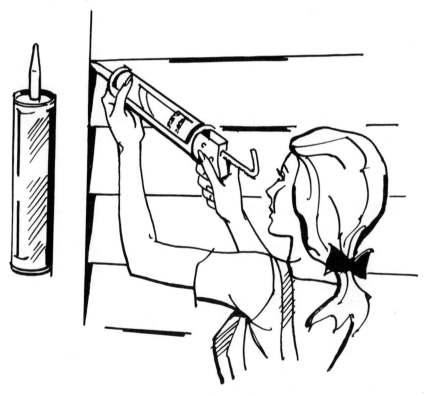

Caulking compound is available in a cartridge form that fits into caulking gun.

The weak point in a brick-veneer wall is the mortar joints. If the mortar was of poor quality the joint will be porous and allow moisture to enter the wall. You can often tell if there is moisture inside the wall because of a white crust, called efflorescence, on the bricks. There are clear waterproofing compounds that can be applied to the mortar joints or to the entire wall, and these will usually correct the condition.

Stucco is a cement mortar used as an exterior finish. It can be applied over masonry block or over metal lath that is fastened to the house sheathing. Stucco applied over masonary block seldom gives any trouble, because it literally becomes a part of the block. But it's a different matter when the stucco is applied to metal lath used on houses framed with wood. If there is any movement in the house framework—and there generally is—the stucco will crack. Hairline cracks can be sealed by painting the stucco with any good-quality stucco or masonry paint. Large cracks will have to be patched either with cement mortar or with a stucco patching compound.

Stucco will absorb and hold moisture, so it is essential that all seams where stucco joins wood are sealed with caulking compound.

DOORS AND WINDOWS

Any cracks in door and window frames, no matter how small, can allow water to get into the wood and cause decay. Keep these frames coated with paint. If the cracks and seams are too large to be sealed with paint, fill them with exterior spackle or white lead. Also be sure that the window sill is well protected by paint.

The putty around window glass will need to be replaced from time to time. As soon as you see that the putty is cracking or that bits have become loose, remove the old putty and replace it. If you don't, the glass may become so loose that air and moisture can get into the house. The moisture can also start the sash on the road to decay.

ROOFS

The roof of a house is usually framed with 2-by-6-inch rafters spaced 16 inches apart. The rafters are covered with sheathing made of plywood or boards, and the roofing material is applied over the sheathing. Strips of metal, called flashing, are used to make a watertight joint where two different roof planes meet to form a valley and where the roofing material meets another surface or material such as a dormer or chimney.

There are a lot of different materials used for roofing, but asphalt shingles are the most common. Asphalt shingles are made of layers of felt with a covering of mineral granules. The life of asphalt shingles will be from 15 to 25 years, depending on the quality. When these shingles get old they dry out and become very brittle. A high wind can tear them up, causing the roof to leak.

You can tell when the shingles on your house are about ready to be replaced because the mineral granules will begin to disappear, exposing the black felt base of the shingles. You may even find accumulations of these granules in the gutters. You can also tell if the shingles are too old by bending up a corner. If the corner breaks off, the shingles are pretty far along and you should get a new roof.

New asphalt shingles can be applied directly over a single layer of old asphalt shingles or even wood shingles. But you should never allow new shingles to be applied over two layers of old shingles, whether they be both asphalt or one layer of wood and one layer of asphalt.

Leaks can occur in what is otherwise a perfectly sound asphalt shingle roof, but these are generally easy to repair. Holes and tears in the shingles can often be repaired with a few roofing nails and some roofing cement. Or one entire strip of damaged shingle can be replaced. High winds often turn up the tabs of lightweight shingles, allowing water to enter. The tabs can be fastened down with roofing cement.

Wood shingles and wood shakes are another common kind of roofing. These will last about 25 years. When old wood shingles are about finished they'll begin to curl up at the edges or at the ends.

Some may even pull loose. You can get a few more years out of the roof if you slip strips of roofing paper under any shingles that are allowing water to get through and if you split and nail down the curled-up shingles. But sooner or later you'll need a new roof.

By the way, always check the condition of a roof on the south side, because this is the one that gets the most sun and therefore the side that will fail first.

Don't ever assume that a roof is tight just because it looks good through a pair of field glasses or even on close inspection. Go into the attic or attic crawl space every few months and check the underside of the roof. If you find water stains on the underside of the sheathing or on the attic floor, check the roof when it rains to see where the water is coming through.

ATTIC LOUVERS

These are vents usually placed at each end of the attic close to the peak of the roof. Their purpose is to allow warm moist air that flows into the attic space in cold weather to flow outdoors. These louvers should never be closed in cold weather. But you may want to screen them to keep insects, birds and rodents out of the house.

GUTTERS AND LEADERS

These can be real troublemakers unless they are properly maintained. If the gutters along the eaves sag or are filled with debris, water will pour over the side of the gutters and down along the side of the house. This can cause the paint on the house to peel and blister, and some of the water may even get to the inside walls. Check gutters during a heavy rain or fill them with a garden hose to make sure that the water in them drains to the end of each gutter section and then down the leader or downspout. Adjust the gutter hangers if necessary.

In freezing weather, snow melting off the house roof can accumulate along the gutters to form ice dams, and these can allow water to back up and leak through the roof. Moreover, heavy accumulations of snow and ice in the gutters can pull them loose.

Increase the life of galvanized iron and wood gutters by coating the inside with roofing cement.

The best way to eliminate this problem is to install a heating cable along the eaves of the roof or in the gutter. You can get these at most hardware stores.

Gutters can be made of aluminum, copper, vinyl, galvanized iron or wood. Aluminum, copper and vinyl gutters don't need any protective coating, but galvanized and wood gutters do. Coat the inside of these gutters with roofing cement. It will keep galvanized gutters from rusting and wood ones from rotting.

Gutters should be cleaned out in the late fall if there are deciduous trees about. It will help to keep leaves out of the gutters if you cover them with gutter guards—screening—and put a wire cage over the opening of the leader or downspout to keep leaves from getting into this line.

THE PLUMBING SYSTEM

This is one area where even a little knowledge can be a good thing and a lot of knowledge is like having money in the bank.

The house plumbing system is divided into two parts—and never the twain should meet. There is the fresh-water system that provides cold and hot water. The water in this system is under pressure so it can be forced to the various fixtures about the house. Then there is the drainage system to carry waste out of the house. This system depends on gravity to carry the waste through the pipes.

For the fresh-water system, water from the city water main or your own well comes into the house through an underground water line. Near the point where the water line enters the house there is a shut-off valve. Close this valve and you turn off all the water to the house. This valve may be located in the basement, in the crawl space, in the utility room or even under the kitchen sink. Find out where the shut-off valve is in your house and tag it so anyone will know its purpose.

Connected to the supply line are several branch lines. Some of these carry cold water to the fixtures about the house, and one goes directly to the hot-water heater. There will be additional branch lines close to the hot-water heater to carry hot water to the fixtures.

Most, if not all, branch lines will have a shut-off valve so water can be turned off to one area without disturbing the flow of water to other fixtures in the house. You can find out which fixtures each of these valves controls by closing the valves one at a time and then seeing which faucets can be opened without any flow of water. Tag each valve so you'll know the fixture or areas it controls.

You will also find separate shut-off valves in the lines to certain fixtures, such as the lavatory, kitchen sink and toilet flush tank. These valves are located directly under the fixture. These are handy because you can turn off the supply to just one faucet if needed. Since the fresh-water system is under pressure, you must turn off the water when making any repairs in the system, such as changing a faucet washer, or you'll end up with a small flood. Although you could shut off the main valve, it is much more convenient to shut off just the valve that serves the faucet or fixture that requires repair.

Fresh-water pipes are generally made of copper, and you can identify them by the reddish color. In older houses you may find galvanized-iron pipes, which are silver-colored. If you have galvanized pipes in any part of the fresh-water system you'll eventu-

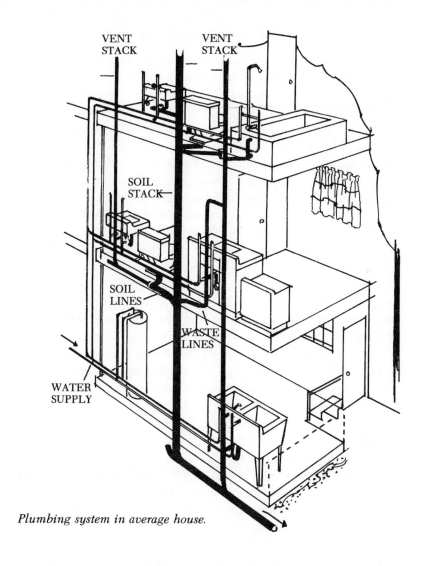

Plumbing system in average house.

ally have to replace them with copper, because rust accumulates on the inside of an iron pipe until only a trickle of water can get through.

Most houses have an independent hot-water heater to provide water for bathing, washing dishes and clothes, etc. If your house is heated by a boiler you may have a coil inside the boiler to provide hot water.

Independent hot-water heaters don't last forever. Gas and oil heaters are good for only about 10 years; electric heaters last a bit longer. There is a thermostat on most heaters so you can regulate the temperature of the hot water. You'll save energy and also prolong the life of the heater if you don't set the thermostat higher than 140 degrees. That's plenty hot for most household jobs.

You will also prolong the life of a heater by draining off the sediment that collects at the bottom of the hot-water tank. There is a drain faucet at the base of the tank provided for this purpose. Don't use any hot water for an hour or so to allow the sediment to settle at the bottom of the tank. Put a pail under the faucet and drain off water until it runs clear. Do this every month or so depending on the amount of sediment that collects in your tank.

The drainage system connects all the plumbing fixtures to a main sewer line that carries waste out of the house to the street sewer or septic tank. The main sewer line extends above the roof of the house to allow gases in the sewer line to escape and to prevent a partial vacuum forming that would prevent the flow of waste through the system. The opening of this pipe above the roof —it's called the vent—must never be covered or allowed to become clogged with debris.

The drain line for each fixture contains a trap which has a water seal to prevent gases from the sewer from coming up through the house drain. The trap on the kitchen sink and lavatory is usually an S-shaped piece of pipe directly under the fixture. The trap in a toilet bowl is built into the bowl. The trap for a bathtub or shower stall is usually not visible. It may be an S-type trap set in the floor under the unit, or a drum trap with a removable lid set flush with the floor.

Drain lines are made of cast iron, galvanized iron, plastic or copper. Most systems installed today are made of plastic, for this is the least expensive material and requires the least labor to install.

Some homes also have septic systems. These are often called "septic tanks" and are used to dispose of household waste where there is no city sewer system. If you have a house in a suburban, rural or vacation area, chances are that you have a septic system.

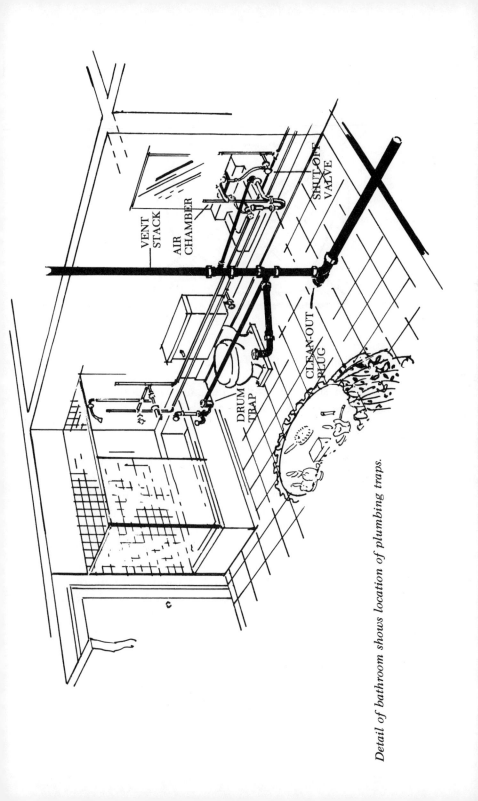

Detail of bathroom shows location of plumbing traps.

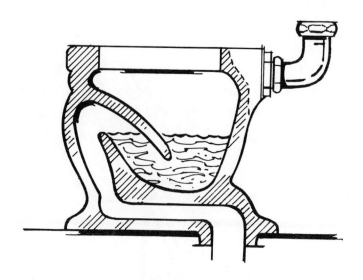

Toilet bowl traps are built into the unit.

If you are not sure, better find out, and also find out the exact location of the system. You can get this information about your septic system from the builder, real estate broker, previous owner, building inspector or your plumber.

A septic system consists of an underground tank made of steel or concrete. It is connected to an underground disposal field made of large-diameter pipe or tile. The tank must be inspected every couple of years and the semi-solid waste in it pumped out if necessary. You'll find firms that inspect and clean tanks listed in the Yellow Pages under "Septic Tanks." If you don't have the tank pumped out as required, the sludge inside will accumulate to the point where there is no room for more waste and your drainage system will back up and make for one horrible mess. And if the sludge flows into the disposal field it can clog up all those underground pipes, and the only way to clean them is to dig them up. This little chore can cost $1,000 or so.

Besides regular cleaning, there are other things you can do to keep the septic system in good working order. Don't pour grease or coffee grounds down the sink drain, and keep paper—except toilet paper—out of the system. Solvents such as paint thinner, cleaning fluids, liquid floor wax and so forth should also be kept out of the system. The septic tank works by bacterial action—bacteria break down solid wastes so that all but a small amount of sludge is liquefied and runs out to the disposal field. If the bacteria in the tank are killed by caustic or poisonous materials, the system won't work properly.

A normal amount of household detergent won't harm the system, but be sure not to use more than recommended by the detergent manufacturer.

Never run lines from roof gutters into the septic system or use it as a handy place to drain water out of the swimming pool.

If you are considering installing a kitchen sink garbage disposer, consult with your plumber or the firm that inspects and cleans the tank before you make the purchase. You want to be sure in advance that the tank is large enough to handle this additional load. The general rule is that the tank should be somewhat larger if a garbage disposer is to be used than would ordinarily be needed. But you can often get along with a somewhat undersize tank if you have it cleaned out more frequently.

THE HEATING SYSTEM

The more familiar you are with your particular heating system, the less chance there'll be of your having an icy cold house some winter's day. And if you understand your heating system, you'll be able to save energy and money.

BURNERS. Gas-fired and oil-fired heaters have burners. These burners should be inspected and adjusted periodically. The gas or oil company that supplies you probably has qualified people who can do this job. Usually an oil company will routinely check your system just before the start of the heating season every year. Gas systems, which burn cleaner, do not need inspection so frequently, but it is not a bad idea to have an annual inspection anyway. You should learn how to relight the pilot light on a gas burner if it should ever go out. There is a plate on most gas burners that explains how this is done, but if there isn't or you are not clear on what to do, find out from the serviceman. You should also learn the location of the gas shut-off valve so you can turn off the gas in case the burner doesn't light or you smell gas escaping.

A properly adjusted burner will produce smoke only for a minute or so when it first goes on. If smoke continues to pour out of the chimney at all times when the burner is running, it means the burner is not properly adjusted. Get it attended to at once because that smoke means you are wasting a lot of fuel. The kind of checking that should be done is described in Chapter 17.

THERMOSTATS. The brain of every modern heating system is the thermostat. There won't be any heat until the thermostat demands it, and it will demand it only when the temperature of the air around the thermostat is below the thermostat setting. Thermostats are sensitive, and they don't last forever. Six years is about the life span for the average home thermostat, so if you've been having trouble maintaining a comfortable indoor temperature it may be that you need a new thermostat.

FORCED-WARM-AIR SYSTEM. This consists of a furnace where the air is heated generally by a gas or oil burner. Inside the furnace is a blower run by an electric motor. The blower forces the heated air through metal or composition ducts to the registers about the house. There is a filter inside the furnace to remove dust and dirt from the air before it is circulated throughout the house.

Furnace filters must be cleaned or replaced when they become dirty. Dirty filters not only waste heat but may allow the furnace to overheat and burn out. If you hold the filter up to the light and can't see light coming through the filtering material, the filter should be either cleaned or replaced. Some filters are designed to be cleaned and reused, and others are designed to be thrown away when dirty.

The furnace blower is generally connected to the motor that runs it by a V-belt. These belts eventually wear out. If the belt breaks, you won't get much heat in the house no matter how long the burner runs. And a worn belt can make a lot of racket. Check the belt at the start of the heating season. Be sure to turn off the

Use finger to check tension on belt of furnace blower. A properly adjusted belt should depress from ½" to 1".

power to the furnace so it can't go on while you are checking the belt. If the belt looks worn, replace it. Most hardware stores stock this type of belt.

CIRCULATING-HOT-WATER SYSTEM. In this system there is a boiler in which water is heated to around 180 degrees. A small pump, called a circulator, pumps the heated water through pipes to the devices that radiate the heat, which may be radiators, convectors, baseboard units or coils set in a concrete slab floor.

A hot-water system must be completely filled with water if it is to operate efficiently. Most modern boilers have a pressure-reducing valve in the water-supply line to the boiler which automatically adds water to the system when it's needed. And there may be automatic valves on radiators, baseboard units, etc. that allow the air inside to escape so there will be room for the water. In older systems, you have to open a valve by hand to add water to the boiler. There is an altitude gauge on the boiler with two needles —one black and one white. The black needle is stationary and set at the proper point when the system is installed. The white needle indicates the true altitude of the water in the system. The white needle should be directly over the black one. If it moves away, it's time to add water.

As a hot-water system contains water, you must protect the water from freezing if you close your house in cold weather or if the heat goes off for any length of time. You will have to have the entire system drained or have antifreeze added to the water. Any plumber can handle either of these chores for you.

STEAM SYSTEMS These are generally found only in older houses and apartments.

Steam is a very simple kind of heating system. Water is heated in a boiler until steam forms. The steam rises through pipes to the radiators. Each radiator has a little air valve at one end. When the steam comes up, the air valve opens up and lets the air inside the radiator escape, making room for the steam. When the steam strikes the air valve, the valve closes to keep the steam from escaping.

Steam boilers are never completely filled with water. There is usually a little glass gauge on the side of the boiler that indicates the water level in the boiler. The water level in the gauge should be about one-third to one-half the height of the gauge.

There will be some loss of water in a steam system, so you must add water to the boiler at frequent intervals during very cold weather. Never add water when the burner is running, as it might damage the boiler.

Every steam boiler should have a low-water cut-off so the burner won't go on if the water level in the boiler is too low. If it did, it could burn out the boiler. If your boiler does not have a low-water cut-off, have a plumber install one. It's worth the money.

The main problem with steam systems is that the little air valves on the radiators don't always work properly. Sometimes they become clogged with dirt and grease, and sometimes they just wear out. If the air valve doesn't work properly, the radiator may never get hot or steam may escape through the air valve into the room. Air valves are easy to replace, and you can buy them at most hardware stores.

HEAT PUMPS. These run entirely on electricity. They operate on the same principle as a refrigerator. In summer the heat pump removes the heat from the air inside the house and pushes it outdoors. In cold weather the pump reverses the action and takes heat out of the outside air and puts it indoors. There are resistance heaters inside the heat pump that provide additional heat if the outside temperature is so low that there isn't enough heat in it to allow the heat pump to operate efficiently.

Heat pumps use the same method of distribution inside the house as a forced-warm-air-system with a furnace and a gas or oil burner. The pumps have blowers, ducts and filters, and these must be cleaned or replaced when they become dirty.

THE ELECTRICAL SYSTEM

You should know the location of the main electric switch in the house and how to use it so you can turn off all electric power in case of an emergency, such as a fire caused by faulty electrical equipment. You should also know the location of the fuse box or circuit-breaker panel and how to reset a circuit breaker or replace a fuse if one of them should blow because of an overloaded circuit or a short circuit.

The main switch along with the circuit-breaker panel or fuse box is located near the electric meter and at a point close to where the power lines come into the house. You may find this equipment in the basement, in the utility room or even in the kitchen.

If you have a relatively new electrical system, you'll have a nice neat circuit-breaker panel with the main switch at the top and under it rows of smaller switches that control individually the various circuits about the house. If you want to turn off all the power to the house, just flick the main switch, as well as the switches for any 220-volt circuits required by the range, hot water heater, etc., off. If there is any problem in one of the house circuits, the switch for that circuit jumps automatically from on to off. After the problem has been corrected by removing the overload or short circuit, you can flick the switch back on. If the switch turns itself off again, there is still something wrong with the circuit and you will have to investigate further.

Older systems have a fuse box instead of a circuit-breaker panel. If you have an electric stove, at the top of the fuse box will be two plastic panels with handles on them. One of these will be marked

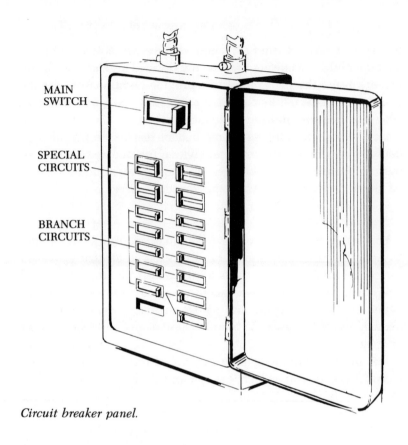

MAIN
SWITCH

SPECIAL
CIRCUITS

BRANCH
CIRCUITS

Circuit breaker panel.

"Main" and the other "Range." Attached to the rear of these panels are two cartridge-type fuses. If you want to cut off all power to the house, pull the panel marked "Main" right out of the box. This pulls out the main fuse and cuts off the power. If you want to cut off power just to the electric range, pull the panel marked "Range."

And if you have a very ancient electrical system, you may find something called a "knife switch" next to the fuse box. The switch is inside a metal box and there is a lever on the side of the box. If you want to shut off the power to the house, pull the lever down to off.

There will be a number of fuses in the fuse box. Each one

controls a separate circuit in the house. These are plug-type fuses that screw into a socket in the same fashion as a light bulb. The capacity of each fuse is measured in amperes—usually abbreviated to "amps"—and you'll find it stamped on the base or on the top of the fuse. Fuses for lighting circuits usually have a 15-amp capacity, while those for appliance circuits may have a 20-, 25- or 30-amp capacity depending on the appliance and on the capacity of the house wiring.

When a fuse blows it must be removed and replaced. Never replace a fuse with one of a higher capacity than the one that has blown. If you do, it can start a fire in the wiring. Keep an assortment of spare fuses on hand so you'll be able to replace a blown one with the correct-size new one. You'll find it helpful to make a chart showing what each fuse or circuit breaker controls.

If you have any doubts or questions about the main switch, circuit breakers or fuse box in your home, get them answered as soon as possible to avoid the inconvenience of not having power and the danger of not being able to deal with an emergency. Your electric utility company may be able to send someone around to explain things to you, or you can call in an electrician.

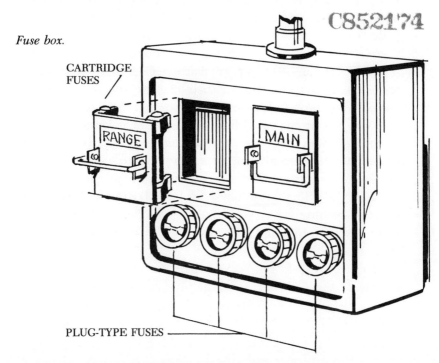

C852174

Fuse box.

CARTRIDGE
FUSES

RANGE

MAIN

PLUG-TYPE FUSES

2

SPRING AND WINTER CHECK-UPS

GIVE YOUR HOUSE A SPRING CHECK-UP

A HOUSE TAKES quite a beating in winter, so just as soon as the worst of it is over you should get going and make a thorough inspection to see what damage, if any, has occurred.

Begin with the exterior of the house. Check the roof to see if there are any torn or loose shingles, sections of flashing that have pulled loose or any other signs of damage. Go into the attic or attic crawl space and check the roof sheathing and attic floor for water stains that indicate a leaky roof.

If you live in an area where there are heavy snows, inspect gutters to be sure that they have not sagged at certain points or come loose. If you can't wait for a heavy rain to see if the gutters are working properly, fill them with the garden hose.

Check the siding of the house for loose boards or shingles. Inspect all painted surfaces carefully. If you find spots where the paint has worn thin and the wood is exposed, prime these areas right away.

Freezing weather can be very hard on any form of masonry, because if there is even just a hairline crack, water will get in and freeze, expanding and making the crack wider. Check the exposed portion of the chimney, the concrete chimney cap and all other masonry surfaces such as siding, walks, driveway and so forth.

Blacktop driveways and walks can be damaged by frost under the paving. You can patch holes with blacktop patching, sold at most hardware stores and lumber yards. If the blacktop surface is dull and absorbs water rather than shedding it, apply a coat of blacktop sealer.

Early spring can mean heavy rains, and this is the time that basements are apt to flood. Check your basement after each rain. If you have a basement sump pump and it has not had to run for several months, better make sure that it will if it is needed. Pour a pail or two of water into the pit where the pump is set. If the pump motor goes on and the pump removes the water from the pit, fine. But if it doesn't operate properly, call in your serviceman right away.

You will want to turn the water on to any outside faucets and other water lines you closed off and drained for the winter. Do this chore carefully to avoid an accidental flood. Inspect the line to be sure there are no joints that were taken apart when the line was drained. Close the faucet at the end and open the shut-off valve slowly so that if there is a leak, you won't get a gush of water.

CHECK FOR MOISTURE, DECAY AND TERMITES

These three enemies will attack your house unless you keep alert. And they can do a lot of damage if you give them just half a chance.

Moisture in the walls of the house can cause outside paint to peel and blister, reduce the effectiveness of insulation and damage walls and ceilings. The most obvious spot for moisture to get in is through the roof, but there are many other less obvious points of entry. Improperly hung and maintained gutters can allow water to enter the house at several points. Unless the joints between siding and window and door frames are caulked, you can expect trouble here. You also need caulking where two different exterior materials come together, such as masonry and wood or wood and metal.

Improper grading of the earth around the house can allow water to get into the basement. The ground around the house should slope gently away for a distance of about 8 feet.

The moisture generated in the house by bathing, washing, cooking, etc. can also cause trouble. The signs of excessive moisture in the house air are sweating windows in cold weather and even moisture forming on the interior surfaces of outside walls. There are only two ways to deal with this problem. One is to reduce the amount of moisture generated in the house, and the other is to get rid of the moisture before it can become a problem. The way to do this is with exhaust fans in kitchens and baths, where most of the moisture is generated. Be sure the dryer is vented to the outdoors, for it produces vast amounts of moisture each time clothes are dried.

Decay is often called "dry rot," but actually there can be no decay unless the wood becomes wet from time to time.

You can expect to find decay in almost any untreated wood that is in direct contact with the earth, is close to the damp ground or thick planting, or is located where there is insufficient circulation of air to dry it out quickly and thoroughly if it should become wet.

Decay is most apt to be found in the exterior wood siding close to the ground, and in any wood posts set in or close to the ground or in concrete set in the ground. It may also appear in window and door frames.

You can't always spot decay just by the appearance of the wood. The way to make sure is to prod the wood with a sharp-pointed tool such as an icepick or an awl. If the point goes in easily, the wood may be damaged by decay. If the damage is not too severe the decay can be removed and the wood patched with a plastic filler.

Paint is not always the best way to protect wood from decay. Any wood that is subject to decay should be treated with a wood preservative. The paint can then be applied as a finish.

Termites can plague homeowners. These little insects require wood for food, and as there can be a lot of termites in a nest they can eat up a lot of wood. It may be wood coming from your house.

Termites build their nests in the ground. The termite worker—the one who does all the damage—travels back and forth underground from the nest to the house woodwork, carrying cellulose from the wood to feed the vast population of the colony.

The termite worker is blind, cannot stand light and needs a damp environment. It travels underground as much as possible, and when it must go above ground to get to the wood, it builds little earthen tunnels. These tunnels are around ¼ inch wide. If you should find them along foundation walls, along posts and piers set into the ground or even on water pipes coming into the house, it means you've got termites.

It's impossible to tell if wood is being attacked by termites just by the way it looks, because the termite worker eats only the inside of the wood and leaves the outside as a shell. If you prod wood that has been damaged by termites the point of the tool may go in with hardly any effort.

The only member of the termite colony that ever makes an appearance is the reproductive. These swarm a couple of times each year—usually in the spring and early fall—and then go underground again to start a new colony or nest. You may see them flying around or find a pile of their wings that they shed before going underground.

The termite reproductive is often confused with the flying ant, but there is a big difference between the two. The flying ant has a wasp waist, but the termite has a straight body. The flying ant has two pairs of wings of unequal length, while the wings of the termite are of equal length.

The way you get rid of termites and prevent them from coming back, or ever arriving, is to poison the earth around the house. Once all the ground has been saturated with the poison, the termite worker can't get back to the nest. The members of the colony die of starvation, and the worker dies for lack of damp soil. As long as the earth contains the poison, no termites will bother you.

If you do find signs of termites, don't go into shock. Take your time and call in several termite-control outfits and get bids from each one. Ask for references and check them out.

It is possible to get rid of termites on your own, but it can be a lot of work. You must make sure that every square inch of soil around and even under the house is treated with the poison— often chlordane. This may involve drilling holes through the concrete basement floor and walks to get the poison into the ground. And if the job is not 100 percent thorough, you'll still have termites.

Make a complete inspection of the outside of the house in late spring after there has been a spell of warm weather. Check the paint on the siding to see if there are any spots where it has begun to blister or peel. The warmth of the sun draws out any moisture that may be in the wood in back of the paint, and this is what causes the paint to blister and peel. If you find these conditions, try to locate where moisture is getting into the wall and correct it. Scrape off the loose paint and prime, then touch up with house paint.

Make a complete inspection for signs of termites. Look for those little earthen tunnels, and also be on the watch for piles of wings left by the termite reproductives. Check the underside of porches and stoops, in crawl space and the basement and on inside and outside of foundation walls.

Get out your pruner and trim back any shrubs and plants around the house. You should keep branches at least 18 inches away from painted wood siding or woodwork.

Replace storm windows with insect screening, but leave the storm windows up on windows that you don't need for ventilation in summer. The storm windows not only help keep noise out of the house but they also reduce heat gain and make the house cooler in hot weather.

GET SET FOR WINTER

Fall is the time of year to make sure that the house and grounds are ready for the trials and tribulations of another winter. Regrettably, this does involve more than just switching from screens to storm windows and putting away the garden hose. That is, of course, if you want to get through the next few months with a minimum number of headaches and with your budget intact.

Remove any dead branches that hang over electric and telephone lines to the house so they won't break off in a bad storm and cut off power. If you live in an area where ice storms occur, better remove even living branches that could fall on these lines or on the house roof.

Newly planted trees that have no protection from strong winds should be given some reinforcement. Drive three wooden stakes into the ground in a triangle around the tree. Attach wire or strong cord to these and fasten to the tree. Protect the bark from the wire or cord with strips of cloth or sections of garden hose, tires, etc.

Foundation shrubs can be damaged by heavy accumulations of snow and ice falling from the eaves of the roof. You can protect plantings by building sheds over them out of plywood or boards.

Evergreen trees and shrubs may need protection from the cold and from the drying effects of strong winds, especially if they are of a variety normally found in a climate warmer than yours. Cover them with burlap and apply about 6 inches of mulch around the base of each plant.

After the leaves are off the trees, clean gutters. Gutters that are full of leaves and debris will hold water, which will freeze, and soon you'll have a gutter that has pulled or sagged or, even worse, a leak in the roof or siding. An old whisk broom is good for this job. Also flush out downspouts, or leaders, with a garden hose. If they are clogged and can't be cleared with the hose, use a plumber's snake.

If you have had trouble in the past with ice dams forming in the gutters or along the eaves of the roof, install a heating cable. It can be either placed in the gutter or strung along the eave, depending on where the trouble occurs. Cables are sold at hardware and electric stores and are not expensive to buy or operate. Be sure to get a brand that comes with installation directions.

It can be a very expensive nuisance to have a septic tank go out of order when the ground is frozen and covered with snow. If the tank has not been cleaned in the past two or three years, have it done in the fall, or at least have it inspected.

Turn off the water and drain any water pipes that might be exposed to freezing, such as those running to a garden pool or to an outlet for a garden hose unless the outlet is the freezeproof type. To drain a line, close the shutoff valve to the line and open the faucet. Then turn the little brass knob on the side of the shut-off valve to drain the valve and pipe. Have a bucket handy to catch the water. A line that can't be drained and will be exposed to freezing should be protected with an electric heating cable. These are wrapped around the exposed pipe and supply sufficient heat to prevent the water inside the pipe from freezing. The better-grade cables have a built-in thermostat so they can be left plugged into an electric outlet and the heating element inside the cable will go on only when heat is required. Heating cables, of course, run up your electric bill, and they don't always offer the same degree of protection as draining the water out of the exposed line or having it set far enough below ground so the water inside cannot freeze.

Use a pair of field glasses to inspect the house roof, and check it out from the attic for leaks. If you find any torn or loose shingles or loose metal flashing around the chimney, dormers, etc., have repairs made at once.

If the roof television antenna wobbles in a high wind, have it reinforced before the winds get stronger and be sure that the lead-in cable is secure so it cannot be lashed by winds and pulled loose.

Store outdoor furniture inside or under a canvas tarpaulin or heavy plastic cover. It doesn't do furniture—or any other outside equipment—any good to be exposed to the weather all winter long.

If the windows need washing, have this done before the storm windows go up (and be sure the storm windows are clean before putting them in place). Also check to see whether the window shutters are secure so a strong wind won't slam them about. If the latch on the shutters won't hold, run a long screw through them into the house siding.

Be sure not to leave any liquids or other materials that can be damaged by freezing in unheated areas such as the garage, tool shed or outside storage bin. Check the labels on containers to be sure. Latex paint, for example, is ruined if allowed to freeze.

Patch holes and cracks in concrete or blacktop drives and walks. If you don't, water will get under the surfacing material, freeze and heave up a large section. Patching materials are available at hardware and building-supply stores. Blacktop drives should also be given a sealer.

Attic louvers should not be closed in the winter. They are there to allow moist air to escape, and if you close them up, you may get a severe moisture problem from condensation on the underside of the roof.

Have your snowplow or snow blower checked out well before the first snow. If you don't and there is something wrong with it, you may have to wait until almost spring before you can get it serviced. Doctors agree that men who live sedentary lives should not shovel snow. If this description fits the man of the house, get a power snow remover or arrange now for someone in proper physical condition to do your paths and drive.

Remove the gasoline from the carburetor of the power lawn mower. If you don't, a gummy substance will form that will have to be cleaned out before the mower will run. The easiest way to drain the carburetor is just to turn off the gasoline supply and let the motor run until it stops.

Keep a few days' supply of firewood indoors, but store the rest outside with some form of cover to protect the wood from rain and snow. If wood is stored indoors in a heated area, it will dry out and burn too quickly and also may bring some unwanted insects into the house.

3

HOW TO PREVENT HOME ACCIDENTS

THERE MAY BE no such thing as a hazard-free house, but there is a lot you can do to make your house safer than it is, indoors and outdoors.

CHILDPROOF LATCHES

Countless small children are seriously injured each year by eating, drinking and handling stuff like chemical drain cleaners, solvents, paints and finishes. And a lot of these dangerous materials are put where a child can easily reach them—in the medicine cabinet or in the cabinet under the kitchen sink. You can keep the kids away from these hazards by installing a childproof latch. These latches are designed so that they can be easily opened by an adult with one hand but are just a little too complex for a child to open. They are not expensive, are easy to install on wood or metal cabinets and are sold at hardware and department stores. You should also put a latch or a lock on the door of any cabinet or room where you store garden sprays, paints, finishes, etc.

BATHROOM

This is probably the most dangerous room in the house. One way to make a bathroom safer is not to allow water coming out of bathroom faucets to be above 115 degrees. Water above this temperature can injure skin and it may make someone jump and take a fall. Either reduce the setting on the hot-water heater or have a plumber install a mixing valve in the hot-water line to the bathroom so that the temperature of the water reaching this area will never be above 115 degrees. You can also have a thermostatic mixing valve installed on the tub or shower so that the water flowing out of the faucet will never be above the setting on the mixing valve.

Shower and tub doors made out of plate glass are very dangerous; if the glass breaks the long sharp pieces of glass can cause serious injury. Replace ordinary glass doors with doors made of tempered glass. Tempered glass is much stronger than ordinary plate glass, and if it does break, it crumbles into particles without sharp edges. Clear plastic is also good for bath doors.

Install no-skid stickers on the bottom of tubs and shower stalls. You can get decorative stickers of this type at department and hardware stores. It's also a good idea to install a grab rail on the bathtub wall, but if you do, be sure it is strong enough to take the full weight of an adult. Make tile floors skidproof by covering them with rubberized mats or carpeting.

STAIRS

Every flight of stairs in the house should have a sturdy handrail. You can buy one for indoor stairs at any lumber yard along with the necessary hardware. They are not too difficult to install. You should also have a handrail on outside steps leading from landing to outside walks. You need metal rails here, and you might need a mason to do a proper job of installation.

Make stairs skidproof by covering them with carpeting, or at least cover the treads with carpeting or rubber mats. An inexpensive way to make attic and basement stairs safer is to paint the treads with any good floor enamel to which you've added a slip-resistant additive. You can get these additives at most paint and hardware stores. You just pour them into the paint, mix and then apply the paint with a brush or roller.

Attic and basement stairs often have open risers, and this creates a hazard, for it's easy to catch your toe on the underside of the tread and take a fall. Close in open risers with sheets of hardboard or ¼-inch plywood cut to size and nailed to edges of the stair stringers.

Open stair rails can be very dangerous if there are small children in the family—it's easy to crawl off the edge of a tread and take a bad fall. Enclose the space between the stairs and handrail with an open mesh material such as decorative metal lath or hardboard.

DOORS

It's easy to put your hand through the glass on outside doors, storm doors and sliding glass doors. And if you do, you may get a very serious cut. Replace ordinary glass with safety glass (tempered glass) or plastic.

Lots of people get hurt walking into a sliding glass door without knowing the door was shut. You can paste little decorative devices at eye level on the glass to warn everyone when the door is shut.

LIGHTING

Adequate lighting can prevent a lot of home accidents. There should be at least one light in every room that can be turned on by a wall switch by the door. This will eliminate the risk of moving about in a dark room trying to find the lamp switch. Every flight of stairs should be well lighted, and the light should have a three-way switch so it can be turned on from the top or bottom of the stairs.

Fluorescent paints can be very helpful when it's not practical to provide all the light you need or to call attention to a particular hazard. These are high-visibility paints in bright colors such as yellow and orange. They can be applied to just about every material. Use them on any object that might be a hazard—the bottom tread of basement or attic stairs, beams, pipes and ducts that you can bump your head on unless you duck in time, sharp corners and so forth.

Fluorescent paints are also great for items that are often left outside the house and can be tripped over in the dark—bicycles, power mowers, garden tool handles, trash containers, etc.

ELECTRICITY

Improperly maintained and improperly used electrical equipment can be a serious home hazard resulting in fire and even fatal electrical shock.

Replace worn or damaged electric cords and plugs immediately. If you receive even the slightest electric shock when you touch any piece of equipment—a metal lamp socket or pull chain, plate on a wall switch or wall outlet, any appliance—turn the power off or disconnect the equipment and don't use it until the cause of trouble has been found and corrected. If a wall switch or outlet plate feels warm to the touch, turn off the power to the circuit and call an electrician.

Any electric device used near water or in a damp location is a potential troublemaker because water and electricity and people don't mix and it is the people who come out badly. Lights in the kitchen, bath and laundry should be controlled by a wall switch if at all possible. The fixtures should be made out of porcelain and not metal. If there is a metal fixture, be sure the pull chain is not made of metal but of cord.

Never use any electric appliance where there is a chance of it falling into water that a person is using. This goes for hair dryers, electric razors, toothbrushes and so forth. Never allow the children to take an electric radio or TV into the bathroom while they are taking a bath. If the set falls into the tub, the child might be killed.

One of the best ways to reduce the chance of someone receiving a dangerous shock while using any portable electric appliance is to have a ground fault interrupter installed. A ground fault interrupter is a very sensitive device—far more sensitive than a fuse or circuit breaker. If there is any problem in the equipment—an open circuit that will not always blow a fuse or circuit breaker but could produce a severe shock to anyone touching the equipment —the interrupter will shut off the current before it can do any serious harm to the individual.

It is particularly important to have a ground fault interrupter in the circuits to the bathroom and kitchen, for these are the rooms where you've got that mixture of electricity and water. The swimming pool is another spot that needs this sort of protection.

You can have a ground fault interrupter installed in the outlet box to protect that kind of circuit or in the entrance panel to cover the entire house. They cost from about $20 up and should be installed by a licensed electrician.

OUTDOOR SAFETY

A couple of well-placed outdoor lights can do a lot to prevent accidents; many accidents occur at night and only because someone can't see well enough to protect himself. Apply skidproof stripping to the treads of outdoor steps and other spots that become slippery when wet. Repair cracks—even the small ones—in walks and driveways. You can get prepared patching material for both concrete and blacktop paving at most hardware stores and lumber yards.

If you have an attached garage make it a fast rule never to start the car motor unless the garage doors are open. If you do start the engine and the doors are closed, carbon monoxide from the exhaust can enter the house, and this is a deadly gas. Many persons have been overcome by carbon monoxide fumes because someone forgot to turn off the engine after closing the garage doors or turned on the motor on a cold morning and neglected to first open the garage doors.

And don't store gasoline in the garage. If you need gasoline for your lawnmower, snow blower or other purposes, store it in a bin or storage shed away from the house.

4

PLAY IT SAFE WHEN YOU DO IT YOURSELF

THERE IS a certain amount of risk involved in practically everything you do around the house and grounds, so get into the habit of playing it safe. There isn't much future, for instance, in saving $5 doing a job yourself if you get hurt in the bargain and spend $25 (or more) to have a doctor repair the damage.

Here are some hints that just might save you a good deal of pain and expense:

Never tackle a job when you are tired. Fatigue increases the chance of an accident, and you'll seldom do your best when you are pooped.

Don't mix alcohol and work. Even one beer can slow you down and increase the chance of an accident.

Always be kind to your back, because backs are tricky and once they get out of order they are hard to correct. Don't try to lift anything that is obviously too heavy. And when you do lift any heavy object, bend your legs and use your leg muscles to lift, not your back muscles.

Wear sensible clothes when you work. Heavy fabric can protect the arms and legs from cuts and scratches. Loose-fitting clothes, flowing neckties, jewelry around neck, wrists or on the hands can be dangerous, especially if you are handling power tools with exposed moving parts.

Wear work shoes with non-slip soles when working in the garden, cutting the lawn, chopping wood or doing any other job where you might slip or where your feet could be injured.

Protect your hands with work gloves when you handle rough lumber, masonry and metal and when handling steel wool or other materials that can cut the hands. Wear rubber gloves when working with caustic cleaners, paint removers and other liquids that can burn or irritate the skin.

Get into the habit of wearing safety glasses. You can get these at most hardware, drug and department stores. Put them on when using spray paints, garden insect sprays, chemical drain and oven cleaners, and solvents, and when you sand or saw with power equipment, when you drill in masonry or metal and so forth. Many tool manufacturers suggest wearing safety glasses even when driving a nail into wood because of the chance of a piece of nail head flying off when it is struck a glancing blow with the hammer.

You'll also be wise to get a face mask—available at drug, paint, and hardware stores—and put it on when you are handling powders and sprays. Be especially cautious when the instructions say "Do not inhale." These masks are also great when you do dusty or dirty work—cleaning out the attic or basement, or sanding a floor.

If you do any work where you might get a knock on the head —chopping firewood, pruning tree limbs, taking down storm windows, etc.—you'd be wise to wear a hard hat.

Read and follow directions. Many of the items we use about the house and grounds can be hazardous if not used correctly. This holds true of such everyday items as drain and oven cleaners, spray paints, insect sprays—not to mention all kinds of power equipment such as snow blowers, lawnmowers, chain saws, table saws, etc. Before using any of this kind of product, read the instructions on the label or in the booklet and follow them.

Be extra-careful with power tools. Any kind of power tool or power equipment with a cutting edge—snow blowers, chain saws, lawnmowers, hand and table saws, electric drills, shredders and so forth—can be extremely dangerous if not used correctly and intelligently. Be on your toes when you use this equipment and don't let anyone come too near you. Even the family lawnmower can toss out a stone or stick of wood with enough force to injure someone standing close by.

Chain saws can be very dangerous to the operator unless they have a chain brake that will prevent the saw jumping up and striking you in the face if the tip of the chain strikes a piece of metal or hard spot in the wood. Many safety experts suggest that if your saw does not have the chain brake you should wear a motorcycle helmet with a shatterproof face mask.

Electric power tools should have a heavy-duty three-wire cord so that they can be grounded. Plug these cords into a three-hole outlet or use an adapter plug with a wire that can be attached to the grounding screw on the standard two-hole outlet. Never use electric power tools in a damp location or outdoors when the ground is wet.

Ladders are essential for work indoors as well as outdoors, but they are a high-risk item unless used correctly.

Don't take a chance with a rickety ladder or stepladder. If it is not in first-class shape, toss it out.

Keep an eye on wood ladders that are left outside, because decay can weaken the rungs where they are set into the rails and you may not know the rung is weak until you stand on it and it breaks. Protect the wood from decay by coating it with a wood preservative. Never paint a wood ladder; paint can conceal splits and breaks.

Metal ladders don't decay, but they are excellent conductors of electricity, so never use them where there is the slightest chance of the ladder coming into contact with electric wiring, such as the power lines connected to the side of the house.

If you set a ladder in front of a door you can bet your last dollar that someone will open the door and set you on your ear unless you've locked the door shut.

There is a right way to set a high ladder against the side of the house. The base of the ladder should be set so that it is about one-fourth the distance from the base of the wall as the wall is high. In other words, if the wall is 12 feet high, the ladder should be set 4 feet from the bottom of the wall. Be sure both feet of the ladder rest securely on the ground. If the ground is uneven, shore up one side or the other with wood planks.

Don't climb too high up on a ladder. Your shoulder should never come above the top rung. Always keep both feet on the ladder and always keep one hand free to hold on with. And don't try to get out of having to move a ladder by leaning over to one side or the other. Face the ladder when you climb up and down—never turn your back to it.

5

NOISE CONTROL AND SAFETY

MANY HOME ACCIDENTS, especially in the kitchen, are attributed to high or unexpected noise levels. The housewife who cuts her finger with a knife, trips over the kitchen stool or knocks over a pan of scalding water is not necessarily awkward or inefficient— she may be subconsciously trying to escape from more din than her nervous system can cope with.

We have only recently become aware of just how damaging noise can be. It has been know for some time that loud noises are harmful to the hearing, but it was not until the early sixties that the New York otologist Dr. Samuel Rosen, a pioneer in noise research, established that prolonged exposure to excessive noise not only can cause progressive hearing loss but has a measurable effect on the circulatory system, causing constriction of the arteries, increased rate of heartbeat and increased flow of adrenalin into the bloodstream. And according to tests made in 1975 at the San Diego Naval Hospital, exposure to prolonged loud noise can result in an increase in blood cholesterol levels.

Noise is often defined as "unwanted sound," but Dr. Chauncey Leake of the University of California, San Francisco, terms it "stressful or unwanted sound"—which is more to the point, for while not all noises are necessarily unwanted, they can be stressful even if we are not consciously aware of the stress. Even sounds that we want and enjoy—music, the roar of a waterfall or the roar of the crowd at the big game—can insult our bodies and nervous systems if too loud and too long.

Sound pressure level is measured by the decibel scale. Zero decibels (db) is the faintest sound audible—a low whisper or the rustle of a leaf. Interestingly, this is a logarithmic scale, so that for every 10 degrees increase on the scale, the pressure of the sound is increased 10 times. A 20-db sound has 10 times as much pressure as a 10-db sound, and an 80-db sound has, incredibly, a million times as much pressure as a 20-db sound.

At 120 db the sound is deafening—on the threshold of physical pain. You get this sort of sound if you stand too close to an amplified rock band, if a clap of thunder comes right overhead or if you are too near a jet engine.

Many authorities on noise feel that prolonged exposure to any sound level over 50 to 60 db—the level of normal conversation—is harmful. Many familiar noises, such as the garbage disposal unit, the electric blender, the power mower, the vacuum cleaner and even the chatter at a large cocktail party, are considerably above that.

In the home there are the normal but unexpected sounds that make us jump, such as the screen door slamming, the sharp bang of a water pipe or the commanding summons of an overloud telephone bell. There are also the noises that we do expect and even initiate as part of a daily routine—the high drone of the vacuum cleaner, the churning of the dishwasher or the shrill whine of the electric blender. Some of these noises we may even find gratifying, for they tell us that a particular piece of equipment is doing its job and saving us time and work.

Added to these are the everyday background noises—the hum of the furnace or air conditioner, the muffled roar of traffic on a nearby street or even the radio or television left on all day to mask more annoying sounds or just to keep us company. Add them all together and it is no wonder that by the end of the day many of us are ready literally to jump out of our skins.

The most important single step in eliminating this kind of unnecessary stress is the decision that you want to do something about it.

If you need to convince yourself further that you ought to start a noise-control program, try making a sound-level check of your own home. At the beginning of the day write down every sound you hear above the level of normal conversation. Put down the time you are exposed to the sound of the dishwasher, the vacuum cleaner, the kitchen exhaust fan, outside traffic and so on. List the number of times you are startled by a slammed door, the telephone, a power mower or other unexpected sounds. And if you'd really like to know just how noisy your kitchen can be, put a tape recorder on the counter and turn it on each time you are working there and are exposed to noises. When you play it back at the end of the day you may wonder whether perhaps you are working in a boiler factory after all.

Once you determine which noises are most disturbing, you can begin to do something about them. Obviously, you can't eliminate all sounds in the home, and you wouldn't want to. But you can do a lot to reduce their volume and get them down to that tolerable 50-to-60-db range.

Some of the steps suggested are easy and cost nothing. Some are more complex and require spending money. How far you wish to go with your noise-control program is up to you, but remember, almost anything you do will be an improvement.

KITCHEN

Usually the kitchen is the noisiest room in the house and a good place to start. You spend a lot of time there and your family probably does too.

Acoustical tile on the ceiling will definitely absorb a lot of kitchen clatter. Washable acoustical tile on walls in back of work counters is also helpful. Foam-backed vinyl is a good choice for floor covering.

Get a few rubber kitchen mats and use them in the sink and on counter tops to absorb noise from pots, pans and dishes. Use these mats under blenders and mixers and you'll be surprised at how much they reduce the whine and chatter.

Cork tile (which is not expensive) can be used on the backs and shelves of cabinets and does a good job of muffling noise when china and glassware are being put away.

Any appliance with moving parts—even a refrigerator, which is usually a pretty quiet helper—can make a racket if it isn't sitting level on the floor. And if it touches another appliance or a cabinet, the sound will be amplified. Make sure all such appliances are level so they can't wobble. It will also help if you put a pad of rubber or other resilient material under the legs or base to insulate the unit from the floor. If your refrigerator is making too much noise, vacuum beneath it at the air-intake area. This will relieve motor strain and cut noise.

Garbage disposal units will make less racket if there is a rubber or neoprene gasket between the rim of the unit and the sink. Sometimes only a thin bed of putty is used to seal this joint and it isn't too effective in keeping the sink from amplifying the sound of the disposer. You can reduce the noise of the disposer if you line the inside of the sink cabinet with acoustical tile or 2-inch-thick fiberglass insulation.

Some kitchen exhaust fans can be very noisy, especially if the blades are coated with grease and dust or if the blades are bent out of proper alignment. If screws or bolts holding the unit in place are loose, the fan will vibrate and make more noise than normal. Excessive fan noise will also occur if the fan unit is in direct contact with metal ducts. Either insulate the unit from the duct with rubber or fibrous gasket or use a length of fiberglass duct to separate the fan from the metal. Instead of turning the fan on high speed, keep it on low when possible. It is usually much quieter and less annoying. And if you are remodeling a kitchen or installing a new exhaust fan, specify the "squirrel cage" type of fan—quieter than the one with blades.

If you are putting in a new kitchen or shopping for new appliances, tell the salesman to show you the *quiet* ones. They may be a little more expensive than the standard models, but you'll be glad you chose them.

Think about yourself first when you're planning your daily schedule and try to put space between yourself and kitchen noises that can't be eliminated. You don't have to be in the kitchen when the dishwasher or washing machine is pounding away—they don't require human companionship. Escape whenever you can and don't forget to close the kitchen door when you leave so annoying sounds don't follow you about.

FAMILY ROOM, GAME ROOM, PLAYROOM OR TELEVISION ROOM

Whatever you call it at your house, it can be as noisy as the kitchen at times—especially when it's inhabited by budding musicians or other offspring who are convinced that the more decibels generated by guitar, drums, record player or television, the better.

You can, of course, eliminate some of this sound if you encourage or, if necessary, bring the full weight of parental force to bear on members of your family to use headsets when they listen to their favorite music or television program (especially if there are several separate dins going on at the same time). It costs around $20 to have a television or radio rigged for headsets, but many of the better radios and stereos come with this attachment. A headset adequate for television costs around $15, while those suitable for listening to music without distortion start at around $30.

If a member of the family is about to take up a musical instrument, look into the possibilities of the soundless (to you) electronic type that can be equipped with a headset so that only the player can hear what's coming out.

So much for headsets. You still have to make your house a home and everybody has to make a certain amount of noise at times to work off steam, especially small children. (Psychologists say it helps them relax!) It's important that there be a room where they can make a certain amount of racket without disturbing the rest of the household.

A good start is to furnish the room with sound-absorbing materials. Use acoustical tile on the ceiling, carpeting or cushion-type resilient flooring, fairly heavy draperies and upholstered furniture. All these will absorb and muffle sound. Noise can also be transmitted through walls and door. The various ways to prevent this are discussed later on.

Basement recreation rooms present a special problem if the walls are of poured concrete, because this material not only doesn't absorb sound but will amplify and distort it. Covering the walls with acoustical tile or insulating board will do a lot of good. Even hanging burlap or inexpensive carpeting on the walls will improve matters. Walls made of concrete, cinder and similar block don't present this problem because they contain a lot of holes, which absorb sound. But don't paint the inside of these walls, because you'll reduce the sound-absorbing quality of the block.

Cover basement floors with a cushion-type resilient material and area rugs, or cover the entire floor with indoor-outdoor carpeting.

Acoustical tile on the ceiling is a big help, but it won't keep sound from going upstairs. To make the ceiling more resistant to the passage of sound, install 3-inch-thick insulation between the floor joists. Over this goes gypsum board, which is attached to the joists with resilient clips, and over this goes acoustical tile. It requires a little effort and money, but you'll have a good place to holler.

BATHROOM

Like basement rooms, the bathroom usually has hard surfaces that amplify and distort sounds. Washable acoustical tile, carpeting on the floor, vinyl wall covering and curtains will help absorb a lot of sound.

Houses built in the last 20 years or so frequently have insulated walls in the bathroom to reduce sound transmission, but openings made for water pipes, heating lines, etc. can still allow sound to escape into other areas. Filling cracks around such pipes with caulking compound or insulation will help.

Everyone deserves privacy in a bathroom, but, oddly, not enough attention is paid to bathroom doors. They are often so poorly fitted that they allow a lot of sound to escape into the rest of the house. If you do nothing else about the bath, make the door as sound-resistant as you can (see section on doors).

BEDROOMS

To protect bedrooms from noise made in other areas of the house, it may be necessary to treat both walls and doors to make them more sound-resistant. Floor-to-ceiling closets, if they run the length of the wall and are full of garments, make a very good sound barrier and will reduce the amount of noise passing through a wall. They should, however, have solid rather than louvered doors to be most effective.

Draperies, carpeting and other sound-absorbing materials will reduce the amount of noise emanating from the bedroom but won't protect the bedroom from sounds made in other areas of the house.

DOORS

Doors allow a great deal of noise to pass from room to room, especially the hollow-core or thin-panel door found in most houses. The solid-core door is far superior as a sound barrier. Even the best door won't keep out noise, however, if there are cracks when it is closed, and all too often there are. Seal these cracks with a weather-stripping type of gasket. If properly installed, it will make the door airtight. An adjustable threshold gasket should also be installed to seal the crack at the bottom of the door.

Lightly constructed hollow-core and panel doors can be made more sound-resistant by covering them on one or both sides with ¼-inch plywood.

To keep outside doors, storm doors and screen doors from slamming, equip them with mechanical closers. Rubber stops can be used on interior doors. To keep doors from striking a wall when flung open, install rubber-cushioned doorstops on the wall or floor.

WALLS

Interior walls in many houses and apartments are so lightly constructed that you can often hear a whisper through them. To make matters worse, they usually contain holes made for plumbing, heating and electric outlets that provide a nice easy route for a meandering sound wave.

Fill the spaces around pipes, as suggested for bathrooms, with caulking compound or fibrous insulation. Use a rubber or fibrous gasket around floor and wall registers to make an airtight seal between the rim of the register and the wall or floor. It may be worth going to the expense or effort of loosening the electric wall-outlet boxes so that insulation can be packed in back of them.

The only way to increase the sound resistance of an existing wall is to increase the thickness. Covering one or both sides with acoustical material is not going to do the trick. A relatively easy and inexpensive way to increase the thickness of a wall is to apply ½-inch-thick sheets of gypsum board over it. The more you apply, the better. If you cover one side with a single layer, it will help. If you put on two layers or one layer on each side, it's even better.

An excellent way to make a wall more resistant to sound is to build another wall alongside it, filling the space between the two walls with insulation. This is a fairly major solution that will also reduce the dimensions of the room by about 4 inches, but if the situation is serious, it's worth it.

A floor-to-ceiling bookcase (filled with books) is of some value in helping soundproof a wall, but the case must have a solid back and the back *must not come into direct contact* with the wall.

FLOORS AND CEILINGS

Sound that comes through a ceiling from the floor above is difficult to control. Putting acoustical tile on the ceiling does no good. The simplest solution is to cover the floor above with carpeting over thick padding or with a cushion-type resilient flooring, which will at least lessen the sound you get from people walking around above. This approach may be easy enough to do in your own home, but if you rent, it may take bit of doing to convince the tenant in the apartment above to go to this expense just for your convenience.

Another method is to make the ceiling itself more sound-resistant by installing a suspended ceiling, made of gypsum board secured with resilient clips, directly under the existing one. The work should be done by an experienced mechanic, for if the installation is not done properly, it will lose much of its value.

STAIRS

Covering these with carpeting or the treads with rubber mats will take care of a lot of the clatter made by people running up and down.

PLUMBING SYSTEM

Noises in the plumbing system can be caused by worn faucet washers, water hammer and even a partially clogged drain pipe. The remedy for these problems is covered in Chapter 21, on basic home repairs.

ELECTRIC SYSTEM

The click of the standard electric wall switch can be very disturbing to a light sleeper. Switches can easily be replaced with a silent type.

Fluorescent lamps often give off a very annoying hum, possibly due to loose or faulty ballast. Check the screws holding the ballast and, if they are loose, tighten them. If this doesn't eliminate the hum, replace the ballast.

Some doorbells and buzzers are unpleasantly loud. If there is no volume control, replace them with something pleasanter, such as chimes.

TELEPHONES

Most modern telephone sets have a volume control on the underside of the case, but it's amazing how few people bother to use it. When you don't need to hear the ring all over the house, turn down the volume.

HEATING SYSTEM

The snap and crackle of a fire in the fireplace is a pleasant sound, but the rattle and crash you get from some forced-warm-air heating systems is not so great. Often these sounds, made in the furnace and conducted all over the house by the metal ducts, are due to nothing more than a worn fan or blower belt. You'll also get an annoying sort of sound if the blower is running at too high a speed. Have your serviceman adjust the furnace so the blower runs more slowly.

Sounds in the furnace can be kept away from the rest of the house if a canvas or fiberglass collar is inserted into the ductwork near the furnace to break the metal-to-metal contact.

Circulating-hot-water systems are pretty quiet unless something goes wrong with the circulating pump. In this case the noise will get around via the pipes. Better have a plumber or heating man over to see what's wrong.

The most common noise in steam systems, found in apartments and older houses, is the pounding in the radiators and pipes when the steam comes up. Often the source of the trouble is the radiator shut-off valve, which is only halfway open. It should be either opened all the way or, if the radiator is not required, closed completely. Pounding is also caused by water trapped in the radiator and connecting pipe. The standard cure for this is to change the pitch of the radiator so that the water drains back to the boiler. This is done by putting blocks of wood under the legs at the opposite end from where the steam pipe is connected. Start with ¼-inch blocks and keep adding until the pounding stops.

OUTSIDE NOISES

Street noises and sounds from your neighbor's house or yard can be muffled or reduced by installing a noise barrier between your house and the source of the noise. The barrier, which can be a wood or masonry fence or a natural planting, should be set as near the noise source as possible and must be relatively high—8 feet or more. It need not be thick, but it must be solid. Boards tightly fitted together are effective, but a louvered fence won't do much, if any, good. A high thick hedge or a row of evergreens set close together is both attractive and effective, but the more open the plant barrier is, the fewer sound waves it will deflect from your house.

6
REDUCE YOUR CHANCES OF BEING BURGLARIZED

MOST OF US, whether we live on a quiet suburban street or in a city apartment, are concerned about the rising number of home break-ins and burglaries. Over the past decade, according to the Federal Bureau of Investigation, residence nighttime burglary has gone up 108 percent and residence daytime burglary has increased a whopping 286 percent. In the majority of cases, the residences were unoccupied at the time of the break-in.

Police officials say that the typical home burglar is usually a small-time operator—a far cry from the international jewel thief of film and fiction. While the professional burglar is by no means obsolete, today's intruder is increasingly apt to be a drug addict who needs money to buy a fix, and he will take anything of value that he, and perhaps a companion, can carry and sell readily. Television sets, radios, guns, furs, silver, credit cards, cameras and sporting equipment, all easy to dispose of, get priority as his favorite loot.

Whether amateur or professional, the home burglar doesn't like trouble and tries to avoid a confrontation with the occupant if at all possible. He much prefers to break into an empty house or apartment, which accounts for the large increase in daytime entries, for this is when most homes are apt to be unoccupied. If he is interrupted in this work, he'll try to escape, but if cornered, he may panic; he may be armed and he can be dangerous.

While there is no such thing as a completely burglarproof home, law-enforcement authorities agree that there are many things you can do to reduce the chances of being burglarized and to assist them in retrieving your stolen belongings and catching the burglar. The six most important things to do are:

- Give the impression that you are at home at all times.
- Make it as difficult as you can for anyone to break in.
- Avoid making your activities or travel plans public.
- Don't broadcast what you own.
- Work with your neighbors to protect each other's property.
- Help your local police help you.

Since the vast majority of burglaries—both daytime and nighttime—occur when no one is at home, it is important to make it as obvious as you can that someone is at home at all times—even when no one is. This isn't too difficult with proper use of lights, sound, the telephone and a few mechanical devices.

When you go out for the evening, turn on all the lights that would normally be burning if you were at home. Never leave just the front entry light on and the rest of the house dark. Pull shades and draperies and leave a transistor radio going. Be sure that all doors and windows are locked.

When you leave the house during the day, make sure the garage doors are closed and locked. An open garage with no car inside is a sure sign that there may be no one at home. Be sure shades are up and draperies are open if this is their normal position during the day. Even if you are just leaving the house for a short while, lock doors and windows. Even if you only go to the backyard, be sure that the front and side doors are locked.

When you go on vacation, do the obvious, such as stopping mail, milk and newspaper deliveries. Don't order merchandise that is likely to be delivered while you are away. Make sure the grounds are properly maintained. If grass goes uncut, if snow is not removed from walks and driveway, if debris collects on the lawn, it indicates that the house is empty. Notify your neighbors and the police that you are away and double-check all doors and windows.

Electric timers to turn lights on and off are an excellent way to make a house seem occupied at night. Never leave lights on in an empty house during the day. A simple timer that you can plug into your lamps costs around $10. One type will turn on the lights at a predetermined time and then turn them off five hours later. It will repeat this cycle every 24 hours. More expensive timers can be wired into the house wiring circuits. There are also timers with a photoelectric cell that will turn lights on in the evening and off in the morning.

The trick in setting a timer is to have it follow the normal lighting routine of the house. For example, use a timer to turn on the lights in the kitchen and living area of the house when it gets dark and turn them off when the family normally moves into the bedroom and bathroom areas. A second timer can turn on the bedroom and bathroom lights later in the evening and turn them off at the time the family normally retires for the night. If it is your habit to leave certain lights on all night, set a timer to turn these off in the morning.

Radios and television sets can also be hooked up to timers, which will help create the illusion that you are at home.

Use a timer for outdoor lights, too, because they are not usually on during the day.

Don't pull the window shades down when you leave a house for a day or longer. If someone sees a house with the shades down during the day, he will assume, correctly, that the family is away.

What should you do about the telephone when you go away? Don't have it temporarily disconnected, because this makes it obvious that you are away for an extended length of time. The best policy is to have an off-premises extension put into the home of a relative, good friend or neighbor. Should someone call you, the relative can answer your phone and make it appear that you are at home but can't come to the phone right now. The cost of such an extension runs from $2 to $4 per ¼ mile a month, plus installation costs, which run about $7.50.

When you are away but there is still someone at the house—the children, the baby sitter or the cleaning woman—instruct them never to say, "Mr. and Mrs. Jones are out for the evening" or "They are away for a few days." Have them say, "Mr. or Mrs. Jones can't come to the phone right now. Let me have your name and number and they'll call you back."

When you are at home alone at night, turn on all the lights that would normally be on if the family were around. Pull the shades and draperies. Play the radio, television or record player. If it makes you feel better, leave a few lights on all night.

Do outdoor lights help? Yes, expecially if they are installed so that all areas of the house—the sides and rear as well as the front —are flooded with light. It's wise to have a switch for these lights by your bed so you can turn them on quickly at night if you hear someone outside the house. Trim shrubs and bushes around windows so that a potential housebreaker can't hide from the light.

When you are at home during the day and want to make it obvious that someone is at home, take the car out of the garage and leave it in the driveway. Turn on the radio or television.

LOCKS

While it may be true that if an experienced burglar wants to get into a house badly enough and has enough time, he can do it, police officials agree that the chance of a break-in can be greatly reduced if all doors and windows are locked. It is a fact that many burglars don't even bother to pick locks—they just go from one house or apartment to another until they find one with unlocked doors.

What sort of locks should you have? Those that are difficult to pick. The spring or snap-fastening lock found on most house and apartment doors can be easily opened with a strip of plastic and not much talent. You should either replace these with a trigger-guard lock or install a dead-bolt lock. A dead-bolt lock is very difficult to pick and can be installed for around $25. It is best to get the type of dead-bolt lock whose keys can be duplicated only by a licensed locksmith.

There is also a wide range of maximum-security locks. Some are combination-type locks and some use a key with built-in magnets. They are very good but expensive, running from $50 up.

You should have a pickproof lock on every outside door of the house as well as on the door leading into the garage and basement, and the basement bulkhead door should have a secure locking device.

On doors where ordinary pickproof locks can't be used, install a good-quality padlock. The more expensive types are made of special steel that can't easily be cut through with a hacksaw. If the hasp is properly installed, they will provide good protection.

There is no point in having good locks if you don't use them. Also they don't do much good if you are casual about the keys. It's never a wise idea to put your house keys on the same chain with your car keys—too easy for them to be stolen or duplicated when your car is at the garage or service station. It's also not a good idea to put your name and address on your key chain, because if it is lost or stolen, a burglar having possession of the keys will know exactly where to find the door they fit.

If you lose your keys, have the combinations on the lock changed or replace the lock at once. If you move into a new house or apartment, do the same to the existing locks. Don't hand out keys if you can help it. It may save you time and bother if the laundry man, the dry cleaner or the cleaning woman has a key to your house, but the more keys around, the more chance that they will get lost, stolen or duplicated.

Apartment-house doors are usually the easiest to open. Have a good-quality dead-bolt lock installed by a locksmith and at the same time have him install a chain guard. You should also have a one-way viewer in the door so that you can see outside before opening the door. Residents in big-city apartments are much more likely than people in private houses to have potential intruders come in when they are at home, because it is hard for the burglars to tell whether the place is empty until they ring the bell.

Always leave the chain guard on if you open the door to a stranger, and check with the superintendent before admitting a workman.

Many local codes require the landlord to install pickproof locks, chain guards and one-way viewers on all doors. If your apartment lacks these, check with your building department, because you may be able to save the cost of installing them yourself.

Sliding glass doors can be a problem, because the latches and locks on lightweight aluminum frames don't offer much protection even when they are locked. The unit is so light it can easily be pried open. There are wedge-type locks you can use on these units, or you can buy a length of ¾-inch wooden dowel, cut it to the right length and place it along the bottom track with the door closed. This will, in effect, jam the track and prevent the door's being opened even if the latch is sprung.

The heavyweight wood and aluminum sliding doors usually have a keyed lock that is adequate. If you want to play extra safe, install a wedge lock or use the wood dowel.

It is worthwhile to put locks on screened doors, for these give an extra degree of protection and can be very valuable in keeping someone out when you are in another part of the house and have the main door open. In any event, when the main door is open, be sure the screen door is at least latched.

Windows are hard to deal with because someone can always break or cut the glass to get inside. However, this makes a noise and takes time. A burglar much prefers an unlocked window that he can open easily, or better still, a window that is already open. Locks on the average double-hung window are the least effective. Keyed window locks are excellent, for the only way to get in is to smash the entire window—glass and frame. Keyed locks, however, should not be used on all windows because you might need the window as an exit in case of fire. There are several types of un-keyed wedge locks that are also effective. You can also install metal grilles or bars on windows, but these are not attractive and you will still need some windows free of them for use in case of fire.

It is certainly wise to put additional locks on windows opening onto fire escapes or onto roofs, ledges, etc. But check first with your local fire department as to the type of window lock they will allow you to use.

If you don't need a window for ventilation, it pays to leave the storm sash up the year around. Anything you can do to make it difficult or time-consuming for a burglar is going to help.

Install shutters or curtains on basement windows so that no one can see what is inside. If you want to play super-safe, install metal grilles or a steel bar across the windows. In any event, be sure your basement windows are solid and locked. It also doesn't hurt to have a good lock on the upstairs door leading to the basement.

HOW MUCH HELP IS A DOG? If it's the typical friendly family dog, its bark may help, but that's about it. If someone knows you have a dog, he will probably bring along some meat to keep it quiet. On the other hand, a dog can sometimes be a deterrent for potential burglars.

BURGLAR ALARMS

Alarm systems may not keep a burglar from trying to enter your house, but they make him leave in a hurry or help get him caught before he can get very far away.

There are two basic types of alarm systems. One is the local alarm that sounds a loud bell when it is set off. This is usually enough to frighten away the intruder unless he knows that there is no one to hear the alarm or that the alarm is not connected to the police office or to a central station. These are the least expensive systems and the most practical in areas where there is no central station or the local police station does not have an alarm board.

The other type of alarm system is connected by telephone wires or special wires either to a central station or directly to the police station. It may have an audible alarm or it may be silent. These are excellent if the house is located near a police station.

Some systems depend on switches around doors and windows to set off the alarm. Others use a radarlike device. One of the best is the ultrasonic alarm, which bounces invisible rays around the rooms. If anyone crosses these rays, the alarm goes off.

An alarm system can cost from $100 up to several thousand dollars depending on the type and the size of the house. Your local police can help suggest a good system for your particular needs.

OTHER PRECAUTIONS

The best locks and the best alarm system won't do you much good if you leave valuable possessions around the grounds where they can easily be picked up. Even if you are at home, it's never wise to leave things like a bicycle, power lawnmower, outboard motor or even the portable television on the terrace where they are easily accessible. A thief who wants to make sure that you are inside while he's grabbing something has only to call your number, and when you go inside to answer the phone, he grabs whatever you left outdoors.

Don't make your name, address or activities public. Don't put your name on the front of the house, for it tells everyone just who lives there. Then it's a simple matter to get your telephone number and start calling to find out whether someone is at home or not. And if a stranger calls on the phone, never give him your name or tell him what your number is.

Keep your travel plans out of the local newspapers. The social notes are must reading for many burglars. They can find out when people are going away on a vacation, a trip or just out for the evening.

Don't broadcast what you own. Don't show your valuable possessions to everyone who comes to your house. Don't talk about what you own in front of strangers or where strangers may hear your conversation.

IF YOU ARE BURGLARIZED

If you arrive home and it looks from the outside as though your house has been broken into, don't go inside. If you locked the door and it is now open or appears to have been tampered with or if there is an open or broken window, stay out. Go to the nearest telephone and call the police. Someone may still be inside.

If you don't discover you've had a break-in until you are inside, call the police at once. Don't touch anything, because you might disturb important clues. It might be best to wait outside or at a neighbor's house until the police arrive. And if you find that the burglar is still inside, get out as fast and as quietly as possible. Call the police from the nearest outside phone. If you are trapped and can't safely get away, stay as calm as possible. If the burglar wants to take possessions from you, don't resist. As soon as he has left, call the police. Then you can have a good cry or a strong drink.

If you wake up during the night and hear someone outside the house, call the police and turn on the lights. This is when it's nice to have a switch by your bed that turns on all the lights. But if you hear someone inside the house, that's a different kettle of fish. Be quiet. If you have a bedside phone, quietly call the police. If the burglar happens to be in your room, pretend you are still asleep. Don't get up or try to frighten the burglar because he may panic and this can make him dangerous.

RETURN OF STOLEN POSSESSIONS. If an article is stolen, there is a good chance of getting it back if you notify the police what was taken and if you can give them a good description of the article. They can circulate this information to other police offices around the country so that even if your stolen article turns up in another state, it can be returned to you. If you have had the foresight to write down the serial numbers of your possessions or put identifying marks on objects that don't have serial numbers, they are more easily traced.

By the way, the average homeowner's insurance policy does not cover items of exceptional value such as jewelry, antiques, fine art, etc. Find out from your insurance broker which items are not covered in your standard policy and what type of coverage you need to protect yourself against loss if they are stolen or destroyed by fire.

COOPERATING WITH YOUR NEIGHBORS

No one wants to be or live near a nosy neighbor, but if you keep an eye on your neighbor's property and he keeps an eye on yours, you will reduce the chance of being burglarized—especially during the day.

If possible, keep each other informed as to when the house will be unoccupied—even if only for a short time. If you are going away and expect deliveries or a call from a serviceman, tell your neighbor whom you expect and at what time.

Call the police if you see a suspicious car, truck or person in the neighborhood. Take down the license-plate number if you can or at least make a note of the style and color of the vehicle.

COOPERATING WITH THE POLICE

Call the police every time you see something that strikes you as suspicious. The police would rather make a call and find nothing than have to solve a burglary case. And something that might seem only slightly suspicious to you may be very important to them.

Be sure to alert the police before you leave for an extended trip.

7

FIRE IN THE HOME

IT CAN happen in your house. Each year about 500,000 houses catch fire. Around 12,000 persons—mostly children and older people—will lose their lives in these fires, and many times that number will be seriously injured by flame or smoke. Even the fire that does little damage to the house can kill and injure.

Fires strike at every kind of house. They occur in expensive new suburban houses as well as in older dwellings on the other side of the railroad tracks. Fires can start anywhere, but 37 percent of them start in the living room, 22 percent in the kitchen, 14 percent in the basement and 13 percent in bedrooms.

While it may be virtually impossible to make a house completely safe from fire, there is a great deal you can do to reduce the possibility of loss of life or injury if one does occur, to reduce the chance of fire striking your house and to keep the damage to a minimum.

GET OUT OF THE HOUSE

The first rule when a fire occurs—regardless of its size—is to get everyone out of the house and get them out fast. Don't waste precious seconds calling the fire department, trying to put the fire out yourself or picking up valuable articles. Get everyone out of the house. It only takes a fire seconds to generate temperatures up to 1,000 degrees or to produce deadly smoke and fumes that will quickly fill the house. Once you've got the family outside, you can then decide whether you may be able to put the fire out yourself and call the fire department.

HAVE AN ESCAPE PLAN

Most home fires occur at night between midnight and six a.m. Nighttime fires are very frightening—especially to children—and it is hard for anyone to think too clearly when they are suddenly wakened from a sound sleep. What you need is a carefully detailed escape plan that has been rehearsed by the entire family so that everyone will automatically know what to do in case of fire, even if they are frightened and half asleep.

Every bedroom should have two escape routes. One of these will be the normal route to the bedroom—out the door, through the hall and down the stairs to the outside. The emergency exit should be planned so that you can get out of the bedroom even if the normal route is blocked by flame or smoke. Unless there is a second door, hall or stairs from the bedroom, a window makes the most obvious emergency exit.

Select one window in each bedroom as the emergency exit. Check to be sure that the window as well as the storm sash and screen can be easily opened by whoever occupies the bedroom. Arrange furniture, if necessary, to provide easy access to the window. Any window of sufficient size will do as an emergency exit from a bedroom on the first floor, but it may be more difficult to find a suitable one for a second-floor bedroom. A window that opens onto an adjoining roof or porch is good, for it makes an easier jump to the ground. If there is no handy roof about, buy an escape ladder. An escape ladder should be stored next to the window from which it is to be hung. Try not to select a window that falls directly over a window of the floor below, because if flame and smoke are pouring out of the lower window, the ladder may not be of any use.

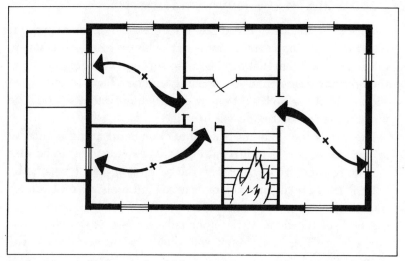

Each room in the house should have two exits in case of fire.

The bedroom windows in some houses are the clerestory type —short windows at the top of the walls. These are not much help as a fire exit for they are difficult to reach and may even be too small for a larger person to squeeze through. If you can't figure out another emergency exit from the room, install a larger window. Basement windows are also not much help in case of a fire. If your basement is used for purposes other than storage so that there is a possibility of someone being down there when a fire occurs, work out some form of emergency exit even if it means putting in a flight of stairs to the outdoors.

Draw a rough floor plan of your house and indicate on it the escape routes from each bedroom, basement, etc. Again, be sure that there are at least two escape routes from all areas—the normal route and an emergency route.

FAMILY INSTRUCTIONS

Once you have your escape plan, sit down with the family and explain what it is all about so everyone understands how it works and what they are supposed to do. Decide on what sort of signal is to be given in case of fire at night. Flame or smoke may prevent you from reaching certain rooms in the house to give the alarm, so you need a signal that can be heard through walls, closed doors and floors. Banging on walls or ceilings can be effective, and so can a loud whistle or bell. Test out your signaling system so you'll be sure that every bedroom will hear it.

The family should be instructed to close doors at night and not to open them in case of fire until they have made a test to be sure that there is no fire or smoke on the other side. Test for flame by holding the hand against the door to see if it feels warm. Look for smoke coming through the cracks around the top and along the sides of the door. If the door fails the test, it should not be opened and the emergency exit should be used to leave the room.

You should decide which members of the family will be responsible for infants and others who may not be able to escape by themselves. Give thought to any pets you may have, too. And you should pick a spot to gather outside of the house so it will be easy to make a nose count to be sure that everyone is out and safe. And make it clear to everyone that once they are out of the house, they stay out. No going back to pick up some special possession.

Select one member of the family who will be responsible for calling the fire department.

FIRE DRILL

Once you have your plan and everyone knows what they are to do, have a rehearsal. It's not a bad idea to have a home fire drill every few months just so no one forgets what he is supposed to do and so everyone will get into the habit of doing the right things automatically. Have your drills at night. Keep them from being scary by making it a game. Have everyone go to his bedroom, select one member to give the alarm and time how long it takes the family to get outside, using the normal escape route. Now repeat the process, but this time have everyone use the emergency routes. Make this drill as realistic as possible without taking unnecessary risks such as having the kids run along a roof or whatever.

After each drill, get the family together and review it to see where it might be improved.

If you are going to be away from home, even if just for a few hours in the evening, be sure that the baby sitter, in-law, grandparent or whoever else might be minding the kids is instructed in the escape plan and knows exactly what to do in case of fire. And if you don't have complete confidence in the ability of the individual to deal with the situation if a fire does occur, get someone who can or stay home. Many children have lost their lives because a young baby sitter or older person could not cope with a sudden emergency.

FIRE-DETECTION SYSTEMS

The earlier you discover a fire, the easier it's going to be to get the family out of the house to safety. And early detection also means a better chance of reducing property damage.

Fires that occur during the day are generally easy enough to spot before they get too far along. It's the nighttime fires—the majority of home fires—that can take the family by surprise. A fire-detection or fire-alarm system will take the surprise out of nighttime fires by sounding the alarm when they first occur.

One of the most popular home fire-detection systems is the smoke detector, which sounds an alarm when there are smoke particles in the air around the detector. These are good because they will sound an alarm even if there is just a smoldering fire that has not as yet produced much heat but is producing smoke.

Smoke detectors should be installed in the bedroom area. A single detector in the bedroom hall might be adequate for some houses, but the ideal would be to have one in each bedroom. The cost for each detector will range from $35 to $100. They can be plugged into a wall outlet or can operate on batteries.

Another type of detection system is set off by a rise in temperature. Heat detectors are not as good as the smoke detectors for small smoldering fires, but they are good where there can be a sudden hot fire as might occur in the basement around the furnace or water heater.

Fire-detection systems are sold at hardware, department and

electrical stores, and you can find retailers listed in the Yellow Pages under "Fire Alarms." Be certain to buy one that is approved by the Underwriters' Laboratories.

FIRE PREVENTION

It's a whale of a lot easier to prevent a fire in the house than it is to put one out. The causes of home fires are almost endless, but here are the primary ones and what you can do about them.

CIGARETTES. These continue to cause numerous fires in the home. If you smoke in bed, or smoke when you are drowsily reading or watching TV and sitting on upholstered furniture, or don't use a proper size ash tray or use one made out of plastic, the chances are that sooner or later you'll start a fire.

ELECTRIC EQUIPMENT. Wiring and appliances are a major cause of fires. Faulty appliance and extension cords, faulty appliances, extension cords tacked to the woodwork or placed under rugs and carpets are all potential troublemakers. And don't you believe that the fuse or circuit breaker will always protect you if the wires or an appliance become overheated. We once had a dandy fire that was started by a radio and the fuse didn't blow until the whole room was ablaze. Replace any lamp or extension cord that is not in perfect condition, and don't use extension cords in place of permanent wiring. If an appliance is not working correctly, don't use it. Have it repaired or replaced.

If your house has aluminum wiring, have it inspected by an electrician or by your building department. There has been some trouble with this type of wiring and it has been responsible for fires.

HEATING SYSTEM: Keep any combustible materials clear of heating unit. Central heaters should be inspected and cleaned at least once a year by a qualified serviceman. Be sure he checks the condition of the smoke pipe between heater and chimney.

Space heaters can be very dangerous unless they are properly installed and maintained. If you don't have the manufacturer's instructions on proper installation and care, get them and be sure to follow them. Portable space heaters can also cause fires if they are not kept clean or are placed near window curtains, woodwork and other combustible materials.

FIREPLACES. Always use a fire screen and never build a roaring fire. Always put ashes in a noncombustible container and put it outdoors—never store hot ashes indoors. Check the fireplace flue once a year and clean it if necessary. Don't build a fire if you are going to leave the house before it has had a chance to burn down.

TRASH. A lot of trash and debris around the house may not start a fire but it sure helps a fire once it gets going. Get rid of debris where fires might occur—in the basement, workshop, utility room and so forth.

FLAMMABLE LIQUIDS. Don't keep a lot of liquids such as solvents, thinners, oil-base paints, gasoline for the mower, etc. around the place. Have only enough for your immediate needs and store them out of the house. Make sure that the container caps are on tight and also that the containers are of metal—never glass.

Always handle these flammable liquids in a well-ventilated area —outdoors is the best—and never around an open flame such as the pilot light on the range or a lighted cigarette.

MATCHES. Children and matches don't mix, so keep all matches away from the kids until they are old enough to handle them properly.

FIGHTING A FIRE

If a fire occurs that doesn't threaten life and is relatively small, you may want to try to put it out yourself *after* you've called your fire department.

The first rule in fighting an indoor fire is always to have an emergency exit between you and the fire so you'll be able to get out in a hurry if the fire gets out of hand. But close the doors to the room, for this will help prevent the fire from spreading quickly.

Stay low as you work, for you'll avoid a lot of the heat and smoke from the fire. Direct the stream at the base of the flame—not at the smoke. Once you've knocked out the high flame, use a side-to-side motion to cover the entire area that is burning. Then sweep from the near edge to the rear and then up vertical surfaces.

Once you've got the fire out, pull apart burned areas to get any hot spots. Be extremely careful with upholstered furniture and bedding, for there can be a smoldering fire deep down in the material that can come alive hours after you considered the fire to be out. If the fire has attacked the house structure, have the fire department check it over to make sure that there is no fire still burning inside wall cavities.

TYPES OF EXTINGUISHERS. The type of extinguisher to use depends on the kind of fire you've got on your hands.

Water is ideal for fighting a fire that is feeding on wood, paper or cloth. And you can't beat a garden hose for delivering a lot of water to the right spot. You can get a garden hose adapter so that the hose can be connected to most faucets about the house. There are also portable water-pump and pressurized-water extinguishers that are handy for small fires of this type.

But never use water on a fire feeding on flammable liquids or on electrical fires. If you use water on flammable liquids it will spread the fire. If you use water on electrical fires you can receive a deadly shock. The types of extinguisher suitable for these kinds of fires are the dry-chemical and carbon-dioxide (CO_2) extinguishers. And both these types can be used to fight fires feeding on wood, paper and cloth as well.

Dry-chemical and carbon-dioxide extinguishers come in a variety of sizes. The dry-chemical type utilizes a powder that coats the burning surface to smother the fire, while the carbon-dioxide type smothers the fire with a heavy gas.

The dry-chemical extinguisher is the most practical for the home because you can refill it yourself after use. Most hardware stores have refills for these extinguishers. The carbon-dioxide extinguisher can also be refilled, but you'll have to take it to a firm that does this sort of work, and they are not easy to find.

Dry-chemical extinguishers have a gauge on them that shows if the unit is properly charged. Charges don't last forever, so it's a good idea to check the unit every few months and have it recharged if the gauge indicates that it is low.

It's a smart idea to have a couple of extinguishers about the house. Put them where they are most likely to be needed—in the kitchen, in the basement workshop or in a centrally located closet. Also keep one in the glove compartment of the car. Be sure that every grown member of the family knows where you've put them and how to work them.

HAVE ENOUGH FIRE INSURANCE

It's bad enough to have a fire that burns your house down or damages it, but it makes matters even worse to then find out that you don't have the right amount of insurance to cover the cost of rebuilding or making the repairs. But this is exactly what happens to countless families each year. They have fire insurance but not enough to provide all the protection they need.

Because of inflation, the cost of building a house has increased considerably over the past few years. This can mean that the house you paid $30,000 for a few years back might now cost $40,000 to replace. But if you have not increased your insurance above the original $30,000 and the house burns down, all you'll get back is the $30,000 and not the $40,000 that you'll need to replace the house. You may also have increased the replacement value of your house considerably by making improvements in it over the years.

The only sure way to know how much insurance you really need is to know the replacement cost of your house. The replacement cost is not the same as "assessed valuation," used for property tax purposes, or "market value," used by real estate brokers. Replacement cost is what it will actually cost today to build that exact house on the same piece of ground. Your insurance agent should be able to tell you who can give you the replacement cost for your house. If he can't, use a local builder, general contractor or real estate appraiser. The charge for this may be from $50 up. Whoever does the job should come over and inspect the house and give you the figure in writing so you can put it in your safety deposit box along with your insurance policy.

Once you know the replacement cost of your house, you can accurately gauge how much insurance you should carry. As a rule it is not necessary to have insurance equal to 100 percent of the replacement cost. The reason for this is that even if the house should burn down, there still will not be a total loss. The foundations may still be standing as well as walks, driveway, underground pipes, etc. But it is absolutely essential that your coverage be equal to at least 80 percent of the replacement cost. 80 percent is the magic figure in home insurance because if you have this amount of coverage you will be paid in full for partial damage to your house. But if you have less than 80 percent of the replacement cost, you will collect only the cost of repairs and replacements *less depreciation.* And this can mean a serious financial loss in the event of fire.

Here is how it might go. The life of the typical house roof is 20 years. If your roof is 10 years old it has depreciated by 50 percent. Now suppose a fire or windstorm completely destroys your roof. If your coverage is for 80 percent or more of replacement cost, you will receive the full replacement cost of a new roof—say, $1,500. But if you have less than 80 percent, you will get back only $750 —replacement cost less depreciation of 50 percent.

This is the reason why it is so important to get today's replacement cost for your house and then be certain that your policy is for at least 80 percent of this amount. And you should make regular increases in your policy to keep up with increased building costs. Some insurance companies do this automatically. Check with your agent to see if your company has this service. If it does not, then be sure you make annual increases in your policy.

8

BE PREPARED FOR LIGHTNING

A BOLT of lightning is a tremendous force—around 15,000,000 volts—and only the foolhardy do not treat it with respect. Some people are terrified of lightning; others really enjoy a good storm. Few of us, though, can remain indifferent when this highly visual and audible drama is in our neighborhood, and there is a feeling of rather special relief when the heavenly theatrics cease and the sun shines once more.

Lightning is erratic and capricious and travels fast—about 100,-000,000 feet a second—as it seeks to spend its astounding power. Even the birds and field mice know that it's a good idea to stay out of its way.

The time to protect yourself and your property from possible harm is before a storm hits your area. You can tell how close a storm is by counting the seconds between the time you see the flash of lightning and the time you hear the thunder that follows. It takes about 5 seconds for sound to travel a mile, so if there is a 10-second interval between the blast and the roll of thunder, it means that the storm is about 2 miles away. Sometimes, of course, you see flashes of lightning along the horizon but don't hear any thunder. This is called heat lightning and is caused by a distant storm reflected by high clouds. If lightning and thunder occur almost simultaneously, the storm is ⅛ mile or less from where you are, and you had better take notice of it.

If you are at home when a storm arrives, stay there. Don't make the mistake of rushing out to rescue your clothes from the line—especially a metal line—and don't allow children to dash out for a favorite toy or to get a bike under cover. Tell your children that lightning is dangerous, but try not to alarm them unduly. Children are not usually afraid of storms unless their parents are, but they must be taught a few common-sense rules.

According to the National Fire Protection Association, some parts of the house are safer than others. Toward the center of the house, where living rooms often are, is probably the best place to be. Kitchens, bathrooms, basements and utility rooms are the least desirable because the plumbing and electrical equipment can become charged with high voltage. So take a break from chores until the storm is over. Keep away from the kitchen sink, washing machine, electric range and appliances such as irons, blenders and waffle irons.

Forget the phone, too, except for real emergencies, especially if there are overhead telephone wires leading into your house. If lightning should strike the wires, or even close to them, you might receive a deafening blast through the receiver.

To avoid possible injury by a side flash of lightning, stay away from windows, outside doors and porches. Chimneys of houses that do not have a lightning protection system are sometimes struck by lightning. While the damage done is usually just to the chimney itself, some experts feel that if the bolt does hit the chimney, the carbon in the flue can conduct some of the charge down into the fireplace. Play safe and don't sit in front of it.

Electrical appliances, equipment and wiring can be seriously damaged during a storm if lightning strikes close to the overhead power lines that bring electricity into the house. If a bolt strikes these lines or even close to them, they will pick up some of the electrical charge and send a momentary surge of high voltage through the house electrical system—often enough to burn out costly electrical equipment and sometimes enough to overheat the interior wiring to the point that a fire occurs.

If this surge does happen, any piece of electrical equipment plugged into the house wiring can be damaged. Even if the equipment or appliance is turned off, the surge of current is often sufficient to jump across the open switch. This is why it is not wise to touch any electrical equipment during a storm.

One way to protect appliances such as washing machines, refrigerators, freezers and toasters from this surge is to disconnect them from the electrical outlets before lightning arrives in your area. Don't do this when the storm is directly overhead, though, because you can receive a fatal shock or a severe burn.

The best way to protect the house electrical system from lightning surge is to have an electrican install a "lightning surge arrestor." This little device costs around $15, plus installation, and is wired into the system at the service entrance where the power lines enter the house. If there is a surge of current, the arrestor will cut off the power to the house for a fraction of a second and allow the surge of current to pass harmlessly to the ground.

Deep-well submersible pumps and swimming-pool pumps should be protected with a surge arrestor even if you don't use one for the rest of the house wiring. Because these pumps are in direct contact with the ground, they make a favorite target for lightning and can be ruined by it.

A surge arrestor is a good investment even if a house is protected by lightning rods, for while these will handle lightning should it strike the house, they don't offer protection against a surge of current coming into the house via the power lines.

Television and hi-fi systems are very delicate, so even if you have a surge arrestor, unplug this equipment at the first sign of a storm. If there is an outside antenna on the roof or some other spot, disconnect or unplug the antenna lead-in wires from the set, for even if the antenna is grounded and provided with a lightning discharge unit, some current might reach the set if the antenna is struck. Antenna lead-in wires are usually connected to the set at the rear.

By the way, an antenna on the roof or chimney does not serve the same purpose as a lightning rod and therefore should not be counted on to protect the house from being damaged by lightning.

LIGHTNING RODS

A properly installed lightning protection system, consisting of rods, connectors and grounds, will prevent a house from being damaged by lightning. Lightning rods will not protect the house from being struck, but they will conduct the bolt safely to the ground.

The cost of a lightning protection system will run between $300 and $500 for the average-size house. A good rule of thumb is to figure the cost of a complete system at about 1 percent of the value of the house. A system for a $40,000 house would therfore cost about $400. If there are large valuable trees around the house, they also should be protected. This will be an additional charge.

A lightning protection system must be installed by professionals. It is no job for the do-it-yourselfer or amateur. If the system is installed by a qualified firm (you can find them listed in the Yellow Pages under "Lightning Protection Systems"), you will receive a "Master Label" issued by the Underwriters' Laboratory. This label indicates that the system meets the Underwriters' requirements. Unless you receive this label you have no guarantee that the system is sound and will offer complete protection. The Underwriters' Laboratory regularly runs a random check on its clients to make sure their systems are in good working order.

Only you can decide whether or not it is worth investing in a lightning system. Most families who live in built-up communities don't have them because the odds on a house being struck are relatively small. Lightning-protection systems are far more common on structures in isolated areas, where it might take a long time for firemen to arrive, and on houses on hilltops and high ridges. They are also often used on structures where the contents of the building or the building itself could not be readily replaced if damaged by fire.

Farms, for example, often have lightning-protection systems, because the destruction of barns and livestock could be a devastating loss to the farmer. The same holds true for houses of historic value or those containing irreplaceable antiques, paintings, collections, etc.

Some families, of course, have a system installed just to give them peace of mind. If you live in an area where electrical storms are frequent or very severe, the feeling of security you will get from a lightning-protection system can more than offset the cost.

Some insurance policies for farm properties are written so that if a lightning-protection system is installed, there will be a small reduction in premiums. Your insurance agent can tell you if this rule applies to your policy.

Part Two
HOME IMPROVEMENTS

There's nothing particularly complicated about making major home improvements if you are not concerned about the cost or whether the improvement is going to add to the market value of your house. All you have to do is to call in an architect or contractor and write checks. But if you do not have unlimited funds with which to add a wing, install a second bathroom, redo the kitchen, finish the attic or basement and so on, then you want to make these improvements as uncomplicated and inexpensive as possible. You want to be certain that you make the kind of improvements that will add value to your property, and you want them made at a realistic cost. The chapters in this section will help you do just that.

9

HOW TO SPEND YOUR HOME IMPROVEMENT DOLLARS WISELY

THE DOLLARS you spend on improving your house can do more than make it an attractive, comfortable and efficient home for you and your family: they can also increase the market value of your property. If you make the right improvements—adding more living space, for example—and you can make them at the right price, you may get back two dollars for each one you've spent, if and when you sell your house. If you make the wrong kinds of improvements—say, an overelaborate and very costly basement recreation room—you may get back only a fraction of each dollar. And if you put your money into something like a superdeluxe backyard brick barbecue when what the house really needs is a downstairs lavatory, you may not get a single penny back.

Of course you can make any sort of improvements you wish and can afford, but if you want your improvements to be an investment, then spend those dollars wisely.

BEFORE YOU IMPROVE

Protect the investment you already have in your house. A modest house that's in tiptop shape is a better investment than a more lavish place in need of essential repairs. So if it's time for a new roof, furnace or hot-water heater, or if your house needs insulation, storm windows, etc., attend to these before investing in improvements.

GOOD IMPROVEMENTS TO MAKE

Some of wisest improvements are those that will bring your house up to the standards of other houses in your immediate area. If many neighbors have a garage or carport, central air conditioning, in-ground swimming pool, fireplace, etc., then these are well worth adding.

Increasing living space is also a financially sound improvement. If your house is short of bedrooms or does not have a family room, a comfortable-size living room or a dining room and you can add space at a reasonable cost, by all means try to do so.

The least expensive way to gain space is to utilize an already existing area. A full attic can give you an extra bedroom or two and perhaps also a second full bathroom. An attached garage can be made into a family room or an extra bedroom with bath. Enclosing a porch can provide another bedroom or family room or extend the living room.

Putting on an extension or addition is the most expensive way to add space, but it can still be a very sound investment and will usually return all your costs.

A basement with one side opening onto grade level can be a good spot for a family room or bedroom. But don't put too much money into the more typical basement that is almost entirely below ground and has only a few small windows to provide natural light and ventilation. Fancy game rooms in basements of this sort are not so popular as they were a few years back.

Simple terraces, wooden decks and fences that enhance the outdoor living area and provide privacy are good improvements. Planting shade trees is also a worthwhile investment. A nice shade tree can add $300 or more to the value of your property, not to mention the pleasure it will give the family. Do not, however, spend a lot on landscaping and planting. An attractively landscaped property is desirable, but today's landscaping must be done with easy upkeep foremost in mind, since few people have the time or money to maintain formal gardens and planting.

IMPROVEMENTS YOU SHOULD AVOID

Highly specialized improvements are not a good investment. The money you spend putting in an elaborate photographic darkroom in the basement probably won't ever come back to you. The same holds true of home gyms, saunas, greenhouses and similar items that have a limited demand. And by all means stay clear of very personalized improvements. You can kiss goodbye to most of the dollars you spend remodeling the recreation room to resemble the main deck of HMS *Bounty* or remodeling the kitchen to duplicate one you saw on a visit to Spain.

An unfinished or unprofessional-looking improvement can be worse than no improvement at all as far as adding value to your property. Doing all or part of the work yourself is a great way to save money, but don't attempt an important improvement unless you are reasonably certain that you have both the necessary skills and time to finish it and finish it right.

Be careful not to overimprove. Overimproving means putting more money into a house than you can realistically expect to get back when you sell. It's one of the most common mistakes committed in making extensive improvements.

The market value of a house is to a great degree dependent on the value of the other houses around it. If your house and the other houses on the block are in the $35,000 range and you put $10,000 into improvements, it means you've increased the cost of your house to $45,000. You'll have trouble getting this amount for it when and if you sell, even though it's a better house than those around it. On the other hand, if you paid $30,000 for your house and the houses around it are worth $45,000, you can spend $10,-000 for the right sorts of improvements and be almost certain to get back all of your investment and maybe more.

There are, of course, cases when owners have overimproved and got back their money, but it's a risky business.

If you are considering making a major improvement, such as

putting on an addition, that might cost a lot—$6,000 or more—it would be wise to get the opinion of a local real estate appraiser or real estate broker. Either of these professionals will be familiar with the market value of houses in your area and can tell you if the addition is a sound investment or if you can expect to get back only a portion of the cost. You may still decide to go ahead with the addition, but at least you'll go in with your eyes wide open. The cost of this type of appraisal usually runs from $50 to $100 depending on the time required.

It's also risky to overimprove one room of the house. If yours is a $35,000 house and you spend $8,000 remodeling the kitchen, you won't have added $8,000 to the market value of your house. All you will have done is to improve the kitchen in what remains a $35,000 house.

Overimproving one room is especially unwise if it is done at the expense of much-needed or more realistic improvements that will have wider general appeal. If there is only one bath in the house, for example, spending money to add a second bath is a better idea than remodeling an adequate but outdated kitchen. Adding the bath and refurbishing the kitchen would be a sounder investment than shooting the works on the kitchen. The market value of a house is based on the total house and not just on one or two rooms.

The rooms most often overimproved are kitchens, bathrooms and basement recreation rooms.

COST IS IMPORTANT

No matter how desirable an improvement, if it ends up costing you more than it should or than it is actually worth on the real estate market (and to a prospective buyer), you are not going to get back all your investment. There is an approximate "worth" to every improvement, based to a great degree on the average cost. For example, the average cost for adding a downstairs powder room might be around $1,500. If you add one that ends up costing $2,500, it's very doubtful that you'll get your money back. The average cost for putting on an addition might be $35 a square foot in one area. If your addition costs $50 a square foot, you will not come out ahead when you sell.

On the other hand, if you can make those improvements at around the average price or less, you stand a good chance to get back your money, and maybe more, when you sell.

FIND OUT THE AVERAGE PRICE IN ADVANCE. A good way to avoid making an improvement that will cost far more than it is actually worth is to find out the average price before you make final plans and call in contractors to bid on the work. Most good local contractors and remodelers know the average price of improvements and can quote them to you over the phone. They may tell you that every job is different and they can't estimate what your job will cost until they see it, but if you push them they can tell you the average price. They can, for example, give you the average cost per square foot for putting on an addition or finishing off the attic. They can give you the average cost for installing a second bathroom, a downstairs powder room, a brick fireplace, a two-car garage and so forth.

Keep the average cost in mind when your plans are complete and you call in contractors and remodelers to bid on the work. The bids will no doubt be slightly higher than the average, but if they are substantially higher, watch your step. Find out why. You may have to trim your sails, or the contractor may think you are the Shah of Iran, or he may not know the business and not be able to make a realistic estimate of what the job is worth.

TRY TO CUT COSTS. Go over the proposed work with two or three contractors or remodelers. Push each one to come up with ways to cut the cost. It may be, for example, that if you changed the location of the proposed second bathroom or the addition, you could save a good deal on both labor and materials.

Check over with the contractors all the materials and products you plan to use to see where you can make additional savings. You want quality products and materials, but you don't have to use the superdeluxe ones.

Be prepared to give up built-ins and other custom touches if necessary. These add a lot to your costs but not much value to the completed project.

Ask your contractors to give you the rock-bottom price on the project and state in writing exactly what it will include. Once you have the project down to the bone, you may be able to build it up with a few extra touches and still keep it at or below the average price.

10

HOW MUCH DO HOME IMPROVEMENTS COST?

MOST OF US have at least one home-improvement project that we would like to get going on but haven't the foggiest idea of the cost. So when we get an estimate (or maybe the bill) for redoing the kitchen, adding a bathroom, making a game room in the basement or whatever the project, it often comes as a severe shock.

It is a fact that making changes or additions to an existing structure is always more expensive than starting from scratch because more labor is involved—often labor to rip out the old and cart it away as well as the labor to fit in the new. There are many home-improvement projects where labor accounts for 75 percent or more of the total cost. The cost of labor varies. It is highest in the Northeast and Midwest, especially around metropolitian areas. It is usually somewhat lower in the Southern sections and considerably lower in rural areas. For example, the hourly rate for a carpenter in a metropolitian area might be $12 or more; in a rural area it might be $5 or less.

The choice of materials also influences the cost of a project. It costs only about 30 cents a square foot to have a wall covered with gypsum wallboard, but if you use the most expensive grades of prefinished plywood, the cost per square foot can be $2 or more.

You can buy a good-quality bathroom lavatory for under $100, but you can also spend over $400 for a deluxe unit.

Even climate will affect costs. Building requirements in warm areas are not as rigid as they are in very cold sections, therefore overall building costs will be less in the South.

The costs given in this section are about the average of what you might expect to pay in 1976 on the more common home improvements. They are based on having the work done by a contractor who provides materials and workmanship of standard quality. But remember, these are rough costs. When it comes to home improvements, each house is different; what your neighbor paid to have a piece of work done is not necessarily what you will pay to have the same work done on your house. Also, estimates from several contractors for the same job will differ, for each one will have his own view of the work involved. That's one reason it's smart to get estimates from at least two contractors on any improvement project. Finally, building costs have been increasing at around 10 percent a year, so the job that might cost $100 in 1976 will perhaps cost $110 in 1977.

ADDITIONS

A bedroom or family-room addition will cost around $30 a square foot. This improvement is covered in considerable detail in Chapter 12.

AIR CONDITIONING

If you have a modern forced-warm-air heating system it will cost around $1,500 to add central air conditioning. But if your house is heated by circulating hot water or electric baseboard units, the cost will be about twice this amount—$3,000 or so.

ATTIC ROOMS

The cost of making a room in an unfinished attic runs about $12 a square foot. A 13-by-19-foot room with 247 square feet will cost about $3,000. Such a room would require one partition to separate it from the rest of the attic and would have a 4-foot-high knee wall along the sides. It would have one large window at one end and an 8-foot-long continuous shed dormer (cost of such a dormer is about $50 a linear foot) along one side. The area would be insulated, with walls and ceilings covered with gypsum wallboard, and heated by electric heat.

BASEMENT FAMILY OR GAME ROOM

The basement can be a relatively inexpensive area in a house in which to make more living space, assuming that it is dry, has a solid concrete floor and is not cluttered with pipes and heating ducts that have to be repositioned to provide space for the proposed room. You can figure the cost of a basement room anywhere from $7 to $12 a square foot depending on whether you utilize the existing masonry walls or install wood-frame partitions. A typical basement game room costs around $4,000.

BATHROOM

The cost of three standard-quality white fixtures—toilet, lavatory and bathtub—including labor to cover installation will be around $1,000 or between $300 and $350 per fixture. This price includes connecting the fixtures into the existing house system and is based on the assumption that the location of the new bathroom is such that these lines can be tied into the house system without too much difficulty.

The cost of carpentry to construct the bathroom will vary depending on the location. If you are going to make a small bedroom into a bath, it might cost only around $500 to frame the recess for the tub, apply ceramic tile around the tub enclosure, put in a new floor covering and add some electric outlets. But if you have to construct a bathroom from scratch, it's another matter. For example, carpentry for a bathroom 8 feet square would cost around $1,000 including partitions, doors, outside window, covering for walls and ceiling, tile around the tub, flooring and electrical work.

The plumbing fixtures can bring the total cost to $2,500 or more.

A half-bath, lavatory or powder room containing two fixtures will cost about $600 for fixtures and plumbing. The cost of carpentry to build a half bath under a flight of stairs will run between $600 and $850.

BOOKCASES

A floor-to-ceiling bookcase with adjustable shelves will cost about $22 a linear foot, so if you want a unit 10 feet long, the price will be about $220. A storage wall with a base cabinet will be about $32 a linear foot.

CARPORT

A carport made of wood with a built-in storage area and floor of blacktop or concrete will cost around $1,700. A metal free-standing unit will cost under $1,000.

ELECTRICAL ADDITIONS

To install the wiring and outlet box for lighting fixtures, wall switches and convenience outlets in existing walls and ceilings, the cost will range from $10 to $25 per box. If the framing is exposed, as would be the case in finishing an attic, enclosing a porch or building an addition, the cost per box will be around $17. The cost to increase the service capacity from 60 amps to 150 amps will be around $350. It costs around $1,000 to rewire the average one-story house.

FIREPLACE

The cost of a brick fireplace with an outside chimney for a one-and-a-half-story house is apt to be about $1,800. This would cover the cost of opening up the wall, masonry and finish carpentry, including the mantel. The same fireplace for a one-story house would be roughly $1,400. Prefab metal fireplaces cost from $400 to $700 installed, depending on the labor involved in bringing the metal chimney through the house to the roof. See Chapter 18 for more information on fireplace costs.

GARAGE

A frame two-car detached garage with concrete floor and overhead doors will cost about $5,000. A one-car detached garage will cost around $3,000. An attached garage of either type will cost about $300 less than the detached garage.

KITCHEN

This is the most costly room in the average house to build and also to remodel. To redo completely, the average-size kitchen can cost between $5,000 and $6,000. This price would include new cabinets and counters, flooring, wiring, new sink and new appliances—range, refrigerator-freezer and dishwasher.

Good-quality stock or custom cabinets and counters will cost around $150 a linear foot installed. This means 1 foot of base cabinet, 1 foot of counter top and 1 foot of above-counter wall cabinet. The cost of cabinets installed plus minor plumbing and electrical work runs around $2,000 for the average kitchen.

A good way to save money redoing a kitchen is to refinish the existing cabinets rather than replacing them. The cost of refinishing cabinets will be around $500.

If you just want to replace the kitchen sink, the cost of a new one installed will be around $150, but if you need a base cabinet for the sink, add another $200.

The average cost for hooking up electric and gas appliances such as a range, washing machine, dishwasher, etc. will be around $50 each. If plumbing or venting is required, add another $25.

A good-quality kitchen exhaust system will cost from $100 to $250 depending on the location of the range. It will cost the least when a range is against an outside wall because a minimum amount of ductwork is required.

ENCLOSING A PORCH

If an existing porch is reasonably well built with a good roof, solid floor and adequate foundations, the cost of making it into a year-round room will run around $13 a square foot. This would include all necessary framing, windows, finish walls, ceiling and floor, electric wiring and heat. If, however, the porch is a rickety affair that is going to take a lot of labor to make solid, the cost to enclose it will be far more than $13 a square foot; it might be better to rip it down and start off fresh.

11

HOW TO REDUCE THE COST OF HOME IMPROVEMENTS

THERE ARE many ways to reduce the cost of home improvements besides doing all the work yourself. The do-it-yourself approach, of course, produces the most dramatic savings, because labor can account for as much as 75 percent of the cost of certain projects. But since many of us haven't the skills, patience, time or inclination to be part-time carpenters, plumbers, painters and masons, we must look for other ways to save money on these projects. Here are some of the ways.

KEEP THE PROJECT SIMPLE. It usually costs less per square foot, for example, to build a square addition than a rectangular one, because the former contains less foundation and outside wall area. An L-shaped addition is very costly because each corner costs money. Anything that breaks up a surface, such as a conversation pit, bay window or roof dormer, adds to the cost.

TAKE ADVANTAGE OF WHAT IS ALREADY BUILT. An attic, basement, attached garage or open porch can be finished or enclosed for no more than half the cost of entirely new construction. So if you need more space, assess these possibilities before adding a new wing. Do not make changes in existing partitions if you can possibly avoid it. The cost of ripping out a partition can run many dollars just for labor (not to mention the mess), and a new one will cost around $15 a linear foot before you are finished. If existing windows can be fitted into your plans, you'll save $250 or so, and another $300 if you can get along with the existing outside door.

DRAW UP PLANS. Even a rough sketch is better than trying to describe to the contractor what you want done. Unless he sees the full scope of the work, his bid or estimate won't mean much. When you go over the plans with him, ask how much you can save by making minor changes. Just moving an electric outlet from one wall to another might save you $20 or so.

SPECIFY LABOR-SAVING MATERIALS. Assume that skilled labor is going to cost better than $10 an hour in most areas, so try to use materials that can be installed quickly, even if their cost is higher than some that take a lot of time to install—provided, of course, that they are more or less equal in quality. Gypsum wallboard, for example, comes in 4-by-8-foot sheets, and a wall or ceiling can be covered with this material for a fraction of what it would cost if you used labor-consuming plaster and lath. A prehung door that includes the frame and hardware costs more than an ordinary door, but by the time you've paid for labor to make and install a door frame and fit the hardware, you'll have paid much more than the cost of the prehung unit. Even if someone gives you a truckload of stone, it will cost more to build a fireplace out of it than out of brick that you have to buy, because building with stone takes an awful lot of labor. It's not just the original cost of the material that is important, it's the installed price that is your chief concern.

STICK TO STOCK ITEMS. Most materials used in construction come in a wide range of stock sizes and shapes. Among these are windows, doors, molding, lumber and so on. These stock items are the least expensive to use. As soon as you ask for something custom-made—especially if it has to be custom-made on the job—your costs soar by leaps and bounds.

Be Sure of What You Want Before You Start. Don't let work begin on a project until you're satisfied with the plans and have decided on all the materials to be used.

Don't Change Your Mind. Once a piece of work has been done, you'll pay three times if you decide to change: once for the original work, once to rip it out and once more to do it all over again.

Don't Keep Upping the Ante. This means don't keep adding items of work after you have agreed to an estimate or bid, for these additions can add up very quickly to a sizable sum. But if you do find it necessary to make additions, find out in advance what they will cost and get this in writing from the contractor before the work begins.

Pick Winter for Interior Improvements. You are apt to get a better price and will certainly get more people to bid on a job if you can have the work done in cold weather when outside construction slows down. Contractors like to have inside work on hand to keep their crews busy. On the other hand, if you insist on having the job done in the busy seasons—spring, summer and early fall—you can expect high bids and may have difficulty getting anyone to do the job at all.

Get Three Bids If You Can. Try to avoid undertaking a project on the basis of what one contractor tells you it will cost. You may have picked one who runs an inefficient operation or is not too experienced and therefore bids high to play safe or simply wants more profit than is reasonable. But if you can get three bids, you will have a pretty fair idea of what the project should really cost.

Be Your Own Contractor. You can save upward of 15 percent (the overhead and profit that a general contractor must charge over and above labor and materials for the job) if you take on the job of hiring the individuals to do the work—carpenter, mason, electrician, etc.—and supervising and coordinating the job yourself.

USE THE TIME-AND-MATERIALS METHOD. If you are sure of the good reputation of a workman—carpenter, mason or whatever—and if you are reasonably sure that the project won't involve unexpected problems, you can save if you pay him just his hourly rate plus the cost of materials needed rather than getting a firm bid on the job. This is because when someone makes a firm bid on a home improvement, he has to make some allowance for the unexpected. If the unexpected doesn't occur, he makes more than otherwise, but he has to keep himself covered.

USE SEMI-PROS. In many communities there are students and young teachers who are proficient at jobs such as inside and outside painting, light carpentry and masonry. While they are not as experienced in all phases of the work as professionals, they are fine for average jobs and may charge only half of what you would pay to have the same job done by a professional. And where hard labor is involved—digging a foundation trench by hand, ripping off an old porch or removing a partition wall—it is hard to beat the price and energy of high school football players who like to keep in condition during vacation.

KITCHEN REMODELING

You can save hundreds of dollars on a kitchen just in the way you plan it. Don't change the location of the kitchen sink unless it is essential, do put the range on an outside wall in order to reduce the cost of installing an exhaust system, and don't make the working area any larger than you actually require. Corner cabinets with lazy Susans are the most expensive (blind corners are not), so plan your work area for a minimum number of such corners.

A single-bowl kitchen sink is less expensive than a double-bowl unit, and one made of porcelain enamel costs less than one of stainless steel. Because it doesn't require an expensive cabinet, a free-standing range is less costly than a built-in oven and counter-top unit.

New cabinets and counters can be the largest cost item in a kitchen remodeling. Even on a modest-size kitchen it's easy to spend $2,000 or more on these fixtures. If the existing units are solid, consider giving them a fresh look with paint or new door and drawer fronts.

As has already been mentioned in the previous chapter, prices on kitchen cabinets and counters range to over $150 a linear foot (this means one foot of base cabinet, one foot of counter top and one foot of above-counter cabinet). The cheapest serviceable cabinets will be about $60 a linear foot. Hardwood cabinets are more expensive than those made of softwood, such as pine, and the ready-mades cost less than custom-made units. Shop around carefully on cabinets before you make a final decision.

ADDING A BATHROOM

The cost of labor and materials necessary to tie the new bath into the house plumbing system can be a major item. If you have several possible locations for the bath, ask your plumber which one is the most practical from a cost standpoint. Colored plumbing fixtures cost up to 20 percent more than white units, and deluxe fixtures may be several times more expensive than the standard units. For example, one manufacturer has a standard white toilet for around $100, while his deluxe unit costs over $350. As the cost of installing either type is about the same, you can save several hundred dollars on a bathroom just by using standard white fixtures.

Ceramic tile is about the most expensive standard material you can use on bathroom walls and floor: it can run to $500 or more. You can cut this amount more than half by using resilient flooring and limiting the use of tile to the walls around the recessed bathtub. If you use fiberglass or plastic panels in this area instead of tile, you save even more.

If you want to replace fixtures in an existing bath, don't ask the plumber to change the location unless you are willing to pay a lot for the extra labor involved. It may take a plumber only an hour or so to remove an old lavatory and connect the new one, but if he has to bring in lines to a new location, it may take him all day to do the job.

12
BUILDING AN ADDITION

BUILDING an addition onto your house—a family room, dining room, larger living room or perhaps a bedroom with a bath—can make better financial sense these days than buying a new and larger house. But an addition is an expensive improvement and it's also a rather complicated one—almost like building a small house. There are a lot of things you should know about additions and the kind of decisions you must make before you go ahead on this kind of project.

COST

A complete addition of standard-quality construction will cost around $30 a square foot at prices prevailing in 1976. At this price, a 12-by-14-foot room will cost $5,000. The price will vary, of course, depending on where you live, the style of the addition and of your house and the kind of room you are building. If you want to include a bathroom in a bedroom addition, for example, figure your cost on the number of square feet of space involved and then add $1,500 or so for the plumbing and bathroom fixtures. If you are adding a family room and want a brick fireplace, add around $1,500 to the base price of the room.

WHERE TO ADD

This depends, of course, on the size and topography of your lot, but as a general rule, the rear of the house is the best spot to add. There is usually more land at the rear of the house than at the sides or front, and an addition there won't change the exterior appearance from the front of the house the way a side or front addition would. Also, a rear addition can be a greatly simplified version of the architectural character of the main house without looking awkward, unfinished or out of place. Finally, a rear addition is apt to afford more privacy and is convenient to outdoor living areas.

CHECK SETBACK REGULATIONS. The location and even the size of your addition may well be decided for you by local setback regulations that give the minimum distance any building can be from the actual boundary lines of the property. Before you begin to plan your addition, check with your local building department. They can show you on a map of your property exactly how much space you have at the rear, sides and front of the house for an addition. They can also tell you whether your plans must be approved by the local zoning board before you can get a permit to build. Ask about any other local regulations you should be familiar with before you start to plan or begin to build.

A TWO-STORY ADDITION

If you need two extra rooms—a family room and a bedroom, for example—a two-story addition can make a lot of sense, especially if you are short of land. A two-story addition takes half the land needed for a one-story addition of equal living space, and the two-story addition will cost less to build because it requires about half the foundations and roof needed for a one-story addition.

Even if you have a one-story house, a two-story addition can be attached with pleasing results if it is well designed. And if you are adding at the rear, you can, if you like, put on a split-level addition so that the roof will not come higher than the roof of the main house.

RELATIONSHIP OF ADDITION TO THE HOUSE

It's best if you can position the addition so there is easy access to it from the main house without making changes in partition walls or disturbing the traffic pattern of the rest of the house. You should be able to reach the addition from the main living areas of the house, not through a bedroom or work area of the kitchen.

Try not to add a noisy family room next to an existing bedroom, or vice versa. But if you must, spend a few extra dollars to have the wall between the two rooms made as sound-resistant as possible, using staggered wall studding and insulation. Also, try to locate the addition so that it won't block off light and ventilation to another area of the house. You will save several hundreds of dollars, by the way, if you can place the addition so it can be reached by an existing outside door of the main house.

PLANNING

Most additions are, or should be, built from detailed plans. These can be supplied by the builder, contractor, remodeler, etc. who is going to do the work. Some of these firms employ a staff designer who will work with you in developing a design exactly suited to your needs. But many builders work from a basic plan that they modify slightly to meet individual needs ("Lady, you can have any style addition you want as long as it's Dutch Colonial").

You can, of course, design the addition yourself and turn your rough drawings over to the builder or to a draftsman who will put them into finished shape.

The ideal way to plan an addition, of course, is to use an architect. An architect will plan the space to suit your exact requirements and he'll also see to it that the addition will harmonize with the main house. He may even be able to save you money by reducing the size of the addition through better use of space and by specifying good-quality but lower-cost materials than you or your builder might select. An architect will charge up to 20 percent of the total construction costs if he takes on all phases of the project—planning, selection of materials, writing specifications on how the work is to be done and supervision of the construction. But you don't have to commission an architect to handle the entire project if you don't want to. Many of them will work on a consulting basis at so much per hour—around $20. With this arrangement you can get professional unbiased help where you may need it most—making improvements in your plans or in the plans supplied by the builder, helping select the best location or style for the addition and so forth. If you are going to make a side or front addition that is sure to make a dramatic change in the appearance of your house from the front, you'd be very wise to get the opinion of an architect on the style of the proposed addition. It is also a good idea to pay him perhaps $100 or so to have him make a simple drawing to show you how the house will look when the addition is in place.

STYLE OF THE ADDITION

The safest approach is to keep the overall architectural style and scale of the addition the same as the main house. Use the same type of siding, the same style and size of windows, cornice, trim, etc. If you are using an architect for help in design, you may want to be a little more daring and put on an addition that does not match the existing house but does harmonize with it. A contemporary-style addition, for example, can be quite attractive with a traditional house if carefully designed with just the right choice of materials and colors. Otherwise, it could become a neighborhood landmark that you may not be very proud to pay taxes on.

You don't have to be half so fussy about style if you're putting on a rear addition, because it is hidden from the street and won't be seen except from your neighbor's back yard. But a side or front addition is going to be right out there where it can be seen by everyone. Any addition, however, should enhance and certainly not detract from the appearance of the house.

By the way, if you have a brick house, use painted or stained wood siding, because new brick won't match the color of the old brick. Also use wood siding on a stone house unless you are willing to pay a lot of money for the high cost of stone.

SELECT THE RIGHT FIRM TO DO THE WORK

The woods are full of builders, general contractors, home improvement contractors and remodelers who handle jobs like additions. But not all of them do good work and not all of them are reliable. Some will charge far more than the job is worth, and a few are not even honest. If you use an architect, he'll be able to give you the names of good people he has worked with on other jobs, but if you don't have an architect, it's up to you to line up the right outfit.

Try to get three good firms to come over and inspect your property and then get an estimate or bid from each one based on exactly the same size, design and quality addition. Established local firms are your best bet. Ask neighbors and friends for the names of people they have used for a major improvement. Look for firms who are members of recognized trade associations such as the National Association of Home Builders or the National Home Improvement Council. Ask your local Better Business Bureau for a list of builders, etc., who have precommitted themselves to arbitration if there is any disagreement between themselves and their customers. The firm that agrees in advance to settle problems by arbitration is probably the one where disagreements with customers are the exception rather than the rule.

The builder who gives you the lowest bid is not necessarily the one to sign up with. Compare all the bids to see exactly what each one includes and what it does not include. That low bid may not include painting and decorating, laying the floor tile or some other vital requirement. A firm that has a staff designer will probably give you a higher estimate than one that does not, but if you want a custom-designed addition and don't use an architect, this is probably the one to choose.

SPECIFY OR APPROVE EVERYTHING. Before you sign a contract with a builder, you must carefully go over the plans and either *specify* your own choice or *approve* the builder's choice of each and every item that goes into the addition. Don't leave the final choice to anyone else, for you have no comeback if you do not like what they have selected. Be certain to specify or approve the brand, model number, design, color, etc. of roof shingles, siding, windows and doors, interior walls and ceilings, interior and exterior trim, paint and finishes, finish flooring, lighting fixtures, bathroom fixtures and wall fixtures for the bath, mantel for the fireplace, all interior and exterior hardware. And also make sure that if it is necessary for the builder to use a substitute product or material because the original choice is not available, you get to approve the substitute before it is installed.

Builders and architects have files of manufacturers' catalogues that give a complete description of almost every building item needed for a dwelling. Go over these files with your builder or architect, make your selection or give your approval and then be sure that all these items are included in writing in the specifications for the work.

THE CONTRACT. You should have a written contract with the builder, and it should be a very detailed one, covering the entire scope of the work including all the specifications for materials and products to be used. It should state the total cost of the addition and method of payment. The general rule, on a job the size of an addition, is to pay 10 percent of the total cost in advance of the work with the balance being paid in one or more installments. But the final payment—and it should be for a considerable amount—should not be due or paid until all the work has been completed and you have had plenty of time—30 days or so—to inspect it and approve it. And you should not be required to make final payment until the building inspector has checked the work and given you a certificate of occupancy.

The contract should state that the builder has all necessary insurance to protect you from any claim or damages arising in connection with the work. It should also state when the work is to begin and the approximate date it will be completed.

And finally, there should be a clause that specifies that if there is any controversy or dispute about any part of the work, it will be settled through the mediation-arbitration program developed by the Better Business Bureau. There is no charge to either party if arbitration is required, but each party must agree to abide by the decision of the board.

Take plenty of time to study the contract before you sign it. And if you have a family attorney, go over it with him or her to see that you are well protected.

FINANCING THE ADDITION

If you are going to have to borrow money to build your addition —and most people do—shop around for the best possible deal. Don't sign up with a builder, remodeler, etc. just because he tells you he can arrange financing for you. If he does, it will cost you more than if you get it on your own and it locks you into using someone who may not be the best choice.

There are several ways to finance the job, and you want to select the one that makes the most sense for you.

Home-improvement loans are popular because they are relatively easy to get if you own your own house, as the house becomes security for the loan. Some states allow you to borrow up to $15,-000 for 15 years with this type of loan. The trouble with home-improvement loans is the high rate of interest—around 12 percent —and the large monthly payments are rough on the family budget.

Increasing your present mortgage loan to cover the cost of the addition can be good if you are already paying somewhere around the prevailing rate of interest and if the lender will rewrite the mortgage without charging you a lot of extra money to do so. The advantage of rewriting the mortgage to cover the cost is that you spread the cost of the addition over the life of the mortgage—20 years or so. This means smaller monthly payments than if you have a home-improvement loan, and it means only one payment a month. But if you have an older mortgage and are paying far less in interest than the prevailing rates, refinancing the mortgage doesn't make very good sense unless it's the only way you can get the money.

Borrowing on life insurance, assuming that the money is there, is good because you pay a low rate of interest. But if you don't pay back the principal at regular intervals along with interest on the loan, it nibbles away at the value of your policy.

13
CONVERTING TO SOLAR HEAT

WOULDN'T YOU like to cut 60 to 80 percent from the cost of heating your house? And wouldn't it be pleasant never to have to worry again about fuel shortages or the rising cost of energy to heat your house and the hot water? Well, quite a few fortunate families have stopped worrying about these matters. Their homes have solar heat systems, and most of the heat for their houses comes directly—and at no cost—from the sun. And each year there will be more such families because, thanks to the energy crisis, solar heat is beginning to get some of the attention and support it deserves, and many people are installing at least a partial solar heat system.

HOW IT WORKS

The common type of system consists of a solar collector, an underground storage tank and a distribution system.

The collector is a series of panels made of glass, metal and insulating material. It is usually mounted on the house roof, where it traps and absorbs the sun's rays and converts them into heat. A fluid—water, oil or water plus an antifreeze—circulates through coils in the collector and carries the heat to the underground storage tank, where it is transferred to standing water or, in some cases, small stones in the tank. A system of pipes, called heat exchangers, removes the heat from inside the storage tank and distributes it throughout the house. A secondary system heats water for household use.

The area of the collector and the capacity of the storage tank varies according to the size of the house, the climate and the percentage of heat the solar system is required to provide. In the New England area a solar heat system designed to furnish about 70 percent of heat will require a collector equal in area to about 40 percent of heated floor space. In other words, if a house has 1,200 square feet of living space, it will need 480 square feet of collector. The storage tank should have a capacity equal to 1 gallon for each square foot of unheated floor space. In warmer climates, you need smaller capacity for both collector and storage tank, and in very cold areas of the country you will need larger.

EFFICIENCY

It is possible to make a solar system efficient enough so it can supply all the heat you need, but the cost of such a system is so high that it does not make financial sense at this time. If the cost of conventional heating energy continues to go up and the cost of installing a solar system goes down, chances are it won't be long before it will be practical to have a 100 percent solar heat system in many areas of the country. At present most systems are designed to provide from 50 to 75 percent of heat required, depending on the amount of solar radiation, cloud cover and fuel costs in an area.

The remainder of the heat must be supplied by a standby or auxiliary heater. In an existing house the central heat system can be used to supply additional heat when it is required. In newer houses designed for solar heat a heat pump is often used, since this can also cool the house in summer. Many solar-heated houses utilize an oversize hot-water heater to furnish stand-by heat. Some

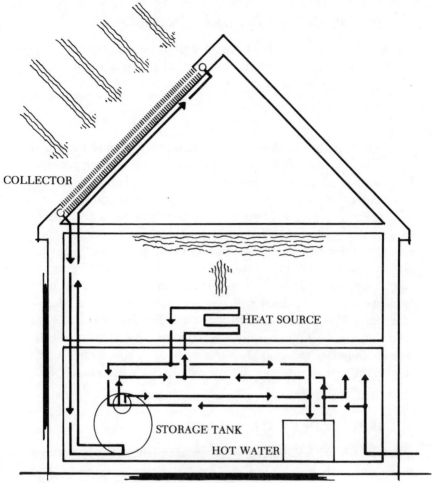

Diagram of typical solar heating system.

solar-heated vacation houses depend only on the fireplace to furnish stand-by heat.

Solar heat will work where winters are very cold because it is the light rays from the sun that provide heat to the collector, not the temperature of the air around it. But since in very cold climates you will need more heat than in milder areas, the capacity of the collector and storage tank must be larger or you must depend more on the stand-by system. You will also depend more on the stand-by system in areas where there is a lot of cloud cover.

Today a typical system may have enough storage capacity to keep the house warm for five or six days, but after that, if the sun does not come out, you'll have to depend on the stand-by heater.

COST

The cost of the average home installation is $4,000 to $5,000 more than the cost of most conventional central heating systems, but manufacturers and designers of collectors and other solar-heat components are working hard to bring these costs down.

At current cost it takes between five and eight years to amortize the cost of installing solar heat. It depends, of course, on the actual cost of the installation and also on what you are currently paying (and will be paying in the future) for conventional heat energy—electricity, gas or fuel oil. Once installation costs have been paid back, your only expenses will be the small cost of operation—electricity to run the small motors that circulate the fluid and distribute the heat plus energy needed to run the stand-by heater.

A good-quality collector should last fifteen years without major repairs, but a poor-quality collector may last only five years before it must be replaced.

SOLAR HEAT IN EXISTING HOUSES

Solar heat can be installed in an existing house, but it may not make financial sense unless you have the right conditions. You must have space on the roof or grounds for the collector, and this space must have an unshaded southern exposure. The existing heating system must be able to serve as a distribution system to carry heat from the storage tank to the living areas. A forced-warm-air system sized for air conditioning will do this, but an electric or hot-water system will not. The house must also be relatively compact and well insulated.

SOLAR HEAT FOR HOT WATER

About twenty cents out of every dollar spent on home energy goes to produce hot water, so it can make good sense to put in a solar hot-water system even in an existing house. According to the Solar Energy Laboratory of the Department of Mechanical Engineering at the University of Florida, there are millions of solar hot-water systems in use throughout the world and thousands in this country. A solar hot-water system adequate for a family of four will cost around $1,200 and might pay for itself in two or three years, depending on what you are now paying each month to heat water. A solar hot-water system does not require a large underground storage unit. Heat from the collector goes directly to the hot-water tank, which may have a capacity of around 100 gallons. The tank has a heating element to supply hot water when there is no sun.

WHO INSTALLS SOLAR HEAT?

Until recently most systems were custom-designed by architects and engineers. Now many builders and developers are also beginning to specialize in this growing field.

There are back-yard solar furnaces that can be purchased as a complete unit to be installed either by a general contractor or as a do-it-yourself project. These have a much smaller collector area than the conventional system, and the manufacturer claims they can produce up to 90 percent of required heat. There are also many firms that sell the various components for a custom-designed system.

The solar-heat field has already begun to attract a lot of shady characters, and you can expect to see more of them about as this kind of heating becomes more and more popular. Watch your step before you buy. Check out any solar-heat outfit with your local Better Business Bureau, your state department of consumer protection and your state energy agency.

14

YOU CAN PAINT PRACTICALLY EVERYTHING

SO MANY advances have been made in paint in the last several years that it's difficult to think of anything inside or outside the house that can't be painted—generally with happy results. All it takes is the right kind of paint, a properly prepared surface and strict adherence to the directions on the label of the paint container.

There is no such thing as an all-purpose paint. Instead you will find a whole range of paints designed for specific materials and purposes. There are paints for wood floors and paints for concrete floors. There are paints for metal—even metal that is subject to heat up to 1,200 degrees, such as the smoke pipe of a stove. Certain paints are ideal for window shades, others for kitchen appliances and cabinets; still others are formulated for tile walls and floors, bathtubs and sinks. There are even paints that produce a terrazzo look on floors or a textured effect on walls.

To make certain you get just the right paint for your particular project you should tell your paint dealer what kind of material you are going to paint—plaster, wood, masonry, metal, etc. Tell him the condition of the material—previously painted with paint in good condition, old paint peeling, etc. Also tell him where and how the material is to be used. A paint that is ideal for interior woodwork—doors and windows, for example—is not suitable for wood floors or for outside trim. A masonry paint intended for walls does not hold up on a concrete floor.

Also tell your dealer the exact area to be covered. If you are painting ceilings, walls and floors, give him the number of square feet involved. For railings, pipes and ducts, give him the length and diameter, and for multiple items such as radiators and shutters, give sizes and number of items involved.

Be sure you like the color selected. You can return unopened containers of stock colors, but most dealers will not take back colors that have been custom-mixed.

The directions accompanying most paints are usually quite detailed and cover surface preparation as well as application. Some manufacturers also provide handy little booklets that you can get from your paint dealer that cover specific projects such as painting a room, the outside of a house, basement floors, etc. Nonetheless, it's still a good idea to read over the directions while you are in the paint store, so if you have any questions or need more information, you can get it right then and there. Also check on any tools or other materials that may be required for a particular type of paint.

PLAY IT SAFE. Many types of paint, along with thinners, liquid-type and paste-type paint removers and other materials you may be using, are flammable, may be irritating to the skin, are dangerous if taken internally and give off harmful fumes that should not be inhaled. These warnings are usually stated quite clearly on the container. Never use these flammable materials in a room or area where there is an open flame. Turn off pilot lights on the gas range, hot-water heater or central heater if you are working around such equipment. It's even wise to disconnect or turn off any motor-driven appliance, such as the refrigerator, freezer, water pump, etc., to eliminate the possibility of a spark occurring while the motor is running.

Also, be sure that the area in which you are working is well ventilated. It is important to keep small children out of the room until the paint or finish is completely dry and you cannot smell any odor close to the floor where toddlers might walk or crawl.

The mist from spray containers is harmful if inhaled, so wear a protective mask when spraying. You can get a mask at many paint, hardware, drug and department stores. For your health's sake, it's worth putting up with any slight discomfort or annoyance while wearing one.

SURFACE PREPARATION

Don't expect paints to conceal all the flaws in a surface. Before you paint, fill holes and cracks with spackle, patching plaster or plastic wood, depending on the material. Sand down rough spots and remove any loose paint. If the old paint is in very poor condition, remove it before applying fresh paint. Also, paint won't hold if applied over a dirty surface. A vacuum cleaner is fine for removing loose dirt and dust, but you'll have to wash a surface to get rid of grime and grease. A household detergent or wall and woodwork cleaner is good for this job.

Paints won't hold over loose rust, so it must be removed before you paint. A wire brush and coarse sandpaper are good for this job, or you can use a commercial liquid rust remover that will also help ensure a good bond between paint and the metal.

Ordinary interior wall paints can be applied over wallpaper if the paper is on tight. The dyes in some papers, however, are water-soluble and may discolor water-thinned paints such as latex. Test the action of the paint on the paper, and if the dyes discolor the paint, remove the paper before painting. You can do this with a liquid wallpaper remover that is added to a pail of water, or you can rent a wallpaper steamer from a tool-rental shop. This will take it off in jig time.

PAINTING A ROOM

If you are going to paint an entire room, do the ceiling first and then the walls. Next do the woodwork, cabinets, radiators, etc.

Start at the top of the room and work down so that the baseboards are done last. If you are painting the floor, this should be the final job.

Use a sash brush or sash tool on windows. You will save time in the long run if you apply masking tape around the edges of the glass to keep paint off them unless you have a very steady hand. It takes a lot of time to apply the masking tape, but not as much time as it takes to scrape bits of paint off the glass. Use a relatively dry brush when painting windows to reduce the chance of paint flowing into the seams and making the windows difficult, if not impossible, to open or close.

You will also save time in the long run if you remove any items of hardware that are not to be painted, such as the plates on electric outlets and switches, door pulls, etc.

Radiators and their covers are dust collectors, so give them a good going over with a vacuum cleaner just before you paint. Radiators should be at room temperature for painting—not too hot, nor icy cold. Spraying is the easiest and quickest way to coat a radiator, but if you use a brush, get a special long-handled radiator brush. A heat-resistant radiator enamel is best for this job, but if you use a latex paint, be sure to first prime any bare metal with a metal primer. If you don't, rust stains will appear through the paint.

KITCHEN

Surfaces in this room are almost certain to be coated with a thin film of grease, so wash down with a detergent or wall cleaner anything that is to be painted—even the ceiling.

Ordinary enamels don't hold too well on the smooth surfaces of kitchen cabinets and appliances, so before you paint, rub the surfaces down with medium-grade sandpaper. This will give the surface just enough "tooth" so that the paint can make a good bond and will not chip easily.

Don't use paints or other products that have toxic fumes on the inside of cabinets; it's impossible to get adequate ventilation in these areas.

The ceilings in many kitchens are of perforated acoustical tile. The best kind of paint to use on these is a casein or oil-base paint because these will not interfere with the sound-absorbing qualities of the tile as much as latex paints. But use a very thin coat—just enough to get the desired color.

BATHROOM

You have a high moisture content in the air in this room, so it's wise to apply a metal primer to radiators, pipes, registers, etc. to protect against rust.

It's best to use an enamel rather than a flat paint for walls as well as woodwork, for an enamel is easier to keep clean and less likely to be harmed by moisture.

EPOXY PAINTS FOR BATHROOMS AND KITCHENS

If you have never used epoxy paints, you will be amazed at some of the results that can be obtained with them. The two-component epoxy paints, for instance, provide the only finish that will hold on sinks, bathtubs, ceramic tiles, and other areas that are extremely smooth and/or exposed to water. These paints produce a hard, durable finish that comes in attractive colors, but they must be handled somewhat differently from other paints.

Two-component epoxy becomes hard by means of catalytic action rather than by evaporation as is the case with ordinary paints. The paint comes in two containers—one with the pigment and the other with the special hardening formula. Once the two components have been combined, they must be used in a matter of a few hours. If not, the paint will become hard even if the container is sealed tight. The special hardener is used to remove spills.

Epoxy paints must be handled carefully. Good ventilation is essential, since they give off toxic and irritating fumes. You should also wear rubber gloves, for they can be irritating to the skin. These paints cannot be applied over other paints or finishes, but can be applied over existing epoxy.

Surfaces must be thoroughly cleaned before applying an epoxy. First wash with a detergent, rinse and then scrub with powdered pumice stone on a clean damp cloth. (You can buy powdered pumice stone at most paint and hardware stores.) After scrubbing, rinse again, using a fresh cloth and clean water, and allow the surface to dry before proceeding.

BASEMENT

This area presents special problems because of the variety of materials present.

The easiest and fastest way to paint exposed ceiling joists and the underside of the floor above is with a spray gun. (It would cost an arm and a leg to do this job with spray containers.) If you don't have a good spray gun, you can rent one from a tool rental, paint or hardware store. You can, of course, apply the paint with a brush or roller, but it will take a lot of time.

You'll need masonry paint for basement walls. A latex masonry paint is very good. If the walls are made of block with a very rough surface, you will save time and paint if you first coat the walls with a latex block filler. This will smooth out the surface.

There are many paints available that are designed to damp-proof or waterproof basement walls. How effective these are not only depends on how carefully they are applied but also on the amount of pressure there is forcing the water through the walls. As a general rule, it's virtually impossible to completely water-proof a basement from the inside simply by coating the walls with a waterproof paint.

Cast-iron drain pipes need a metal primer before you apply a finish coat. Pipes and heating ducts made of galvanized iron will usually require a primer, and it should be one recommended for galvanized iron. Copper pipes don't need a primer and you don't have to remove the tarnish from them. You should, however, wipe them with a solvent to remove dirt and grease. Also remove any green discoloration with steel wool.

Be careful about painting cold-water pipes, because they may be damp from condensation of moisture in the air. Cold-water pipes often sweat during warm, humid weather, and the moisture on them can ruin your paint job. If you can't keep the pipes dry until they are painted and the paint is dry, wait until the weather becomes dry or until you turn on the central heater. This usually dries out the basement air.

Use heat-resistant enamels on any surface that gets hot. You will need the high-heat-type enamels that can stand temperatures up to 1,200 degrees for the heater vent and stovepipes, jacket on the furnace or boiler and all other surfaces that become extremely hot. For water pipes and most heating ducts that don't get this hot, an enamel that can take 200 degrees is adequate. Don't try to paint any item made of galvanized iron that gets over 200 degrees because the paint will not stand up.

Concrete basement floors must be cleaned before painting, and any grease or oil stains must be removed. Check the directions to see which cleaner the paint manufacturer recommends and follow his directions.

You may find that with certain concrete floor paints, the surface must be "etched" with acid if it is very smooth. Most paint manufacturers recommend a 20 percent solution of muriatic acid, which you can get at most paint and hardware stores. Handle it carefully, for it is very strong stuff. Wear old clothes, rubber gloves and protective goggles. Apply it with a long-handled brush and do not let it splash on any finished surface. If you must mix the acid to get the proper-strength solution, add the acid to the water, *never* the water to the acid, for if you do, the solution will boil and splatter.

You may not be able to get all the specialized paints you need at your local paint or hardware store, because few dealers stock all the various paints that are available. But your local dealer can generally tell you where you can get a particular item, or he may be able to order it for you.

OUTDOOR PAINTING

Any article that is exposed to the sun and rain takes a real beating. The way to keep outdoor furniture, fences, children's outdoor play equipment, storm windows, trash containers, window boxes and so forth looking bright is to protect them with the right kind of coating. And if they are protected, they'll last for many years.

Be sure that any paint or finish used on outdoor work is designed to withstand the weather. Paints and finishes used for indoor work won't hold up if used outdoors. Always check the label, and if it does not state that the material is suitable for outdoor work, don't waste time using it.

ALUMINUM. This is a very easy metal to paint. First wipe the metal clean with a cloth and then coat with any good exterior zinc-chromate metal primer. When the primer is dry, apply two coats of outside enamel.

If you like the natural silver color of aluminum, and wish to restore the color and keep it that way, make it bright by removing the gray discoloration. First, wearing rubber gloves, wash the metal with a commercial metal conditioner containing phosphoric acid (available at paint and hardware stores). Wash the conditioner off with water and polish the metal with fine-grade steel wool. Wipe clean with a paint thinner and then coat with a clear nonyellowing acrylic or butrate lacquer. That's all there is to it.

Use these same techniques for painting or restoring any aluminum article exposed to the weather—storm doors and windows, furniture, trash containers, mailboxes and so on.

IRON AND STEEL. This is easy to paint if the old finish is in perfect condition—no peeling paint, cracks or rust. Rub the old finish down with fine steel wool or sandpaper. Wipe clean with a cloth dampened in paint thinner and then apply one or two coats of outdoor metal enamel.

If the old finish is in poor condition, it will take a bit more work to make things right. Remove all the cracked and peeling paint with steel wool or a stiff wire brush. Sand the edges of the surrounding paint to produce a feathered edge. Remove rust with medium steel wool and/or medium-grade sandpaper. Very heavy rust accumulations may have to be chipped off, navy-style, with a hammer and cold chisel. Get the metal as bright as you can and then coat with a phosphoric-acid metal conditioner—the same as used on aluminum. Wash the acid off with water and dry the metal. Coat with a metal primer, and when this is dry, apply at least two coats of outdoor enamel to these spots and then give the entire piece one or two coats.

When the old paint is in bad shape, remove it with a paint remover and apply a primer followed by at least two coats of enamel.

These same methods can be used for repainting outdoor furniture, iron and steel outdoor railings, fences, bicycles and other articles used outdoors. When painting bicycles, power mowers and other mechanical equipment, be sure to remove all traces of grease and oil before painting.

GALVANIZED STEEL. Most people call this "galvanized iron." It is actually steel with a thin coating of zinc, and when it's new it has a silver color. Many mailboxes are made of galvanized steel, and it is also used for window boxes, trash containers, gutters and downspouts.

As long as the thin coating of zinc remains intact, this material won't rust, but in time the coating wears off and then the steel will rust.

Most galvanized-steel articles contain an inhibitor that makes it difficult to paint when the metal is new. But after it has been exposed to the weather for six months or so, the inhibitor disappears and paint will stick.

Prime the metal with a special primer designed for galvanized steel. The most common one contains 80 percent zinc dust and 20 percent zinc oxide. Follow this up with two coats of enamel and be sure that the enamel is the type that will get along with the zinc primer.

WOOD. If the wood is painted and the paint is in good condition, just roughen it up a bit with sandpaper or steel wool, wipe it clean and paint. If there are spots where the old paint has cracked or is peeling, scrape or sand off the bad paint, feather the edges of the surrounding paint, prime the exposed wood and apply a coat or two of paint to these areas before repainting the entire piece. If the old paint is in poor condition—cracked, peeling or blistered—strip it off with a paint remover, prime and then follow with two coats of paint.

If the wood was varnished and the varnish has started to crack or flake or is discolored, take it off with a paint and varnish remover. Sand the wood smooth and then apply two or three coats of exterior or spar varnish. Remember, however, that varnish is not an ideal finish for exterior woodwork; it does not stand up too well under the weather, and when it begins to fail, it must be removed before fresh varnish can be applied with good results. If you don't wish to paint the piece but want a clear or natural finish, you can use clear or pigmented exterior penetrating stain or sealer. These are applied to the bare wood and are easy to renew when they begin to fade—just wipe the surface clean and apply a fresh coat. You can also paint the wood, but you should remove all the old varnish before doing this.

Wood furniture that has had no finish soon becomes discolored from the weather and from spills of food and liquids. Stains and discolorations can usually be removed by sanding, but deep stains may have to be bleached out with a commercial wood bleach sold at paint and hardware stores. Once the wood has been restored to its natural color, keep it that way by coating with a sealer. It will also prevent the wood from absorbing stains easily.

BAMBOO, RATTAN AND WICKER FURNITURE. It is a lot easier to paint these with a spray container or spray gun than with a brush. If it is a painted piece, work it over with a stiff fiber brush—a floor brush is fine—to remove any loose paint. Wash it down with warm water and a household detergent. Rinse with a garden hose spray and allow to dry thoroughly before repainting.

If the piece has a varnish finish in poor condition, the old varnish should be removed with a paint and varnish remover before fresh varnish is applied. An easier solution is to scrub off as much of the loose varnish as you can with a fiber brush and then paint with an enamel.

CANVAS AWNINGS. If these are a solid color, they can be painted with a special canvas-awning paint that comes in several colors. It can be used, however, only if the canvas is porous and has not been treated with a waterproofing compound. Hold the material up to the light. If you can see light through the weave, chances are the canvas will take and hold paint. Before painting, scrub the canvas clean with warm water and a detergent, rinse with a garden hose and allow to dry. Canvas awing paint can also be used for renewing the colors on canvas deck chairs, cushions and so forth.

WOOD WINDOW BOXES. The paint on the outside of window boxes usually peels and blisters because water from inside the box penetrates through the wood and pushes the paint off. Before repainting, remove all the old paint from the outside of the box with a scraper, paint remover or sandpaper. Clean out the inside of the box and then allow the wood to dry thoroughly. Put it in a warm dry place and let it sit for a week or so. When the wood is dry, coat the inside of the box with an asphalt-base tree-dressing paint. Give the inside a nice thick coating to be sure that every speck of wood is coated. The asphalt paint will protect the wood from moisture from inside the box. Give the outside of the box a coat of exterior latex primer and then a couple of coats of latex enamel.

WOOD FENCES. Wash the surface with a garden hose and a brush. The lower portion of fences and posts usually pick up a lot of dirt, so be certain to get it off the wood. Use a standard house paint on fences—the self-cleaning or chalking type of house paint. If the fence is made of solid boards, a paint roller can be used, but if it's a picket fence, the job will have to be done with a brush or with a spray gun.

Fences that are unpainted or have a natural finish should be wiped or washed clean and then coated with an exterior wood sealer.

Part Three
SAVING MONEY ON REPAIRS, SERVICES, UTILITIES AND HEAT

Back in the good old days, the chief money worry for most homeowners was getting together each month enough cash to make that payment on the mortgage. Today's homeowners have all kinds of money worries that can frequently add up to several times the amount of the mortgage payment. Monthly heating bills, for instance, have become a true horror for many, often more than the mortgage payment. Service for equipment is another devourer of our money. A serviceman comes over and spends ten minutes tinkering with the dishwasher and we end up with a bill for $40 or more. The plumber and his helper spend a morning trying to locate and fix a leak in a pipe, and that costs another $75. And let's not forget those charges for utilities—electricity, gas and water—that seem to be on a very special inflationary spiral.

You can lie awake at night worrying over these expenses or you can do something to cut them down. And, as you'll find in the various chapters in this section, there are literally hundreds of things you can do that really will help reduce the financial burden of operating a home in today's economy.

15

HOW TO CUT YOUR GAS, ELECTRIC AND WATER BILLS

DID YOU know that one leaky hot-water faucet can cost you $25 or more a year just for the energy to heat the wasted water? At that rate it's not hard to see where the expression "money down the drain" may have originated.

More money down the drain could also be that old refrigerator you keep in the basement to cool beverages and make extra ice. It may be adding $30 a year to your electric bill. And the ornamental gaslight in the front yard—burning 24 hours a day—is using more gas in a year than the kitchen range.

As energy supplies get smaller and utility bills bigger, there's no escaping the fact that we must stop squandering our resources and our money. If we can't cut the rates, at least we can cut our consumption.

The largest share of our home-energy dollar goes for heat in winter, and, in warm climates, for central air conditioning in summer. So it's obvious that we must take all steps to reduce waste in this area by insulation, storm windows, etc. (Chapter 17 explains in detail how to reduce heating costs, whether you use oil, gas, or electricity.)

What's left of our energy dollar goes for normal household activities and conveniences—cooking, lighting, hot water for washing and bathing, television and electrical appliances. It is in these areas that we can make substantial savings if we really want to, once we become aware of how much energy we are wasting. Over the period of a year such savings can add up to hundreds of dollars for the individual and, for the nation, can mean enormous savings in natural resources.

REDUCING HOT-WATER COSTS

More of your home-energy dollar goes for hot water than for anything else except heat. The cost of hot water will vary, depending on what you are paying for energy—electricity, gas or oil. In the Northeast, where no form of energy is exactly cheap, it can cost up to 1½ cents to heat 1 gallon of 40-degree water to 140 degrees. (We'll use ½ cent a gallon for our cost figures. If you pay less than this, good. If you pay more, you've got a lot of company.)

A typical household will use about 26 gallons of hot water each day per member, according to figures supplied by the Connecticut Energy Agency. This would mean that a family of four will use about 104 gallons of hot water every day, and at ½ cents a gallon it will cost them 52 cents a day, or $189.80 a year. More extravagant families, according to this report, use as much as 68 gallons of hot water per member each day. These families are spending $1.36 a day for hot water, or almost $500 a year.

Most of the hot water is for bathing; as much as 30 gallons for a full tub bath but only 10 to 20 gallons for a shower—depending on the shower-head design and the length of time you stay under it. So switch to showers—brief showers at that. You'll also be wise to install a low-flow shower head that allows only around 4 gallons a minute to come through rather than the 6 to 10 gallons a minute you get through many ordinary shower heads.

If you can cut just 10 gallons from every bath per day, you'll save 40 gallons of hot water with a family of four. This means in a year you'll have saved 14,600 gallons of hot water. At ½ cent a gallon this comes to $73.

You'll also save on hot water by fixing leaky faucets and not allowing it to pour out of the faucet while you wash your hands and face, shave or shampoo your hair. And each time you can do the wash with cold instead of hot water you'll save around 10 cents.

Insulate hot-water pipes where possible so that the heated water in them won't be wasted. Keep your water heater set at around 140 degrees—adequate for most households. For each 10 degrees you increase the temperature over 140 degrees, your hot-water costs go up 3 percent.

REDUCING ELECTRICITY BILLS

The average household uses between 650 and 700 kilowatts of electricity a month and pays for it at so much a kilowatt hour (kwh). One kwh is equal to the amount of electricity needed to light one 100-watt bulb for 10 hours. The charges per kwh vary in different parts of the country, but the national average, according to the Edison Electric Institute, is 2.92 cents. For the sake of convenience we'll round this out to 3 cents and use it as our base for cost figures.

The vast majority of the electrical appliances in the home require relatively little electricity or are operated so infrequently and/or for such a short period of time that whether you use them or not won't affect your electric bill to any great extent. (Of course, they add to the total amount of energy we consume as a nation.) Some specialized appliances, however, actually do help conserve energy. The electric coffeepot, toaster-oven and skillet perform their tasks more economically than the kitchen range.

You can make substantial savings, however, on those items that take a lot of power and are in constant or frequent use—the refrigerator, clothes dryer, color television, room air conditioner, etc. Include electric lights, too, because there are so many of them about the house.

Turning off unnecessary lights is an easy way to cut your electric bill. One 100-watt bulb burning 10 hours a day costs $10.95 a year.

If you have 20 100-watt bulbs and cut the time they are on each day by just one half-hour, you'll save that $10.95.

Fluorescent lights, by the way, use 75 percent less electricity to produce the same amount of light as incandescent bulbs. You might want to install fluorescent fixtures if you redo the kitchen or fix up the basement, since both these areas take a lot of lighting.

Refrigerators and freezers are big consumers of electricity. A 16-cubic-foot frostless refrigerator, for instance, takes around 5 kwh a day. At our rate of 3 cents a kwh, this adds about $4.50 a month to your electric bill. A manual-defrost unit with the same capacity requires one-third to one-half less electricity, assuming you get rid of the frost before it becomes thicker than ¼ inch.

If your frostless refrigerator has a switch that turns off the defrost heater when the humidity is low, it reduces your operating costs by around 16 percent.

To reduce the cost of running any type of refrigerator or freezer, make sure the inside temperature is low enough for safe food preservation but not so low as to overchill the contents, thus increasing your operating costs. A temperature of 0 degrees is adequate for the freezer compartment, 38 to 40 degrees for the food-storage area.

You can also reduce operating costs by keeping the condenser clean, replacing door gaskets when they become worn (a worn gasket allows warm air to seep into the freezer and food-storage compartments) and limiting the number and length of times the door is opened.

That old refrigerator in the basement or garage that we mentioned earlier may be costing you $5 a month unless it's in tip-top shape, and even then it's adding another $2 or $3 a month to your electric bill.

Dishwashers require about 1 kwh per load—about 3 cents—plus around 14 gallons of hot water. They actually use less total energy than it takes to do dishes by hand, assuming you rinse under running water, but you can still cut $10 or so a year off your electric bill if you operate the dishwasher once rather than twice a day. To reduce costs by 50 percent, turn the washer off before the drying cycle. Open the door and let the air dry the dishes.

Washing machines use around 1/3 kwh per load plus 18 to 30 gallons of hot water. You can save around $10 a year if you wash with cold water for even two loads each week. And naturally, you'll save if you stick with full loads whenever possible rather than half loads.

Electric clothes dryers take about 3 kwh per load—9 cents or so a load. That isn't very much, but if you run a load through the dryer five times a week, you've added $18.54 to your annual electric cost. The way to save here is to run the dryer only when absolutely necessary and with full loads (but not overloaded) when possible. It will also help reduce costs if you set the dryer for as short a drying cycle as the weight of the wash permits. When the sun is shining, hang the wash outside.

Television, radio and stereo account for a little over 3 percent of the electricity in the home. Television consumes the most. It's not that so much power is required—a tube-type color television draws about 1/3 kwh per hour—it's that the set is on for so many hours a day. The average television is turned on somewhat over six hours a day. This means it will cost around $21 a year to run a color television set. But if there are a couple of sets around the house or if one set goes twelve hours a day—not unusual—you've added another $40 to your electric bill for the year. This sum, of course, does not include what it may cost to operate a couple of radios and a stereo, although these take relatively little power.

Color televisions with instant-on circuits consume the most electricity because they continue to draw electricity to keep the circuits warm even when the set itself is off. Disconnect the set from the wall outlet when it's not going to be used for any length of time and save around 6 percent on operating costs. Some of the newer sets have a switch so you can turn off the instant-on circuit when the set won't be needed for a period of time. A new 30-second-on set requires less electricity than the instant-on and comes on faster than the old regular set.

Solid-state television sets need about 50 percent less electricity than those with tubes—something to keep in mind when you buy a new set.

The obvious way to save money is to turn off the television when no one is watching it and certainly if no one is enjoying it. It's costing you around $12 a year to fall asleep watching the late-night movie.

An efficient room air conditioner with a cooling capacity of between 8,000 and 10,000 Btu's per hour consumes around 860 watts per hour. A less efficient unit with the same cooling capacity, however, may use 1,500 watts per hour.

If an 860-watt unit runs for 1,000 hours a season—about average for a climate like that of St. Louis, Missouri—your annual cost will be $25.80. If you got stuck with an inefficient unit that takes 1,500 watts to provide the same degree of cooling, those 1,000 hours will cost you $45.

Since your air conditioner is costing you around 3 cents an hour, the obvious way to save is not to turn it on unless it's really needed. If it is in the bedroom, turn it on an hour before you retire. This should give it ample time to cool the room. If you are away from home during the day and want to come back to a cool living room, get an electric timer. Plug the air conditioner into the timer and set it so it will turn the unit on an hour or so before you come home.

The very best way to keep the cost of running a room air conditioner down is to buy one with a high energy-efficiency rating (EER). An EER of 6 to 7 is fair, 8 to 9 is good and 10 or more is excellent. The EER is marked on all new models.

REDUCING GAS BILLS

You pay for gas by the therm or by the cubic foot. One therm is more or less equal in heating value to 100 cubic feet of gas. The cost of natural gas varies depending on where you live, but 14 cents a therm is the national average, so this is the rate we'll use for our figures.

Since there are relatively few gas appliances in the home, there are fewer ways to save here than with electrical equipment. Aside from the hot-water heater, which we discussed earlier, the most common gas appliances are the range, clothes dryer and ornamental outdoor gaslights. Gaslights that burn 24 hours a day use around

180 therms of gas a year (18,000 cubic feet) according to a recent report made for the Department of Housing and Urban Development. If you are paying 14 cents a therm, then each gas lamp will cost you around $25 a year. That's more than it costs to run the average range. If you need light for security, you may save with an electric light that can be turned off during the day.

The pilot light on a kitchen range uses around 30 percent of the gas required by this appliance—slightly over 100 therms a year— but turning off the pilot light is not always feasible or without certain hazards. One manufacturer of gas ranges now has a unit that uses an electrical ignition system instead of a pilot light, and he claims this reduces the gas consumption for the range by 30 percent.

REDUCING WATER BILLS IN GENERAL

The total water used for the average household of four runs around 7,500 gallons a month. This includes water used for bathing, washing clothes, cooking, washing dishes and flushing toilets.

The cost for these 7,500 gallons each month can be over $10 in some areas, and that means a water bill of $120 a year. Even if you don't pay very much for water, you should try to conserve it, because at the rate we are using water, we may be short some 50 billion gallons of underground water by 1980, according to a study made in late 1971 by *National Wildlife* magazine.

Leaky faucets, as mentioned earlier, can waste a tremendous amount of water. So can leaky garden-hose nozzles and connections. According to one water company, just one leaky faucet can waste up to 15 gallons a day, and that comes to about 5,475 gallons a year—down the drain.

Leaky toilet flush tanks are also a big water waster, and often we don't know the fool thing is leaking. The way to make certain is to put some food coloring in the tank. If the coloring comes into the bowl before the tank is flushed, the tank is leaking. You should either adjust the flush mechanism or replace it.

The average flush tank may use 5 to 8 gallons of water per flush, and a family of four will use 880 gallons of water each week just to flush toilets, according to the Department of the Interior. You can save right here by not using the toilet bowl in place of a wastepaper basket for facial tissue or in place of an ashtray for cigarettes. Many products now on the market are designed to reduce the amount of water required to flush, and some appear to have considerable merit. But before you buy and install one, check with your local building department to make sure they are approved for use in your area.

The newer-type flush tanks, by the way, are designed to use a lot less water than the older types—3 gallons or less per flush.

During the summer a tremendous amount of water we use goes for watering lawns and gardens. In Denver, Colorado, for example, around 40 percent of summertime water use is for this purpose. Heavy mulching for flowers and vegetable gardens will help the soil retain moisture. Also, you'll lose less by evaporation if you water gardens and lawns early in the morning or late in the day.

CHECK YOUR UTILITY BILLS

You can save money if you check these bills carefully.

Keep a record of your monthly utility statements. Note the amount of electricity, gas and water you used—this information is given on the statement—and the amount you paid. When a new bill arrives, compare it with your records of previous statements. If the amount of the new bill is higher than average, find out why.

An unusually high bill can be a warning that you are wasting a lot of electricity, gas or water. It can also mean that some of your equipment is not operating efficiently because of age or some minor problem. High water bills are often due to a leak in an underground water pipe.

But usually when a particular bill is high it is because it contains an error. Maybe someone did not read a meter correctly, or maybe the computer that made out the bill was out of whack, but one thing is almost certain: the error won't be in your favor but rather in the favor of the utility firm. Check the bill. Compare the amount with the amount of electricity, gas or water that you have been previously using. Multiply the amount used by the rate to see if you arrive at the same figure as that given on the bill. If you find the bill incorrect or you doubt you used that amount, get off a letter. Send it to the president of the firm by registered mail, return receipt requested. That should get some action.

16
HOW TO GET BY WHEN THE ELECTRICITY GOES OFF

"OH DEAR! There go the lights!" This is the standard opening line to an exciting little drama entitled *There's No Electricity*. And what it means is that not only are there no lights, but everything else in the house that runs on electricity—the kitchen range, refrigerator, dishwasher, water pump, heating system (which usually has an electric ignition and other components even if it's an oil- or gas-fired system), air conditioner, coffee maker, television, clock, razor and even the toothbrush—takes an unexpected vacation and leaves you to cope as best you can.

Power failures can and do occur in every part of the country. Sometimes the power will be off just a few minutes or a couple of hours, but if the area has been hit by a bad storm, electricity may not be restored for several days.

Electricity is so essential in the home that even a few hours' interruption can be a great inconvenience, and a failure that lasts a day or more can be serious, especially in cold weather.

Since you can do nothing to prevent a power failure, prepare your house so that when and if one does occur, you'll get through

144

it with the least amount of inconvenience or damage to your house and equipment.

BE PREPARED

Have emergency equipment and supplies always on hand and in one place. Be sure to keep them just for an emergency. If you and other members of the family use them whenever it is convenient, chances are that when you really need them, they won't be around or in working order.

Every home will need some type of emergency light. Candles are attractive and okay in a pinch but not too practical. Flashlights and battery-operated lamps are both safe and dependable—if the batteries are fresh. Check these units every month or so and replace the batteries when you notice the light is a little dim.

Kerosene, gasoline and propane lamps and lanterns give off excellent light, but they are something of a fire hazard, especially if used around small children.

If you have an electric range, you'll need something to heat food and water, unless you are willing to go on a diet of sandwiches and cold drinks. Don't forget that it's more than the electric range that is out; it's also the toaster, electric skillet, waffle iron, electric hot plate and all the rest of your small appliances. A portable one- or two-burner gasoline, propane or alcohol camp stove is a good investment and will get you through those three hot meals a day if you stick to simple dishes. In a pinch you can even cook over the fire in the fireplace if you have some sort of grill to hold pots and pans. You'll do better with a charcoal fire (be sure that the damper is open until the fire is completely out) instead of wood.

Keep some emergency rations in a special section of the cupboard. Select items that can be prepared with a minimum amount of cooking time. One-dish meals, such as canned stews or canned spaghetti with meatballs, are best. And be sure that you have an old-fashioned can opener handy. You can feel very foolish with a well-stocked supply of canned goods that can't be opened because the electric can opener isn't operating.

You'll want to have a supply of paper or disposable plastic plates and cups on hand. Unless you have a gas hot-water heater, there won't be any hot water during the power failure, and if you have your own water pump, there won't even be any water. And certainly no dishwasher.

Have at least one battery-operated radio with fresh batteries on hand. If the phone is also out, the radio will be your only means of keeping in touch with the world and learning when you may expect the electric power to be restored.

If you have a fireplace or woodburning stove, always keep several days' reserve wood or fuel supply on hand. You'll welcome a nice steady fire if you have a power failure in cold weather or on a wet day, and the children will have fun toasting marshmallows or hot dogs over the coals.

PAY ATTENTION TO ADVANCE WARNINGS

The vast majority of lengthy power failures are caused by severe storms—wind, ice, snow—and usually there is some advance warning, sometimes a day, as to when the storm is expected to hit your area. Use this advance-warning time to your advantage, rather than just sitting around worrying. Check over your emergency equipment and supplies. Do any last-minute shopping. You don't have to hoard, but the time to buy flashlights, batteries, fuel for a portable stove, etc. is before there is a general power failure. Once it has occurred, stocks of these kinds of items are rapidly depleted.

If you have a lot of dishes to do or clothes to wash or dry, now is the time to do them, while you still have electric power. This is also a good time to do some advance cooking—a roast, for example, or a cake.

If your water supply is provided by an electric pump, fill clean containers so there will be water available for drinking and cooking. Also fill the bathtubs. This will provide a good supply of water so the family can at least wash. It will also be handy for flushing toilets. To do this, lift off the top of the tank, and using a handy-sized pail, pour water from the tub into the tank until it reaches the correct level—where the discoloration on the inside of the tank stops. The toilet can then be flushed. It's a good idea to put the tank cover in a safe spot until the normal water supply has been restored. Tops are heavy and fragile, and if they are accidentally dropped, they will break.

If the power goes off, call your local power company at once and report the failure. Just because the power is out in your house and perhaps your neighbor's, there is no reason to assume that there has been a general power failure unless you heard so over the radio. It may be a very local condition, and the faster the power company learns about it, the quicker they can fix it.

When the lights do go out, it's a good idea to disconnect or turn off any motor-driven electrical equipment, such as the water pump, refrigerator, air conditioner, and oil burner, and keep it off until the power has been restored and the lights are burning bright and steady. The reason for doing this is that when power is being restored, there can be a sudden surge of voltage or a very low level of voltage, either of which could be harmful to a motor.

If the power goes out during daylight hours, be sure to leave a light or radio turned on so you'll know the minute the power has been restored.

When there is a serious disruption of power because of a bad storm, even the power company can't say for sure just how long it will take to get things back to normal, so prepare for the worst.

PROTECT YOUR FROZEN FOODS

Don't open your freezer or freezer compartment of your refrigerator if you can possibly avoid it. When you open the door, warm air flows inside and speeds up the thawing of the food. A fully loaded freezer cabinet will keep food frozen for about two days, but if it is only partially filled, the food may remain frozen for only about one day. Naturally, thawing will occur faster in warm weather than in cold.

Make sure that the gasket on the door of the freezer or refrigerator is in good shape, for if it is worn, warm air can flow inside even with the door shut. If the inside of the cabinet frosts up quickly, it may mean a worn gasket. You can also check by closing the door on a dollar bill and then trying to pull the bill out. If it comes out easily the gasket is worn and should be replaced.

If frozen food becomes soft to the touch, it should never be refrozen. It can, however, be cooked immediately. After cooking, the food can be refrozen if power is restored within a relatively short time. If you have a lot of frozen food on your hands that has begun to thaw, this might be a good time to invite friends and neighbors over for a feast—if you have some means of cooking and if somebody else hasn't invited them first.

The correct temperature in the freezer can be maintained with dry ice if you can find some, but it's usually hard to get, especially during a power failure. Dry ice must be handled with great care because it can give you a nasty burn. Always wear heavy gloves when handling it.

If you live in an area where power failures occur rather frequently and have a freezer loaded with several hundred dollars' worth of food, you might want to consider buying a standby generator. These will be discussed later on.

WHAT TO DO ABOUT HEAT

A power failure when the temperature is below freezing is a real headache. Electric and oil-fired heating systems won't work at all. Some gas burners will run, but as there is no power to operate the blower or circulator, the heat will not be distributed through the house.

As soon as the power goes off, conserve what heat there is in the house. Be sure all windows are closed tight. Don't open outside doors unless absolutely necessary, and then for as short a time as possible. This is no time to allow the family cat or dog to stand in an open door trying to decide whether to come in or go out.

If you use electric blankets, you'll be wise to have some ordinary ones set aside in case of emergency. An old-fashioned hot-water bottle or two can come in pretty handy, too, if you've got a few extra drops of water and a means to heat it.

A good fire in the fireplace will add welcome warmth and cheer if you can keep it going all the time, but if it's just a puny little fire, it is allowing more heat to escape up the chimney than it is providing. And a huge roaring fire also wastes more heat than it produces because it must consume so much of the heated air in the room. The best kind of fire is a brisk one—not too little and not too big. And when there is no fire, be sure the fireplace damper is closed tight. There are, by the way, many products that will increase the heat output of an ordinary fireplace; these are discussed in Chapter 18.

With the outside temperature well below freezing, even a well-insulated house will not remain warm long. In about 24 hours the inside temperature may drop to around 40 degrees unless you have a fireplace or stove to provide sufficient heat. When the inside temperature does get to 40 degrees, it's time to worry about pipes freezing. This is serious, because if they do freeze, they may split and then leak when they thaw out.

If you happen to have city water, slightly open all faucets above the basement level. If the water is moving in the pipes, it won't freeze as readily as when standing still. If your water supply comes from your own electric pump, this remedy isn't going to work. What you may have to do is have the plumbing system drained. If you have a hot-water or steam heating system, this also must be drained. And don't forget that if it's cold enough inside the house for the pipes to freeze, it's cold enough for almost anything to freeze—canned goods, bottled goods, etc. This is about time to think about closing up the house and taking a long winter vacation.

FLOODING

Heavy rains that often accompany storms can cause flooding, especially in basements. If flooding appears inevitable, shut off the electrical supply to all equipment and lines likely to be affected. If you haven't taken this precaution before flooding, don't wade through the water, but call your utility company or electrician to check any potential hazard. Of course, when there is no electricity, the basement sump pump can't do its job unless you have one of the new and rather expensive kind that runs on batteries when the power is off. Call your local fire department. They are usually pretty good about coming around to pump out a basement, but if they can't, a local contractor may have the equipment to do the job. But get someone over before the water reaches some of your expensive heating and laundry equipment.

STANDBY GENERATORS

Many families who have experienced the inconvenience of a prolonged power failure or the costly loss of food in their freezers have purchased these units to provide temporary electric power until regular service has been restored.

Most electric generators designed for home use are powered by

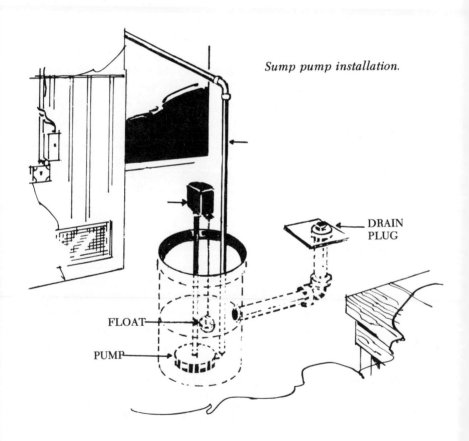

Sump pump installation.

DRAIN PLUG

FLOAT

PUMP

either a gasoline engine or one that runs on natural or propane gas. The gasoline types are the least expensive and are used when the unit can be set away from the house in a detached garage or outbuilding. The gas types can be placed inside the house in the basement or in an attached garage.

Diesel-powered home generators are also available. These can operate on the same fuel used to run the oil burner.

The cost of a home generator depends on its electrical output. For under $200 you can get one that will handle the home freezer, refrigerator, water pump and oil burner, but not, of course, all at the same time. For around $1,000 you can get one that will handle all the normal needs of the average house—except electric heat.

If you are interested in buying a standby generator, figure out what your minimum electrical requirements really are. For most families, the essential equipment is the heating system, water pump, freezer and refrigerator. A 3,000- or 4,000-watt generator, costing around $500 to $700, would handle this load along with one burner on the electric range.

Standby generators can be purchased through electrical contractors. You can also buy them direct from other sources, such as the large mail-order houses. But the equipment should be installed by a licensed electrician. If you do get standby equipment, don't just let it sit around month after month and then expect it to run when you need it. A gasoline-powered generator should be started and run for a short time two or three times a month; a natural-gas or propane-gas type, about once a month.

It may be stretching things a bit to say that doing without electricity for a few days can be fun, but if you are well prepared for such a situation, it can be a very interesting experience and even a pleasant one for some members of the family—especially the children.

17

HOW TO CUT HEATING COSTS BY OVER 30 PERCENT

FEW of us today can afford *not* to do everything under the sun to reduce the cost of heating our homes. Energy for heating has been going up at a pretty alarming rate for the past few years, and there is every indication that it will continue to increase in the years to come. So even if heating your house hasn't broken your bank account, just wait. It will, unless you do a few things to reduce heating energy requirements in your home.

There are a lot of ways you can cut your heating costs, and cut them by as much as 30 percent or even more. Some of the steps you can take will only save you nickels, dimes and quarters, but these add up. Others will save you nice crisp dollars. Some require no outlay of money, while others, such as insulation and storm windows, require an initial investment that will be repaid in two, three, five or six years. After that, the savings are all gravy. And if your house is air conditioned in summer, many of the steps you take to cut down winter heating costs will also lower the cost of operating the air conditioner.

152

SAVE WITH THE THERMOSTAT

Whether you use electricity, gas or oil for heating, you can save around 3 percent on your heating costs for each degree you lower the thermostat below the setting you have normally used in the past. If, for example, you've been keeping the thermostat at 72 degrees and you lower it to 68 degrees, you'll reduce your heating costs by 12 percent for the year. And once you get used to 68 degrees, you might try 64 degrees, at least during the daytime when the family is either not at home or is active. This low setting is not too bad if you dress properly. Wear warm clothes and be sure that arms and legs are covered. And be sure that everyone wears heavy socks or stockings, because if your feet are cold, you feel cold all over.

In any event, try to keep the normal thermostat setting well below 72 degrees, for once you pass this point, your heating energy consumption and costs go up at a rather alarming rate.

When there is a sudden drop in outside temperature, you may, of course, have to move the thermostat up a degree or more from its normal setting. The colder it is outside, the higher the inside air temperature has to be to reduce body-heat loss and keep us comfortable.

If your house is well insulated and you have storm windows, you can save a little money by lowering the thermostat to 60 degrees at night when the outside temperature is *above* freezing. But don't try this when the outside air is very cold, because you'll use all of the heating energy you saved during the night, and possibly more, to get the house warm again in the morning.

USE "SPOT HEAT"

You'll find it easier to live with a lower indoor temperature if you use small portable electric heaters to give you instant heat when and where you need it. Use them to warm the area for dressing and undressing, to take the chill off the bathroom in the morning and so forth. If these heaters are used for only a short length of time, they will not add much to your electric bill and will make it much easier and more comfortable to keep a low thermostat setting all winter long.

You'll also find that electric blankets can pay for themselves by allowing everyone to be comfortable at night in a cool bedroom.

REDUCE HEAT LOSS FROM RADIATION

If you sit near an outside wall or window, you will often feel chilly even when the temperature of the air around you is quite warm. This is because the surface temperature of these areas is usually lower than the temperature of the air in the rest of the room, and heat from your body is being drawn off just as though the cooler surface was some sort of magnet. Even if the walls are insulated and you have storm windows or insulating glass, these outside surfaces will be cooler than the air in the room. The common solution to this problem is to increase the air temperature in the room by pushing up the thermostat, but this is wasteful because the rest of the room and house then becomes overheated. A more economical solution is to arrange the furniture in winter so that no one has to sit too close to a window or outside wall. Another solution is to cover the windows and cold areas with draperies. When these are pulled, they will reduce body-heat loss from radiation.

USE FREE HEAT FROM THE SUN

You'll be happily surprised at how much heat the winter sun can pour into your house if you raise the window shades and open the draperies as soon as the sun comes up in the morning. And every degree of heat you get from the sun is going to save you money. In winter it's the south side of the house that gets the most intense heat from the sun, but sunlight from any direction can be a big help. Even if you have storm windows or double glazing, the heat from the sun will get through. A relatively small amount of heat will get through if you have applied sun-control film, however, so maybe you might want to strip it off.

If you are at home during the day, try to remember to pull the shades or close the draperies when the sun moves away from the window.

SHRINK YOUR HOUSE TO SAVE HEAT

Close off any area of the house that doesn't require heat all the time. Some families have cut their heating cost by as much as 20 percent just by closing off a couple of rooms—an extra bedroom and the family room, for instance. In very cold weather it can make sense to close off a room or rooms for just a couple of days. It's easy enough to close off a room. Turn off the radiator or close the warm-air register about two-thirds of the way. Leave the cold-air-return register open. If the door to the room doesn't fit tightly, apply weatherstripping or seal the edges with masking tape. Check the room every few days to make sure that the temperature doesn't get below 45 degrees or so.

DON'T TRY TO HEAT ALL OUTDOORS

In the average busy household vast amounts of heat are donated to the great outdoors. Leave an outside door open for just a few seconds, and heat and money flow away. Some heating authorities claim that each child and housebroken pet increases heating costs by around 5 percent because they are constantly coming in and going out. And often the door remains open for a long time while they stand on the threshold trying to decide whether they really want to go out or come inside. One family installed a loud buzzer that rings when any outside door is opened and keeps buzzing until the door is firmly closed. Another family has a strict law that a door can be left open only for 10 seconds.

If you have more than one outside door—and most houses do—use the one that faces away from the prevailing winter winds. Seal the other door or doors up tight with weatherstripping or masking tape. If there are storm doors, pack some insulation in between the main door and the storm door.

A storm porch can be a very worthwhile investment, for it keeps cold blasts of air from coming into the house each time the door is opened and also makes a convenient place to take off wet overshoes and heavy coats.

The doors of attached garages should be kept closed, and it's smart to weatherstrip them.

Kitchen and bathroom exhaust fans waste a lot of heat, so don't use them except when it is absolutely necessary. The fan in the average-size kitchen will remove all the air in the kitchen that you paid to heat in about three minutes. Also, when the fan is running it creates a slight suction that pulls cold air from the outside into the house through cracks. If the fan has an automatic damper, be sure it closes tight when the fan is not running. If you can't get it to close tight, or if there is no automatic damper, forget about the fan during winter. Seal up the exhaust with masking tape or insulation and keep the fan out of use until warm weather arrives.

The fresh-air fiend who loves to sleep with the windows wide open in an icy bedroom can be a menace to the heat budget unless properly controlled. If you have one of these around, make him shut his bedroom door and turn off the radiator or close the register before retiring at night. If heat to the room has been turned off several hours before bedtime, the room may be cold enough so that our fresh-air fiend may not need to open the windows to get a good night's sleep.

There are, of course, many ways for heat to escape from a house that are less obvious than through open doors and windows. One of these exits is the fireplace. If the damper is not closed when there is no fire burning, as much as 20 percent of the heated air inside the house can escape up the fireplace chimney. If your fireplace does not have a damper, have one installed or seal up the flue and don't use the fireplace. If there is a damper but it does not make a tight fit when it is closed, have it repaired.

If there is a fire burning in the fireplace—even just a smoldering one—when it is time to go to bed, you can't very well close the damper. But unless you do something, once the fire is out warm air will flow up the chimney until the next morning, when the damper is finally closed. One way to handle this problem is to set a large sheet of aluminum or asbestos board in front of the fireplace opening when you go to bed. This will keep the air in the room from flowing up the chimney. A better approach is to install either a glass fire screen or a metal roll-up screen that can be pulled across or pulled down to close the opening. This is discussed in more detail in Chapter 18.

CAULK CRACKS AND JOINTS

Someone has figured out that the heat loss and cold-air-infiltration in the average house from cracks and joints around windows and doors are equal to one window being left open all the time. Sealing these cracks and openings can reduce heat loss from 10 to 30 percent. You can check the situation inside your house by holding a lighted candle around the edges of doors and windows.

Remove old caulking and then replace with fresh caulking.

If the flame flickers, warm air is flowing out or cold air is coming in, and neither is good.

Lots of cold air gets into the house through seams where the siding joins window and door frames, where the woodwork joins the foundations or even around outside electric outlets and the exhaust outlet of an exhaust fan. All these seams should be filled with caulking compound. It may be that many of these seams were caulked, but check the condition of the caulking, for it may be old and brittle and no longer effective. If you find that it is, remove it with a sharp-pointed tool and replace it with fresh caulking. It will pay you to use the more expensive latex or butyl caulking compounds, for these last from five to six years while the less expensive kinds last only a year or so.

If you have a lot of seams to caulk, use the type of caulking that comes in a cartridge that fits into a handy little caulking gun. Be sure that the seam you are filling is clean and dry and that the compound is at room temperature—it doesn't flow easily when cold.

USE WEATHERSTRIPPING

Weatherstripping seals the joints around window sash; you need it even if you have a storm sash. You need it urgently if you don't. And you also need it on all outside doors.

There are many types of weatherstripping available for use on wood or metal windows and doors.

The easiest kind of stripping to apply is caulking cord. This comes in a roll, and all you have to do is to press the cord into place and it will stick and make a tight seal. It's handy to use on windows and doors that don't have to be opened, and it holds well on metal. It's not very pretty, but it can be painted.

Hair felt stripping is very inexpensive and can be installed on wood units with tacks or staples. It does not wear very well, so you can't expect it to remain effective for more than a couple of years.

And it looks pretty terrible, so use it where appearance doesn't count.

Metal-backed felt is also relatively inexpensive and easy to install, and it looks a lot better than the hair felt. It can be used on wood and is installed with tacks or small nails.

Adhesive-backed rubber or plastic foam stripping is easy to apply—just peel off the protective covering and press it into place. It's excellent for use on metal windows.

Vinyl-covered foam is easy to install and stands up pretty well. And it blends in with white painted woodwork.

Wood and metal rigid strips are excellent but more expensive than the other familiar kinds of stripping and more difficult to apply.

The very best kind of weatherstripping is the spring bronze. This is very durable, will last forever and does an excellent job of sealing joints. But it is very difficult to install; usually the job must be done by a carpenter. All the other kinds of weatherstripping you can install yourself. They are generally available at most hardware stores and usually come with installation instructions.

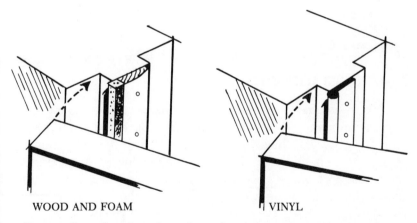

WOOD AND FOAM   VINYL

Foam and wood strip and vinyl weatherstripping are effective and easy to install.

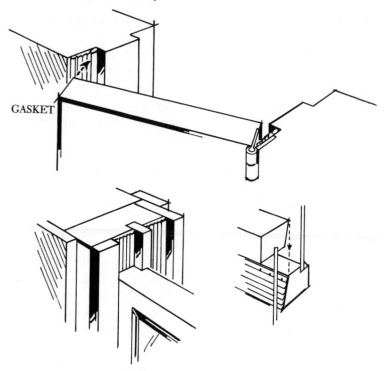

GASKET

Spring bronze weatherstripping is long lasting and effective but difficult to install.

USE STORM WINDOWS

Next to adequate insulation, storm windows are the biggest heat and money savers. They will substantially reduce heat loss through window glass, and they will also reduce by half the difference in temperature between the room and the window glass, making it more comfortable to be near a window. Every window in the house that is not made with insulating glass should have a storm window if you live in the colder regions. And if you live in an area where winters are very cold, it can pay to use storm windows even on those units made with insulating glass.

The most efficient kind of storm windows are those that fit on the outside and are made of aluminum or wood. The wood units are the more efficient of the two but far less convenient than the combination aluminum storm window that is permanently installed and can be switched over to insect screening in the summer in a matter of seconds. When aluminum storm windows are used on aluminum or steel primary windows, it is important to have a "thermal break" of plastic or wood to separate the frame of the storm window from the primary window frame. Unless there is this thermal break, cold will be conducted to the inside metal frame and therefore reduce the overall efficiency of the installation and also cause moisture to form on the metal.

You can use exterior-mounted storm windows on double-hung and sliding windows, but they won't work well on a casement window that swings out unless you don't need to open the window during the cold weather. The more practical way to protect these windows is with a storm panel that fits on the inside of the window rather than the outside. If you use a storm panel, be sure to weatherstrip the primary window. And if you are troubled with condensation forming on the glass of the primary window, apply masking tape or weatherstripping around the edges of the storm panel.

Good-quality aluminum combination storm windows cost around $35 installed. Wood units for the standard-size double-hung window cost around $20, but you can often pick up used ones at garage sales and from building-material salvage yards. You may have to do a bit of carpentry before you can get them to fit your particular window.

Heavy-gauge clear-plastic sheeting can be used to make an inexpensive but very effective storm window. You can buy a roll of it with enough plastic to do all the windows for the average-size house at lumber yards for around $15. The plastic can be installed on the inside or outside of the window. It should be set a few inches away from the window glass so that a dead-air space is created, for this is what provides the insulation value and reduces the heat loss. Fasten the plastic in place with tacks or staples. If it is applied to the outside of the window frame, fasten wood strips over the edges of the plastic to make a tight seal. If it is applied to the inside of the window, masking tape should be used to prevent entry of moist indoor air into the space that is formed.

Wood storm doors with a minimum amount of glass can be very effective in cutting down heat loss through doors, but efficiency drops as the amount of glass area is increased. Metal doors are less effective than the wood units, and, of course, the larger the glass area, the less heat they will conserve.

INCREASE YOUR INSULATION

Insulation is the biggest heat and money saver of them all. The amount of heat required to make an uninsulated house comfortable is almost twice what it takes for an insulated house.

Most houses in areas where central heating is needed have some insulation, but generally it is inadequate and sometimes it is omitted in critical areas.

The U.S. Department of Commerce recently revised house insulation standards to help homeowners deal with the tremendous increase in heating costs that have occurred in the past few years. The new approach to insulation indicates that it can make financial sense to upgrade attic insulation to a value of R-30 even if you live in the milder climates. (The R-value is the unit used to measure the effectiveness of all kinds of insulation. R-30 is equal to a 10-inch-thick layer of mineral wool—the most familiar kind of insulation used in attics.) If you live in the colder regions of the country, it can pay you to insulate up to R-38 (equal to 12 inches of mineral wool) or even as high as R-60 (which means 19 inches of mineral wool).

Most of us, of course, have not in the past had anything close to the 10 inches of mineral wool now suggested even for milder climates. This is because most houses were built when heating energy was relatively inexpensive and 6 inches of mineral wool or R-19 was considered quite adequate. Many so-called "fully insulated" houses have only 3 or 4 inches of insulation in the attic —and there are still thousands and thousands of houses that don't have any at all.

ATTIC INSULATION. If the insulation has been placed between the joists in the attic and there is no attic flooring, it is easy to measure the thickness of the insulation you do have and add more if needed. All you have to do is pile insulation on top of what you already have.

Attic joists are usually no more than 8 inches deep, which means that an 8-inch thickness of insulation is the maximum you can install without spilling above the top edge of the joists. This is okay and no drawback if you have just attic crawl space, but if you have a full attic and plan someday to put down a floor, then you will want to add only enough insulation to bring it flush with the top of the joists. It may not be all the insulation you'd like to have, but it's all you will have space for when a floor is nailed over the joists.

A good type of insulation to use when adding in this manner is the loose-fill kind. This comes in a bag and you just pour it over the existing insulation and level it off with a piece of board. Insulation batts can also be used. These are short lengths of insulation that come in different widths so they'll fit snugly between the joists. They also come in several thicknesses. If you use batts, measure the distance between the joists so you can order the correct width. And *don't use batts with a vapor barrier* if you are adding to insulation you already have. If, however, there is no insulation at all, between the joists, you do want to use the kind with a vapor barrier. The vapor-barrier side should face down so it is contact with the ceiling material of the room below.

When you are working in the attic, be careful not to step into the spaces between the joists, for you can damage the ceiling material nailed to the underside of the joists. Place a wide board so that the ends are supported by the joists and use it to stand and kneel on.

If the joists are covered with flooring, life is not so easy. You'll have to rip up one piece of flooring to see how much, if any, insulation you have. And if you decide to add more, you'll have to rip up a good many more boards so the batts can be slipped into place. If ripping up most of the attic flooring and then putting it back down after the insulation is in place doesn't appeal to you, you can have an insulating firm come over and blow insulation in between the joists without the need to remove the flooring except for a few boards here and there. This will cost a good deal more than if you do the job yourself, but if you have no attic insulation or only 2 or 3 inches, you'll probably pay for the cost in fuel savings in a relatively short time.

You can also insulate an attic by applying the insulation between the roof rafters. This is a good approach if you are going to finish off the attic into a room or rooms. But it is not a wise way to handle matters if you are going to use the attic just for storage, for it will mean that you will be heating all that space below the insulation.

FLOOR INSULATION. The underside of any floor that is above unheated space, such as basement crawl space or the underside of a winterized porch, needs 6 inches of mineral wool or insulation with an R-19 value.

Applying insulation to the underside of a floor is often a very dismal job. If you are lucky, you'll have enough room to kneel, but usually it means having to lie on your back because there isn't even enough headroom to kneel.

Use roll or blanket-type insulation for this job. This comes with a stapling flange so you can secure it to the sides of the joists with a heavy-duty staple gun you can borrow or rent from your dealer. If you are adding to existing insulation, be sure to use the kind of insulation *without* a vapor barrier, but if you are making an initial installation, use the kind with a vapor barrier and, in this type of installation, be sure that the vapor barrier faces *up* against the underside of the flooring of the room above. Many workmen install insulation on the underside of floors with the vapor barrier facing down because it's easier to install this way. If you find that your insulation has been installed in this manner, have it all removed and put in correctly—even if it means having to do the job yourself. If you leave it as it is, you may have a serious moisture condition that can cause the floor to warp or buckle.

WALL INSULATION. You can tell if the outside walls of your house are insulated by running the palm of your hand over the inside surfaces in cold weather. If the wall feels cold, it probably is not

WATERPROOFING INSULATION

FURRING STRIPS

Condensation of moisture on basement walls can be corrected by insulating the walls.

insulated. There is only one way that existing walls can be insulated, and that is to have a firm come in and blow insulation into the wall cavity.

It can also pay to insulate the basement walls—at least down to the local frost line. Two inches of mineral wool on these walls will reduce heat loss in the basement by more than half.

While you are in the insulating mood, be sure that all heating ducts which run through any unheated area such as basement or attic crawl space are fully insulated. Old standards called for 2 inches of mineral wool but today you should have a 4-inch-thick layer. Mineral-wool batts are good for ducts; you just wrap the stuff around the ducts and secure it with strips of wire.

IS IT WORTH THE COST?

Buying storm windows and adding insulation—even if you install it yourself—is going to cost a good many hundreds of dollars.

The question you will naturally ask is whether you'll save enough in heating energy to get back your investment in a reasonable number of years. And this depends on where you live, how much you are paying for energy, how well your house is presently winterized and how much it will cost to fully winterize it. There is a U.S. Government booklet which you'll find most useful in helping you decide how much and where to invest in energy-saving measures, how much it will cost to make these improvements and how much you can expect to save. It is called "Making the Most of Your Energy Dollars in Home Heating & Cooling." It costs 70 cents and you can get a copy from the Superintendent of Documents, Government Printing Office, Washington, D.C. 20402.

MAINTAIN YOUR HEATING SYSTEM

A poorly maintained heating system can waste a lot of energy. It's often possible to cut the cost of heating your house by 40 percent just by getting the system to operate at peak efficiency.

RADIATORS, REGISTERS AND BASEBOARD UNITS. Keep furniture and draperies clear of these units, for they will block the free flow of air and reduce heat output.

Even a thin coating of dust on a radiator or baseboard unit acts as insulation and wastes heat. It also can give off an unpleasant odor. Dust and vacuum these surfaces frequently, and don't forget radiators under enclosures.

Metallic paints such as aluminum or bronze will reduce the heat output of a radiator, thereby wasting heat. You don't have to remove the metallic paint to restore the efficiency; just apply a coat of radiator paint or enamel over the metallic paint.

Heat output of hot-water radiators or baseboard units will be reduced if they contain air, preventing them from being completely filled with hot water. Bleed off the air by opening the air valve on the unit as water is added to the boiler.

Steam radiators, too, will fail to heat properly if the air valve is not working. Replace faulty valves with new ones.

The heat output from a radiator next to a cold wall can be

increased if a sheet of aluminum or even aluminum foil is fastened to the wall in back of the radiator to reflect heat back.

THERMOSTATS. The thermostat is the "brain" of every modern heating system, and if it is not working properly, the heating system cannot run efficiently. The next time your heating serviceman is at your place, have him check out the thermostat. If it is over six years old it may have to be replaced. Make sure that the thermostat is in the right location and have it moved if it is not. It should not be placed on a cold wall or where it will be subject to cold drafts. Either of these can make the thermostat demand heat when it isn't really required, and this will cost you money. You also don't want it located where it might receive heat from other sources, such as the fireplace, TV set, wall lamp, etc.

OIL BURNERS. These should be inspected, adjusted and cleaned at least once a year—generally just before the start of the heating season. An improperly adjusted oil burner operating at only 50 percent efficiency can be wasting almost 40 percent of all the oil it consumes. You want your oil burner to have an efficiency of around 75 percent, which is considered good. You need a qualified man to service a burner. Most fuel-oil delivery firms have men with the necessary experience.

The serviceman should make a draft test to make sure that there is good combustion and that you are not losing too much heat up the chimney. He will also make a smoke test to determine if the burner is properly adjusted so all the fuel is being cleanly burned. One of the most important tests he should make is the CO_2 test, which helps him determine how to adjust the burner so it isn't using too much air. And finally he should make a stack-temperature test to measure the amount of heat going up the chimney. After he has made these tests he can then make the necessary adjustments to achieve proper efficiency of the burner. If you have an old burner that can't be adjusted to provide reasonable efficiency, you might consider getting a new one. This will cost several hundred dollars, but it may pay for itself in a single heating season on the money it will save you in fuel.

The serviceman should also give the interior heating elements of the boiler or furnace a good cleaning with a vacuum. A 1/50-inch coating of soot on these surfaces can reduce heating efficiency by as much as 50 percent.

GAS BURNERS. These are less complex than oil burners, but they should be inspected and adjusted, if necessary, every couple of years. You can generally see for yourself if the burner is properly adjusted, for if it is the flame will be blue with just a touch of yellow or orange. Your gas utility can usually send a man over to inspect and adjust the burner.

FORCED-WARM-AIR HEATING SYSTEMS. The air filters on these must be cleaned or replaced when they become dirty. If they are not, the flow of heat to the room registers will be restricted, and it is even possible that the furnace will become overheated and be seriously damaged. How often a filter must be either cleaned or replaced depends on the amount of dust and lint in the house. If there is a lot of it, or if you have a long-haired pet, it may be necessary to at least inspect the filter every month or so. You can tell when a filter is too dirty by holding it up to the light. If you can't see light through it, it's time to clean or replace it. There is usually some indication on each filter as to whether it can be cleaned by vacuuming or must be replaced when dirty. And if you don't know how to find the filter, check your instruction booklet or ask your serviceman to show you where it is and how to take it out.

BALANCING THE FORCED-AIR SYSTEM. The overall efficiency of a forced-warm-air system will be improved if it is properly balanced so that you get an even flow of heat to all the registers in the house and not a great blast to those close to the furnace and little, if any, to those some distance away from the source of heat. Your heating serviceman can balance the system for you, but you can do it yourself by a trial-and-error method. You'll find dampers installed in the ducts that run from the furnace to the room registers. The dampers are usually set in the ducts close to where they come off the furnace. By opening or closing these dampers you can regulate the flow of warm air to the various room registers. Do this job when the furnace is operating and have someone stand near the register you're trying to control so they can yell when there is just the right amount of air coming through.

Continuous Air Circulation for the Forced-air System. This is called CAC and it means that the furnace is set so that the blower operates all or most of the time even when the thermostat is not demanding heat. Most heating experts agree that while this method of operation will increase your electric bill somewhat because the blower motor is running, the cost of electricity is more than offset by the fuel saved by improved efficiency of the furnace. CAC will also eliminate many of the problems you may be having with your system, such as hot or cold pockets of air in certain rooms.

Many furnaces have a switch on them so you can set them to a "continuous" or "automatic" setting. Your serviceman or furnace dealer can adjust the equipment for CAC if there is no such switch.

Hot-water Systems. As already explained, you waste money on these if any of the radiators contain air, which prevents them from being completely filled with water. You can tell when the unit contains air because only a portion of it will be warm to the touch. The way to remove the air is to open the little air valve at one end of the radiator with a screwdriver or radiator key. Have a small pail handy and hold it under the valve until water begins to flow out, which indicates that all the air inside has been replaced with water. Close the valve immediately. You usually have to bleed a radiator at the start of each heating season, and it may be necessary to repeat this process every few months. Each time water is added to the boiler, a certain amount of air will be released into the system.

Some of the newer radiator valves are automatic and will bleed off the air without having to be opened manually.

Balancing the Hot-water System. A hot-water system needs to be properly balanced so that all radiators receive heat at about the same time. Balancing the system is done by opening or closing valves located in the pipes near the boiler. You can do this yourself using the same trial-and-error approach as suggested for forced-air heat systems, or have it done by a plumber.

STEAM SYSTEMS. You'll find a little air valve on each radiator. The valve is designed so that it opens when steam begins to come up to allow the air inside the radiator to escape. When steam fills the radiator and strikes the air valve, the valve closes so the steam can't escape. If the air valve is stuck, it won't allow air to escape, so the radiator won't fill with steam and will be cold. You should replace the air valve; you can get new ones at most hardware and plumbing-supply stores. The best kind of valve to buy is the adjustable type which can be set so the system can be balanced, allowing steam to reach the distant radiators before it gets to those close to the thermostat.

18

USING AN EFFICIENT FIREPLACE

A FIREPLACE may not be the most necessary piece of equipment in the house, but most of us find the special warmth and cheer it provides worth the fuss and bother. And today many families are turning to their fireplace as an auxiliary source of heat, as they have when a winter storm caused a power failure.

DON'T LET YOUR FIREPLACE WASTE HEAT

Many fireplaces waste more heat than they produce. If the damper is not closed when there is no fire, heated air inside the house will flow up the chimney. The typical chimney flue is 10 by 12 inches, so this can mean a lot of wasted heat. If there is a fire burning when you go to bed so that the damper cannot be closed, either put a sheet of aluminum or asbestos board over the fireplace opening or install a glass fire screen which can be closed when you go to bed. If you don't make one of these provisions, heat from inside the house will flow up the chimney until the damper is closed in the morning. And someone may forget to close it, which means heat will be wasted all day long.

Even when a fire is burning it can waste more heat than it

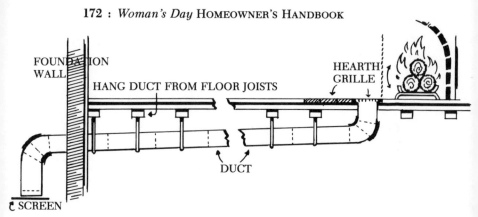

A fireplace won't waste much heat if it is fed with air brought in from the outside rather than using the warm house air.

produces, because a fire needs a lot of air to keep burning. It generally uses the air in the house. And as it pulls the air out of the house it creates a slight suction which draws cold air into the house through minute cracks around windows and doors. An excellent way to eliminate this problem is to bring in air from the outside to feed the fire. This can be done quite easily in most houses. A register is installed in the floor in front of the fireplace and then is connected by metal or asbestos ducts that run to an opening cut in the outside walls or foundations. The ducts should have a slight downward pitch so that moisture will drain out, and the register should be the type that can be closed so there won't be a cold draft of air coming in when there is no fire. With this arrangement, you won't be using the warm air inside the house to feed the fire and you'll also eliminate the cold drafts of air when you stand or sit near the fireplace.

HOW TO INCREASE EFFICIENCY

The average fireplace is pretty inefficient as far as the amount of heat it produces from the fuel it burns. A properly adjusted gas or oil burner is around 75 percent efficient. Electric heat is 100 percent efficient. A fireplace is about 15 percent efficient. That's not very good if you are paying $50 or more per cord for wood.

There are several ways you can increase the efficiency of your fireplace to get more heat from the fuel it burns. One good method is to install one of the several types of heat circulators. These units are made of metal tubing and are set inside the fireplace. Air from the room is drawn into the tubing, where it becomes heated and then is discharged back into the room. Some of these air circulators are designed to take the place of the andirons or grate, while others can be suspended inside the fireplace opening directly above the fire. The cost of these units ranges from around $50 up.

Some homeowners have made or have had made their own air circulators out of a series of 1-inch iron pipes bent into the shape of a C.

Another way to get more heat is to line the rear of the firepit with a sheet of steel or cast iron.

The very best way to make a drastic improvement in fireplace efficiency is to install a stove in it or directly in front of it.

Stoves are many times more efficient than fireplaces. They can be used to burn coal and short lengths of wood not suitable for a fireplace.

There are many different types of stoves suitable for use with a fireplace. The most familiar one is the Franklin stove, and this is still hard to beat for efficiency and looks. But there are several other types which the manufacturers claim are even more practical and more efficient than Dr. Franklin's invention. You'll find stoves at local stores that handle fireplace equipment and stoves.

FUELS FOR FIREPLACES AND STOVES

Hardwood—oak, maple, hickory, etc.—that has seasoned for nine months is the best fuel for fireplaces and is also good for stoves. Well-seasoned hardwood burns briskly, and gives off a lot of heat with little smoke. Green hardwood and all softwoods such as pine and fir do not make good wood for fuel. They give off a lot of smoke, burn too quickly and don't give off much heat.

Commercially sold firewood comes in several lengths up to 24 inches long. You should use logs that are about 4 inches shorter than the width of the rear of the firebox. Wood for a stove must not be so long that it cannot be placed horizontally in the firebox.

The least expensive way to buy firewood is by the cord. A cord is 8 feet long, 4 feet high and 4 feet wide. A cord of well-seasoned hardwood can cost from $35 to as high as $100 depending on the location and availability. If you buy a cord, or a fraction of a cord, be sure that you are getting what you are paying for—the correct amount of well-seasoned hardwood with no decayed logs, no softwood and no logs under 3 inches in diameter.

You'll save some money by getting your wood supply in early before demand pushes up the price. You can also save by buying green wood far enough in advance so it will be seasoned by the time you are ready to use it—six to nine months. You can also save if you buy your wood in 8-foot lengths and cut it yourself to size for your fireplace. All you need is a sturdy sawhorse, a good saw —hand or chain—and a little muscle.

It's sometimes possible to get firewood for little or nothing by taking down marked trees in state parks or on privately owned tracts of standing timber. Check with your county agent to see if there are such sources in your vicinity.

It's best not to store a large quantity of firewood indoors because. it can bring in wood-boring insects and also becomes so dry that it will burn very quickly. Keep a few days' supply indoors, but leave the balance outdoors, covered to protect it from rain and snow.

There are, of course, other fuels you can use in fireplaces and stoves. Among these are artificial logs made of pressed wood chips or sawdust. These are sold at supermarkets, hardware stores and garden-supply centers. Many are made so they don't require any paper or kindling wood to start the fire—just light the paper covering on the "log." Compared to cordwood, these are expensive, but they are convenient for an occasional fire or for those who live in apartments or in houses where there is no room to store a large amount of firewood.

Charcoal, as any outdoor cook knows, makes a good hot fire, but it's expensive. It's the best fuel to use if you want to cook directly over an open fire in the fireplace, but *never use charcoal in an unvented device* such as an outdoor grill or hibachi unless you put it in the fireplace. Charcoal, by the way, is good for starting a cold fire in a fireplace or a stove.

Cannel coal is a relatively soft coal that comes in large chunks that can be broken up if necessary. It is sold by the bag. It can be burned in a fireplace in a grate. It produces a very hot fire and a cheerful one, but it also makes a lot of smoke and soot.

Hard coal is ideal for a stove; once you get the hang of it you can keep the fire burning overnight. It's not a very satisfactory fuel for a fireplace.

Cannel coal and hard coal are not always locally available, and many communities restrict their use because they do cause air pollution.

Newspapers and magazines can also be rolled up and used as fuel for a fireplace. There are several devices on the market designed to help you turn out these paper logs at a pretty fair clip.

SMOKING AND OTHER FIREPLACE PROBLEMS

There are many reasons why a fire will smoke or burn improperly. Sometimes it's the fault of the fire tender, and sometimes it's the fault of the installation or construction. But if you can find the cause of the problem, chances are it can be corrected.

A fire must have a good draft to carry the smoke up the chimney and to pull in air so that the fuel will burn. To have a good draft you must have a hot fire. A smoldering fire or one made of green or wet logs is almost sure to smoke. Also be sure that there is enough air in the room. If you close off the room in which the fire is burning, the supply of air will soon be exhausted as far as the fire is concerned. Keep doors to other parts of the house open to ensure plenty of air.

Every fireplace has, or should have, a damper, and if this is closed or only partially opened, the fire is going to fill the house with smoke. Before you light the fire, always check to make sure the damper is wide open. After the fire has been going a time and is burning briskly you can try closing down the damper a little to slow down the blaze, but have it wide open when you start the fire.

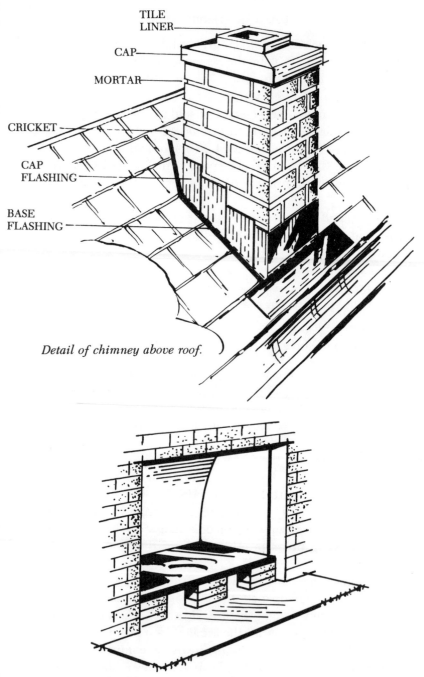

TILE LINER

CAP

MORTAR

CRICKET

CAP FLASHING

BASE FLASHING

Detail of chimney above roof.

Raising the hearth can be one way to correct a poorly designed fireplace that smokes or fails to burn properly.

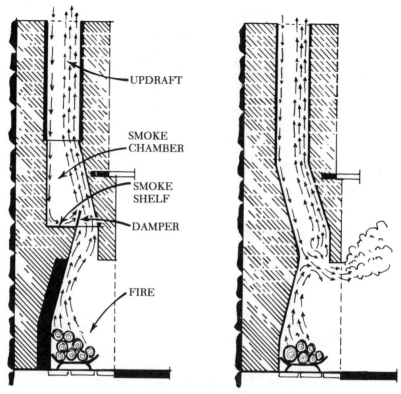

Improperly built fireplace at right has no smoke shelf to prevent downdrafts.

Smoking may also be caused by a downdraft, which usually involves the chimney. The opening at the top of the chimney should be at least 2 feet higher than the highest point on the roof. If it isn't, the roof can create a downdraft that blows smoke into the room. The solution is to extend the top of the chimney. A downdraft can also be caused by a tree branch too close to the top of the chimney or even by a chimney-mounted television antenna.

Fireplaces will also smoke if they were not built to the correct proportions so that the fireplace opening is too large for the size flue. There are several ways to reduce the size of the opening. If the height of the opening is too great, this can be corrected by installing a metal hood the length of the opening. If the opening

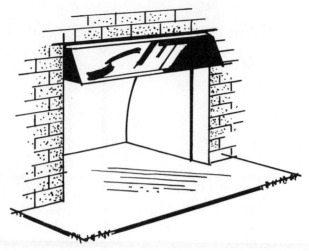

Installing a metal hood is another way to correct a smoking fireplace.

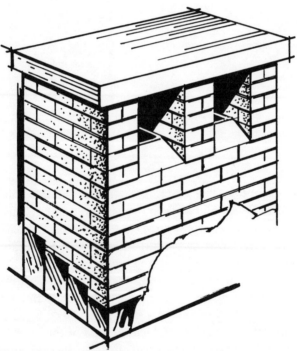

A properly designed chimney cap can eliminate downdrafts that cause smoking.

is too wide, firebrick can be laid up along each wall to decrease the width. This job should be done by an expert—a mason who really knows fireplaces—and only after he has made tests using sheet metal to check out his solution to the problem before putting in the permanent masonry.

CHIMNEY FIRES AND CHIMNEY CLEANING

A chimney will catch fire if the flue becomes heavily coated with carbon contained in the soot, and the fire in the fireplace is hot enough to ignite the carbon. If this occurs, sparks and even flame may pour out of the top of the chimney. If the chimney is well constructed and in good condition, a chimney fire, while spectacular, is not dangerous except that the sparks coming out the top could ignite a combustible dry roof, or dry brush adjoining the house.

Chimney fires seldom occur when well-seasoned hardwood is burned, for this produces little soot. They are more likely to occur when soot producers such as soft coal and green or softwoods are burned.

If you do have a chimney fire, call the fire department just to play safe. While you are waiting for them, toss a heavy dose of baking soda or salt on the fire. This will slow down the fire. And if the weather has been dry, you can get out the garden hose and wet down the roof and nearby brush and vegetation.

It is smart to inspect a chimney flue once a year, and if there are heavy accumulations of soot inside, to clean or have it cleaned. You can inspect the flue on a bright day by looking up it with a mirror, or go on the roof and look down with the aid of a flashlight. If there are large deposits of soot clinging to the sides of the flue, better get rid of them. Professional chimney cleaners charge around $50 to do this job. You can do it yourself if you don't mind dirty work and climbing around on the roof.

To clean a chimney by hand, open the damper of the fireplace and seal the front opening with plastic and masking tape so that the soot and dirt falling down won't get all over the house. One way to clean is to put a few stones or bricks in a burlap bag and then fill the bag with excelsior. Tie a rope to the top of the bag and let it down the flue and then pull it up. Repeat this a few times and you will loosen all the soot so it falls down into the fireplace opening, where you can then shovel it out or push it down into the ash pit.

If your chimney has a cap on it so that you can't get a bag down the flue from the top, use an old tire chain. Tie a rope to the chain and lower it down and rattle the chain around to loosen the soot. Don't rattle too hard or you may crack the clay flue pipe.

BUILDING A FIRE

You must have a fire starter to get a decent fire to burn. Odds and ends of dry softwood make good kindling to start a fire, and so do empty milk cartons, for they contain a lot of wax which produces a very hot fire. The Cape Cod lighter, solid petroleum starter cubes and the propane and electric fire starters are all good and do away with both kindling and paper to start a fire.

Never use a liquid charcoal fire starter or any other flammable liquid such as gasoline, kerosene or paint thinner to start a fire in either a fireplace or a stove.

If you are using kindling wood, put a couple of sheets of crumpled newspaper on the hearth between the andirons or on the bottom of the grate. Lay a few pieces of dry kindling criss-cross over the paper.

It takes three logs to build a fire and keep it going. Set the largest log of the three you have over the kindling at the rear, leaving about ½ inch of space between it and the back of the fireplace. Put the second log next to the first and leave a space of about 2 inches between them. Now add the third log. Some experts set this log right on top and between the other two logs so they form a pyramid; others prefer to set the third log at an angle across the bottom two logs. Use either method you prefer.

Once the fire is laid, check to make sure that the damper is wide open. Fires are likely to smoke when first lighted, and the way to avoid this is to warm up the air in the flue so there is a good draft.

To do this, put a piece of crumpled newspaper over the top of the logs or push it up into the fireplace throat and light it. When the paper begins to burn down, light the paper under the kindling. A fire starter—Cape Cod lighter, electric or propane starter or the fire starter cubes—eliminates the need for both paper and kindling, but it's still wise to warm up the draft with a piece of crumpled newspaper so that there won't be any smoke when the logs first begin to burn.

A fire screen cuts down on the amount of air reaching a fire, so don't put the screen up until the logs begin to catch fire. But stay close at hand in case the kindling begins to shoot out sparks. Once the fire gets going, replace the screen and keep it there at all times there is a fire.

If your kindling burns out and your logs don't ignite, add more crumpled newspapers and kindling under the logs.

Once the logs are blazing briskly you can control the rate of the fire by adjusting the damper. If the damper doesn't have a handle so it can be adjusted from the outside, use a poker.

When fireplace logs are still burning and you don't need the fire, use the tongs to stand the logs up on end at the rear corner of the firebox. The logs will soon go out and they'll be ready for a fire on another day.

ADDING A FIREPLACE

If you don't have a fireplace or a stove, you don't have to feel left out in the cold. You can acquire a fireplace for less than $200, plus the cost of a prefabricated chimney and the labor—your own or a professional's—to install it. The price can go up to $4,000 for a masonry fireplace built into a house wall, but there are many options in between, including efficient and decorative stoves for under $200.

There are three basic types of fireplaces. The built-from-scratch masonry one is expensive. The other two—the factory-built metal fireplace that you wall in and the free-standing or wall-hung metal fireplace that you just connect to a chimney—are economical and practical to install, even for the do-it-yourselfer.

A masonry fireplace is built traditionally of brick or stone but can also be constructed of concrete block. It must be erected on a substantial foundation, so if one is added to an existing house the only practical spot for it is on an outside wall on the first floor. Of course, if you are building a house or putting on a family room and want to include a fireplace it can be set either on an outside or an inside wall.

Masonry fireplaces can be built in many shapes—traditional front-opening, two-sided (one side and the front open), curved to fit into a corner and even open on all four sides. But if you want a fireplace that will produce the greatest amount of heat, stick with the style with a single opening at the front.

The cost of a masonry fireplace depends on the size, shape and materials. A front-opening brick fireplace costs between $1,200 and $1,800; in stone it costs $4,000 or more.

Almost any mason can build a fireplace; not all of them can build one that will work properly and not fill the room with smoke each time you light a fire. You can find masons that specialize in fireplaces under this heading in the Yellow Pages. Ask the mason you contact to give you references, and take the trouble to check them out.

A good mason with a helper can build an average fireplace in about three days.

Factory-built fireplace units to enclose in a wall are made of steel and contain all the basic elements of a masonry fireplace—firebox, throat, damper, smoke shelf and smoke chamber. Some of these units must be covered with a veneer of masonry, but others don't need it unless you wish to add it for appearance instead of other kinds of wall facing such as plaster or gypsum wallboard.

The great advantage to these fireplaces is that they are carefully proportioned so there is no chance of smoking or not burning correctly if they are properly installed according to the directions. And they are great for families who want to put in their fireplaces themselves.

Another advantage to the units that do not need masonry is that you can install them practically anywhere in an existing house if you use a metal prefab chimney. These units don't require any foundation and can be set directly on any solid subfloor. They can be placed safely on an inside wall, used in the center of a room, built into a wall or installed on an upper floor. The only consideration in determining the location is that there be a practical way to get the prefab chimney to the roof without having to go right through the middle of someone's bedroom or the bath.

The prefab chimney is made with double or triple walls of sheet metal with insulation between, which allows the chimney to be set safely as close as 2 inches from combustible materials. It is so lightweight it can be suspended from the house framing or secured to an outside wall with metal brackets. The chimney comes in a complete package with everything needed for installation and takes only a matter of hours to assemble. The cost is less than half that of a masonry chimney.

The circulating-warm-air fireplace is a special kind of factory-built unit with an air space between the outside and inside shell of the firebox that allows warm air to circulate when a fire is burning. Cold air enters through two openings at the base, is warmed and then flows out through two openings at the top. This warm air can be discharged into the fireplace room, or the outlets can be connected to ducts to carry the warm air to other areas of the house. This type of fireplace is popular in vacation houses to warm one or several rooms during cold weather and is useful also in year-round residences when the central heating system is not in operation or additional heat is needed.

Factory-built fireplaces are often sold as a complete package that includes the metal prefab chimney and all other elements required for installation (masonry or other material to enclose the fireplace would be extra). Prices for a package start at around $350 and run to about $600. Where one of these units is to be enclosed in masonry and connected to a masonry chimney, the final cost—unless you do all the masonry yourself—will be about the same as for a standard masonry fireplace, $1,200 or more.

Free-standing and wall-hung metal fireplaces are complete ready-made fireplaces with a porcelain finish in colors such as gold, green, red, copper, black, and white. The units are constructed of two layers of steel with insulation between the two surfaces so that the outside surface does not get too hot.

These colorful fireplaces will burn logs—some models will take logs up to 27 inches long—cannel coal or even hard coal. As they weigh only about 150 pounds they can be set almost anywhere in the house. They are often sold as a package with a metal chimney, and the average price is around $400. They can be assembled all ready for a fire in a matter of a few hours.

STOVES

Stoves are much more efficient heat-producers than any fireplace, so if heat is more important than atmosphere and you want to get the most heat from your wood or coal, get a stove. One family with an electrically heated house installed two wood-burning stoves and cut the cost of heating their home by two-thirds.

There are a lot of different styles of stoves to choose from. There is the Franklin stove mentioned earlier that is a combination of metal fireplace and stove and puts out a lot of heat. It can be set in front of the fireplace and connected into the fireplace flue, or can be placed somewhere else with its own metal prefab chimney.

There are other types of stoves designed to fit right inside the fireplace firebox.

Then there is the parlor stove in many designs; this is the one that was popular in the days before central heating. Many of today's models are of the same design that made a big hit with our great-grandparents. These cost around $270. The potbelly stove, also called the cannonball, is a truly utilitarian stove—simple and functional—and in its day it heated many a house, general store and railroad station. These cost around $180.

Many stoves that have been popular in Norway are being imported and sold in this country. As the Norwegians depend on stoves to heat their homes, these stoves are somewhat more efficient than many U.S.-made stoves; they produce more heat for the same amount of fuel. These stoves range in price from $200 to $500.

Every stove needs a noncombustible hearth; this can be of metal, sand, pebbles or brick surrounded by a wood frame.

19

KEEPING A COOL HOUSE WITH LESS ENERGY

IF YOU don't have central air conditioning, you'll definitely want to do all you can to make the house as cool as possible in hot weather and at little cost. If you have air conditioning, you'll probably be interested in taking steps to reduce operating costs to a minimum. Fortunately, most of the steps you take to make the house cooler will also reduce those monthly bills to operate the air-conditioning equipment.

There are three basic steps you can take to make the house cooler and less expensive to cool. First, keep the heat outside from getting into the house. Next, reduce the amount of heat generated in the house. Finally, remove the heat from the house.

KEEP HEAT OUT OF THE HOUSE

Keeping heat out has a high priority because it's the radiant heat from the sun that drives indoor temperatures up. The important thing here is insulation. If the walls and especially the roof are adequately insulated, the heat gain (the amount of heat that gets into the house) may be reduced by about 50 percent. It may be too complicated or too expensive to insulate the outside walls, but the attic floor or the underside of the roof is another matter. A tremendous amount of heat gets into the house through the roof, and this is a relatively easy area in which to install insulation, even for the do-it-yourselfer. So is the attic floor or crawl space if the joists are exposed. For the roof or the attic floor you need at least 6 inches of mineral wool or some other form of insulation with a value of R-19 (R-values are explained in Chapter 17). If you already have insulation and it's not at least 6 inches thick—and it usually isn't—you can add more. The extra insulation is also going to make the house more comfortable in cold weather and cut down your fuel bills. The area above the insulation should be vented at each end with louvers so that the air between the insulation and the roof can flow out as it becomes warmer than the outside air and not just sit there getting hotter and hotter as the hours go by.

The air temperature in the attic often gets above 140 degrees, and even with insulation some of this heat will seep down into the house. You can remove this superheated air with an attic exhaust fan. A good type to buy is a model with a thermostat that will turn the fan on when the attic temperature gets around 100 degrees and will turn it off when the attic air temperature gets down to 90 degrees.

By the way, dark roofs and dark siding absorb heat, whereas white and light colors reflect it away from the house. If you have a dark roof or a dark paint job and you plan to reroof or repaint, consider white, the light grays or pastels. A white roof absorbs only about half as much solar heat as a black roof.

WINDOWS AND GLASS AREAS. These allow a great deal of heat to enter the house, especially those that face east, west and south. Standard window glass won't keep heat out, and even insulating glass, which prevents heat loss in winter, won't keep out the sun's rays, which change to heat once inside the house. There are various ways to stop the rays from getting in, such as:

• Awnings can reduce solar heat gain by up to 80 percent. Light-colored awnings, because they reflect heat, are more effective than dark-colored ones, which tend to absorb heat. It's best

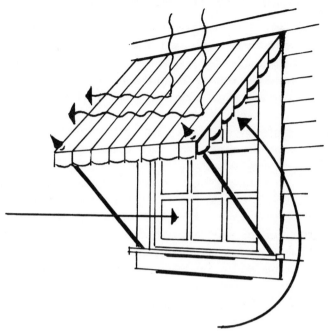

Awnings will keep sun away from windows.

not to use the type of awning that has side panels because these trap air under the awning and build up heat, which will be absorbed by the window glass. Open awnings, however, should extend far enough on each side of the window or door to compensate for loss of shade from the side panels and to protect the lower part of the glass area against the early-morning and late-afternoon sun.

• Window shades can reduce heat gain by 35 percent or more if properly fitted and pulled down (or up if mounted from the bottom) before the sun gets to the window. Room-darkening shades, especially if white on the outside, reflect more heat than translucent shades, but because they also shut out light completely, they are not practical in living areas during the day. Translucent shades come in many distinctive colors and textures and, depending on weight, can be helpful in cutting glare and reducing heat gain. Any window shade is better than none.

Several new types of thermal window shades are designed to

reflect heat away from the glass. One such shade has an open weave that allows air and light but not heat to enter. You can look out through these shades, but no one can see inside during the day. Primarily designed to reduce the operating cost of air conditioning, thermal window shades are also excellent without air conditioning.

When using window shades as room coolers, pull the shades on the east and south windows the first thing in the morning before the sun has a chance to heat up the rooms. When the sun is high enough so it can't shine in the windows, lift these shades and pull those on the west side of the house. An afternoon sun can be very hot, so get the shades down before it starts pouring in and keep them down until the sun gets below the horizon. If you have thermal window shades, you can keep the shades pulled all the time, because the light filters through, giving a pleasant cooling effect.

• Blinds will also help keep the house cool. Use either horizontal or vertical blinds. The outside of the blinds should be white or light-colored. Adjust blinds at intervals during the day to allow for maximum ventilation and minimum sun.

• Sun-control film is a relatively new but effective way to handle solar heat gain through glass. This thin plastic film has a reflective coating that permits light to come through but reflects back about half the solar heat. You can apply it yourself to any size glass area. It is available at some hardware stores and from most plate-glass firms.

• Storm windows should be left on windows that are not needed for ventilation. Storm windows and insulating glass won't keep out the sun's rays, but they will keep heated outside air out of the house, and this can be a big help.

Sliding glass doors can be something of a problem because of their size and because the opening shouldn't be blocked. Coating the glass with sun-control film is probably the most convenient solution. If the doors open onto a terrace, you might want to install some sort of eggcrate or lattice roof that will provide shade for the terrace and keep the sun's rays from bouncing off the terrace and through the glass doors. Room-darkening or thermal shades are good for sliding glass doors, but don't try to cover the entire unit with one shade, because such a large shade not only is awkward to raise and lower but allows a lot of heat to get inside each time it is raised. Use several shades, arranged so that it is necessary to raise only the one covering the door.

KEEPING HEAT AWAY FROM THE HOUSE. Some heat from the sun hits the house directly, and some is reflected onto the house by surrounding surfaces. The ideal solution to both problems is a nice big deciduous shade tree, such as a maple or an oak, and a stretch of lawn. The tree will shade a good portion of the house in summer, and after the leaves fall, will allow the sun to reach the house. And grass will not absorb or reflect much heat (the same is true of other live ground covers, such as myrtle or pachysandra). During the day when the air temperature is, say, around 80 degrees, grass will be about the same, but a section of blacktop will be around 120 degrees. After the sun goes down, the grass will cool

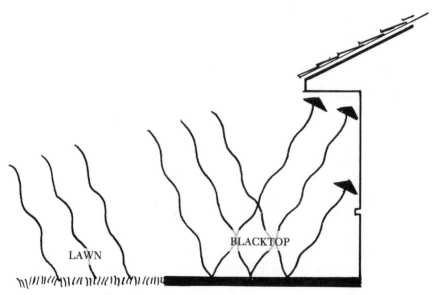

Grass remains relatively cool in hot weather and does not reflect heat into the house as blacktop will.

off very rapidly, but not the blacktop, which will remain hot for hours and hours.

Since we're not always fortunate enough to have a nice shade tree, a good substitute is a louvered fence that won't block off any breeze heading toward the house. A row of tall shrubs is also good for shading. Keep the shading devices as far away from the house as practical so they won't block off movement of air around the windows.

DON'T MAKE HEAT

Not all the heat in the house comes from the hot sun and outside air. A lot of it is generated right inside the home. There are many ways you can reduce this home-generated heat.

• Turn off any energy-using equipment when it is not in use. This includes the television, radio, record player and even electric lights. If you have ever touched even a 25-watt light bulb after it's been burning awhile, you know how hot it can become.

• Go easy on hot water. Drawing quantities of hot water produces a chain reaction—the hot-water heater has to run more frequently, causing the pipes throughout the house to become warm, causing heat to escape into the house. Running hot water also produces uncomfortable humidity—a good reason to switch to cool or lukewarm showers and to use cold water in the washing machine.

• Prepare as many dishes as possible on small specialized electric appliances such as skillets, roasters, grills and waffle irons, for these generally produce less heat than the oven, broiler or surface cooking units of the range would in preparing the same dish.

• Plan meals ahead so that several dishes can be cooked in the oven at the same time. When the oven is in use, open the door as infrequently as possible.

• If you have a self-cleaning oven, wipe up oven spills before they harden so you won't have to use the self-cleaning feature more than occasionally.

• Whenever possible, put lids on saucepans. This reduces cooking time and steam, thus reducing humidity.

- When roasting or broiling, use your outdoor grill or barbecue as often as possible. You don't have to eat outdoors to cook outdoors.
- If you have a microwave oven, you can eliminate perhaps as much as 75 percent of the heat produced in cooking.
- Use your kitchen exhaust fan frequently to clear heat out quickly.
- A dishwasher produces a lot of heat, so try to use it just once a day and in the evening when the outside temperature is relatively low.

KEEP THE HUMIDITY DOWN. A lot of moisture in the air makes high indoor temperature more uncomfortable. You can avoid high indoor humidity in several ways.

- Keep moisture generated in the kitchen and bathroom out of other areas by closing doors and turning on the exhaust fan; even opening a window helps.
- Unless a clothes dryer is vented to the outdoors, it will pump heat and moisture into the house. If it's impractical to vent the dryer to the outside, hang wash outside. Sun-dried clothes smell wonderful.
- Mop floors only when absolutely necessary, using a damp, not wet mop.
- Try to do chores that produce heat and humidity during the coolest hours—early morning or late evening, when windows can be opened to dissipate heat and humidity. These are also good times for baths and showers.

NATURAL COOLING

If you operate the windows and shades correctly, you'll be able to keep your house more comfortable than if you do it on a hit-or-miss basis. In the very early morning the air inside the house is usually cooler than the outside air, so close and pull shades on east and south windows, because as the sun rises, this is where the heat is starting to build up. At midmorning or by noon the air inside the house will be about the same temperature as the outside air, so windows can be opened to catch any breeze that happens along and to allow any heat building up inside the house to escape.

FANS FOR COOLING

While not as effective as air conditioning, fans can make hot weather more comfortable. They are inexpensive to buy and to operate. For example, a 20-inch window fan costs around $40 and requires only 250 watts. A medium-size room air conditioner costs close to $200 and requires 1,000 watts.

• Circulating fans—floor, tabletop and pedestal types—cool by moving the air around you, so the rate of evaporation of moisture on the skin is increased. This makes you cooler.

• Exhaust fans mounted in windows also cool by circulating the air, but in addition, after the sun has gone down, they exhaust hot air out of the house and draw in the cool outside air. The 20-inch portable window fan is the most common type of exhaust fan. It can be mounted permanently in a window or set on the windowsill so it can be moved from room to room as required. Most of these fans have two or three speeds and can be reversed to exhaust air or draw it in. Some have thermostats or timers so they will go on and off automatically.

A 20-inch fan can cool several rooms if used properly. To do this, open all the windows after the sun has set and turn on the fan to exhaust. This will draw all the hot air toward that fan and out of the house. The last room to be cooled, however, will be the one where the fan is located, so try to place the fan in a room that is not in immediate use.

• Attic fans—usually larger than 20-inch—are used to exhaust air from the attic space, but they can also be used to cool the entire house. During the day the fan should be operated at short intervals to remove hot air from the attic. After the sun has set, turn the fan on and open windows on the first floor. Air at ground level cools first, and the fan will draw this cool air up through the house. When the family retires, close all windows but those in the bedrooms. Leave bedroom doors open. Have a timer on the fan so it will turn off automatically before dawn.

AIR CONDITIONERS

Everything you can do to keep heat out of the house and reduce heat and humidity generated in the house will help improve the efficiency of air conditioners—room or central—and reduce the cost of operating them.

Use awnings, window shades, draperies, sun-control film, etc. to reduce heat gain through glass areas.

Keep windows and doors closed when air-conditioning equipment is running. If you have storm windows, leave them up on windows that you don't need to use for ventilation.

Insulate the attic or underside of the roof if possible. You should have from 6 to 9 inches of mineral wool at the top of the house, depending on whether you live in a temperate or very hot climate. And be sure that there are windows or louvers above the insulation so that the hot air can escape outdoors. If the ventilation is poor, install an attic exhaust fan that will automatically go on when the air temperature gets above 90 degrees.

ROOM AIR CONDITIONERS. These should be installed so that there are no leaks between the unit and the window frame. If there are, seal them with caulking compound or caulking tape. Several other measures will improve efficiency:

• Change or clean the filters once a month.

• The best location for the unit is on the north or shady side of the house. If the air conditioner is exposed to direct sun, shade it with an awning, but don't allow the awning, plants, fences, etc. to obstruct the free flow of air around the outside cooling element.

• If there are wall or floor registers in the room, close them so the cold air won't flow down into the heating ducts.

• Adjust the air-conditioner grilles so the air flows upward. Keep furniture and draperies clear of the unit.

• Keep the air-exchange control closed so the machine won't draw in hot outside air.

• If the machine is large enough to cool several rooms, use a small fan to help circulate the air.

BUYING A ROOM AIR CONDITIONER. Make sure you get the right size. If the machine is too small for the space, it won't do a good job of cooling, but if it's too large, it won't remove the moisture from the air, creating a damp, uncomfortable room.

The safest way to get the right size is to fill out a cooling-need worksheet, available from most dealers. You write down on the worksheet all the factors that determine the capacity of the machine required—size of area, number and location of windows and doors, number of people normally using the room and so forth. From this information the dealer can tell you the best size unit for your needs.

Keep down operating costs by selecting a machine with the most efficient operation. Efficiency is determined by the number of Btu's (British thermal units) per watt-hour. The higher this figure is, the better. All units today have this figure printed on the outside of the machine. It is called EER for Energy Efficiency Ratio. Buy a machine with an EER of over 8.

CENTRAL AIR CONDITIONERS. The best way to reduce operating costs of central air conditioners is to turn up the thermostat. The setting suggested by most air-conditioning authorities is between 78 and 80 degrees. If you leave the house for a few days during the cooling season, don't turn the air conditioner off, because you'll use more energy trying to get the place comfortable when you return than you'll have saved. Set the thermostat at 80 and leave it there until your return. Other measures to increase efficiency include:

• Close off any room in the house that doesn't require cooling.

• If windows are to be opened to let fresh air into the house, close doors and shut all registers of rooms involved when the unit is running.

• Insulate cooling ducts that run through areas that don't re-

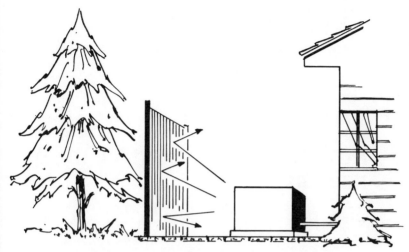

A solid fence will deflect noise from an outside air conditioner condenser from outdoor living areas. Shrubs and trees shade unit and reduce operating costs.

quire cooling, such as the attic crawl space. Four inches of mineral wool will be adequate for this purpose.

• Change the filters on the air conditioner when they become dirty. If you hold the filter up to the light and can't see light coming through it, it's time to replace or clean the filter.

• Remove garden debris from around the outside condenser, and be sure there are no plants or fences that block the free flow of air around this unit.

20
HOW TO AVOID EXPENSIVE HOME REPAIRS

YOU HARDLY need to be told that when something around the house needs fixing or an appliance breaks down, you can sometimes be in for a series of delays, disappointments and frustrations. Whether it's a color television that's gone psychedelic, a washing machine that won't wash or a garage door that refuses to budge, the man to fix it is sometimes awfully hard to pin down for an appointment, and when he finally does turn up, he may not be quite the craftsman you had hoped for. But craftsman or clown, he will undoubtedly present a bill that can be an unexpected and not too pleasant surprise.

How to beat the system? Here are some of the ways.

BEFORE YOU BUY

Because you are still in the driver's seat and can shop around with "quality service" high on the list of requirements, this is the optimum time to be concerned about future service, especially with those items that are likely to need repairs and adjustments from time to time. Check with friends and neighbors for the

196

names of dealers (preferably local) who have good reputations for servicing the equipment and products they sell. While there may be relatively small differences in cost and quality of the actual items themselves, there can be a wide difference in the quality of service. Some dealers, for example, have their own repair and service departments, which usually means prompt and efficient service. But others farm out repairs of the equipment they sell, and this can mean some long delays.

Most durable goods—appliances, oil burners, television sets as well as roofing, siding, etc.—come with a guarantee or warranty. Read these carefully before you buy, and if you have any questions, ask the dealer to explain the wording or the fine print. Remember, it is the *intent* of the manufacturer, distributor or dealer that gives the guarantee or warranty its true worth. Some of these documents may sound fine, but unless those responsible live up to them with promptness and efficiency, the words have no meaning. All warranties and guarantees should cover the equipment for a reasonable length of time; a 30-day or 60-day guarantee, for instance, is not of great value to the buyer, since an appliance is not apt to break down so quickly.

Check to see if labor, as well as parts, is included under the terms. It is the cost of labor that puts the high price tag on most repairs and services. The major cost of putting on a new roof is for labor, so the guarantee you may get from the manufacturer of the asphalt shingles is not worth much unless you also get a guarantee from the roofer that covers the actual installation of the shingles.

And if you do have a guarantee or warranty, use it. Read it over and be familiar with the terms so that you won't be charged for any adjustments or repairs that are covered under the terms of the agreement.

AFTER YOU BUY

If possible, have the dealer from whom you buy the equipment do the installation, because he is then responsible for its proper performance. If it doesn't work properly, he can't blame it on someone else's poor installation. If he does not do installation, ask him to recommend a firm.

Try to be on hand when the equipment is installed. If there are installation instructions, read them over and keep your eyes open to be sure that the men install the equipment in strict accordance with the manufacturer's instructions. Don't take their word that certain recommended steps can be omitted—call up the dealer or their boss and ask him.

Have the men who do the installation show you the correct method of operation. This also gives you the chance to see whether it is performing properly. Ask about proper maintenance. The more you know about the correct use and maintenance of a product, the less apt you are to have trouble later on. Be sure to get a copy of the manufacturer's instruction and maintenance guide. If none is available, get the necessary information from your dealer and write it down for future reference.

A good time to read the instruction guide is while the installation is going on. If you have questions or don't understand certain points, the men should be able to straighten you out. In any case, don't let them get away without checking out the equipment involved.

Don't make a final payment or sign a certificate of completion on anything until you are as certain as possible that it has been installed properly and is working correctly. If a new dishwasher doesn't run properly, if water seeps out around the base of a faucet on the new kitchen sink or if it takes two strong men to open the sliding glass door you've just put in the living room, age will not improve matters. Sad but true, there are many in this world who lose interest in their work or their merchandise after they have been paid in full. Take the time to inspect and check out each piece of work carefully.

Operate all equipment in strict accordance with the manufacturer's instructions. This advice may seem a little dated, but it's worth remembering because it's one of the best ways to avoid future troubles. Most mechanical and electrical equipment requires a certain amount of maintenance—cleaning and perhaps oiling with the right grade of oil. And if the equipment is not properly maintained, the chances of it going on the blink will be increased.

HOW TO SHOP FOR REPAIRS AND SERVICES

While you can reduce the need for service by careful buying and proper operation and maintenance of equipment, sooner or later you will need someone to fix something. The time to find the right person or people is before the need arises. Cost of repairs can often go up and quality down when you are faced with an emergency and have to grab the first outfit that pops out of the telephone book.

Anyone who lives in a house will sooner or later probably need a plumber, an electrician, a carpenter, an appliance repairman, and so forth. Line these people up before you need them. Get friends and neighbors or local storekeepers to recommend good men or concerns. If possible, use people within your area, because if someone has to drive clear across the county to get to your place, you'll be charged in one way or another for all that travel time. Your repairman is also more likely to drop over to make some minor repair or adjustment for you if he is fairly close.

If you have bought or are buying a used house, get the names of the people who have worked on it from the previous owner or the real estate broker. A plumber who is already familiar with a particular system is generally able to do a repair job faster and for less money than one who will have to spend time figuring out how the system was installed. Remember that his time is your money. If you are buying a new house, find out from the builder whom to contact for plumbing, heating and electrical work.

And once you get hold of a good service or repair firm or individual, don't switch. Let them know that you depend on them and that you recommend them to friends and neighbors. Don't try to save a dollar or two on certain work by calling in someone else. You may save a few dollars but you'll take the chance of spoiling your relationship with a good reliable outfit.

Many gas, electric and fuel-oil concerns have their own service departments. These are often very good and relatively inexpensive because the primary intent is not to make money out of service and repairs but to keep the customers happy with a particular type of energy—gas, electric or oil, whichever the case may be—and with the firm that supplies it.

In some communities there are home maintenance and repair organizations that you can join for a small annual fee. These will supply you with men to do various jobs, such as carpentry, plumbing, electrical work and painting. Some of these outfits are very good and can furnish you with screened, qualified men at a reasonable cost. If you would like to find out if there is one in your area, check with some local real estate brokers, for they often require services of this type for a client.

Service contracts are another way to reduce the cost of repairs. These are offered by many retail dealers as well as by gas, electric and fuel-oil companies. These contracts cover durable goods such as appliances and are similar to an insurance policy. You pay so much a year, and when something that is covered by the policy breaks down, the work is done at no extra charge to you. There are many types of service contracts. The least expensive might just cover yearly inspection and cleaning plus some minor adjustments. The more expensive contracts will cover labor and parts for almost anything that might go wrong.

GET AN ESTIMATE

Always get a firm estimate on what a repair or service job will cost before you give the go-ahead. A good repairman or repair center should, in most cases, be able to tell you what is wrong and how much it is going to cost to fix it. You may be better off in some instances if you buy new equipment rather than put a lot of money into repairs, but you should have an idea of the cost of repairs so that you can make an intelligent decision.

The rule of thumb is that if the cost of repairing is over 50 percent of the cost of a new item, you are probably better off to buy new rather than repair the old. But a lot depends on the age and relative cost of the equipment. It certainly does not make much sense to spend $20 to repair a 15-year-old toaster if you can buy a new one for $25, but it might be smart to spend $75 to repair a relatively new sewing machine if you were assured that it would be as good as new and might last as long as 24 years.

Each appliance has an approximate life span, and knowing the number of years of service you can expect from each item can help you decide whether it's worth fixing.

Item	Average years of service
Clothes dryer	14
Clothes washer	11
Freezer	15
Hot-water heater	10
Range	16
Refrigerator-freezer	16
Sewing machine	24
Toaster	15
Vacuum cleaner	15

You should insist on an estimate in *writing,* and it should cover the cost of labor as well as new parts. You'll also be smart to have the service firm sign a statement to the effect that if it turns out that the job will cost more than the estimate, you will be notified before the work is done so you can decide if you still want to go ahead. If you don't have this sort of protection, the repairs may turn out to be far more than the cost of a new piece of equipment, and you'll be stuck with a whopping bill.

Insist on getting a detailed bill that covers the cost of each new part installed as well as labor. And ask to have any of the old parts that the service firm claims to have replaced.

On any major home repairs or improvements, such as putting on a new roof, adding a bathroom, painting the house, etc., you should get two or three estimates before you settle on any one particular firm.

IF YOU HAVE A COMPLAINT

If you are not satisfied with the kind of service you get—if you believe you've been overcharged, that you've been charged for

unnecessary parts or if the equipment still does not run properly
—make a lot of noise. Call the service manager or the boss of the
shop. If this doesn't do the trick, go down and see them in person.
If you are dealing with an outfit that is the authorized service
agent for a particular brand, write to the president of the firm that
manufactures the equipment and send a copy of your letter to the
local service manager. Write or call your local Better Business
Bureau and your state department of consumer affairs and protection. Many local radio stations have consumer-complaint departments, and these can often help you get satisfaction on a com-
plaint.

DEALING WITH SERVICEMEN

Repairmen and servicemen get paid by the hour, so every minute they are at your place is costing you money. Do all you can to
make their visit as short as possible.

Be sure that there is someone at home who is familiar with the
problem when the serviceman arrives. You can't expect efficient
service if you leave the job of explaining the problem to someone
who is not familiar with the situation—the baby sitter, the cleaning
lady or the next-door neighbor.

Get out all the manufacturer's literature and have it on hand
when the serviceman arrives. This can save you a lot of money
because it may save him a lot of time.

Once the serviceman goes to work, leave him alone. Try to keep
the children out of his hair, because this can't help him to concen-
trate on the problem, and that's exactly what you want him to do.

It may be the gracious thing to offer the serviceman a cup of hot
coffee when he's finished work, but if he sits in your kitchen for
15 minutes drinking coffee it is probably adding around $5 to your
bill.

WHAT TO CHECK BEFORE CALLING THE
SERVICEMAN

Always check the obvious before you pick up the telephone and
yell for help. Anything that runs on electricity—and most equip-

ment in the house does—won't operate properly unless it is getting the right amount of current. No modern heating system will deliver heat if the thermostat is not set high enough to demand heat. The best automatic dishwasher or washing machine won't work if it isn't getting water. When something doesn't work, don't immediately assume that the trouble is complex. It could be very simple.

You can save a lot of unnecessary service calls if you use your head. When you do have to call for service, don't just leave your name with whoever answers the phone and say you want a serviceman to come over. Ask to speak to the service manager or one of the servicemen. You may be able to learn enough from him to fix things yourself. Have all the facts on hand when you call for service. If you are having trouble with an appliance or other equipment, give the service manager the name of the brand, model and serial number. Tell him as clearly as you can what seems to be the trouble. Tell him that you have already checked the obvious—the switch, the cord and plug, the fuse, the faucet, etc. If the trouble is minor and you give enough factual information over the phone, the service manager may be able to tell you how you can correct the problem yourself. But even if you do need a serviceman, he will at least know which parts to bring along to make the necessary repairs. In any event, giving the necessary information is going to save you money.

Learn as much about your house and the operation of the equipment in it as you can. If you don't understand how the plumbing system works, ask the plumber the next time he is over to explain the system. Have him point out the location of the shut-off valves so you can turn off the water supply if there is a leak in the system. Find out if you have a septic tank and where it is located. It should be inspected once a year and cleaned if it needs it.

Ask the company that furnishes the energy for your heating system to have one of its men drop in to explain the proper operation of the system and what you can do to reduce the need for outside repairs and services.

Get into the habit of making regular inspections of your house every couple of months with an eye for trouble spots. Both inside and outside there are usually signs of trouble before there is a complete breakdown. If the motor on the refrigerator runs more frequently than in the past, if the water pump keeps going on and off when you're not running water, or if a section of a roof gutter has begun to sag, it means that something is wrong. The faster you act, the less chance there will be of really costly repairs.

Remember that things around a house seldom if ever get well by themselves. A good night's sleep may be all you need to get rid of a headache or the sniffles, but when you see rusty water oozing from the bottom of the hot-water heater, bed rest won't help and the situation can only get worse.

Emergencies are not only inconvenient but often the most expensive of all repairs. You won't have the time to shop around to get the best deal on the work, you may have to settle for a more expensive or inferior product, and you may have to pay a higher cost for labor because many servicemen get overtime if they must work nights, Sundays and holidays. The time to do something about that hot-water heater is when you first notice that it has begun to leak, not after it breaks down.

Appliances are responsible for the majority of service calls. Many of these calls are quite unnecessary. Some authorities claim that about 40 percent of all service calls on appliances are unnecessary and they cost homeowners about $8,000,000 a year. The way to avoid these unnecessary and expensive calls is first to check out the obvious reasons why the equipment won't work and perhaps correct the problem on your own.

ELECTRIC EQUIPMENT. Every appliance and practically every piece of equipment in the house requires electric power. If it doesn't get the power, it won't run. So, when anything doesn't run, the very first thing to do is to make sure that it's getting electricity. Here are the six points to check.

• Plugs and cords. Make sure that the plug is firmly inserted in the outlet. If it is not pushed all the way in, there won't be electrical contact. If the prongs of the plug fit loosely in the outlet, they will not make good contact. Use a pair of pliers to bend the prongs outward just enough to make them fit tightly. If the prongs are coated with dirt or corrosion, clean them with a piece of fine sandpaper. (Never use steel wool on electrical work; the fine strands of steel that may remain could cause a short circuit when you put the plug back in the outlet.) If the wires in the cord are secured to the plug with screws, check the connections and tighten the screws if the connections are loose. Inspect the cord for signs of wear or breaks. Breaks often occur at the point where the cord joins the plug, because this part gets a lot of flexing. Don't try to patch or repair a worn or broken cord—get a new one.

• Fuses and circuit breakers. See if the fuse or circuit breaker has blown. If it has, replace the fuse or reset the circuit breaker. If it blows again and you can't locate the short circuit or overload, call your serviceman. Sometimes the main house fuse or circuit breaker blows, and that means there won't be any power throughout the house. Don't bother calling a serviceman on this—call an electrician or your electric power company.

• Switches. If there is a switch on the appliance or on the appliance circuit, check to be certain that it is on. Some switches are so delicate that while they may appear to be on they are just a fraction away from making contact. Flick them off, then on again. Some equipment, such as an oil burner, will have a switch some distance from the burner, and this may have accidentally been thrown to the off position.

• Wall outlets. Sometimes a lamp or appliance won't work because of a faulty connection or failure inside the convenience outlet into which it is plugged. Plug in an appliance or lamp you know is working. If it doesn't work, call your electrician and have him repair or replace the outlet.

• Overload protectors. Motor-driven appliances such as clothes washers, disposal units, etc. have an "overload protector" on the motor. If the appliance is overloaded or if the motor becomes overheated, the protector cuts off the power so the motor won't be damaged. After the overload has been removed, or the motor has had a chance to cool down, the switch on the protector can be reset and the appliance will run again. These switches are often in the form of a little red button and all you have to do is find them somewhere on the outside of the motor and press down. If the button stays down, the motor will run.

• Power failures. Sometimes the reason an appliance won't run is that there is a local power failure. These do occur during the daylight hours when you may not be aware of them because you don't require lights. If there is a power failure, don't waste money calling your serviceman. Call the power company.

If an appliance is getting electricity and it still won't run, it may be due to one of the following problems—most of which you can correct yourself.

• Automatic clothes dryer. If dryer won't run, check to be sure that the door is securely latched, and check the position of the controls to be sure they are on the correct setting. If the dryer works but clothes do not dry in proper time, it may be that the dryer is overloaded, the lint trap has not been cleaned (it should be emptied after each use of the dryer), or clothes were too wet when placed in the dryer.

• Automatic clothes washer. If water does not run into the washer, check to be sure that faucets are open and that there is no kink in the supply hose. If water does not drain out of washer, check for a kink in the drain hose and straighten it out if you find one. Loud noises in the water pipes when the washer is running are caused by water hammer and this you may be able to correct yourself, as explained in Chapter 21.

• Dishwasher. A dishwasher will not operate unless the door is securely latched and the cycle control is at the proper setting. If the light is on, indicating that the washer is getting power, but it does not fill with water, it may be due to low water pressure in the pipes. This can sometimes happen if you try to use the washer at the same time that water is being run for a shower, clothes washer, etc. When the motor hums but the dishwasher doesn't operate it means that something is jamming the impeller or spray arm. Turn off the power and remove the object.

• Garbage disposer. If the motor stops while the disposer is running, turn off the power to the disposer and wait three to five minutes for the motor to cool. Then press the overload protector button on the motor. If the disposer jams on some metal object, turn off the switch. Check the manufacturer's directions on how to remove the jam.

• Gas appliances. If a range, hot-water heater, boiler or furnace fails to operate, check the pilot light. They sometimes go out. If you have the manufacturer's instructions for lighting the pilot, you can do it yourself. If not, call your gas company.

• Electric range and oven. If a single surface unit does not heat, there may be a loose connection or broken wire to the unit. Turn off the power to the range at the fuse or circuit-breaker panel. Lift up the heating element and reflector to see if one of the wires is broken at the terminal screw. If it is, clean the end of the wires with fine sandpaper and then connect them to the terminal screws. If the wire is broken at some point other than at the terminal screw, call your serviceman. The most common reason for an oven failing to heat is that the timer is set to Off or Automatic. Reset the timer to Manual or set the selector to Bake.

• Refrigerator and freezer. Sometimes all that is wrong is that the temperature control has accidentally been set to Off or Defrost.

HEATING SYSTEMS. It's no joke to be without heat in cold weather —even for a couple of hours—so most of us pick up the phone and call for emergency service the minute we notice that the heating system isn't working. But, like appliances, most calls for heating service are unnecessary. Here are some of the things you should do yourself before calling for help.

• Check the thermostat. Is the thermostat turned up high enough to demand heat? Remember that if the thermostat is getting heat from some other source—the fireplace, TV set, light or even a candle—it may not demand heat when it is required. Sometimes a speck of dirt prevents the thermostat from working properly. Try moving the dial back and forth a few times. A light tap with the hand may also help.

• Electric power. Every modern heating system needs electricity. Check the fuse or circuit breaker on the heater circuit to be sure it has not blown. If you have an oil burner there will be an emergency switch with a red plate located some distance from the burner—at the top of the basement stairs, outside the utility room —and it is quite common for some member of the family to flick this switch off by mistake.

• Gas burner. Is the pilot light out? Instructions for lighting the pilot light are usually printed on the metal plate attached to the heater. If the pilot light won't light or if you smell gas, turn off gas and call your gas company.

• Oil burner. Is there oil in the storage tank? Even in this day and age of automatic delivery it's possible for a tank to go dry. Inside tanks usually have a gauge so you can tell how much oil there is in the tank. The way to tell if there is oil in an underground tank is to remove the cap on the fill line and stick a long rod down into the tank. Also, check to see that the recycle switch is on. This is a little switch on a metal box attached to the pipe that runs from the heater to the chimney. For one of several reasons, it may cut off power to the burner. Usually all you have to do is flick the switch and the burner will start. Sometimes a speck of soot or dust gets inside the recycle switch and keeps the burner from running. A smart slap of the hand on the recycle switch box may do the trick and get things running.

• Hot-water or steam boiler. Is there enough water in the boiler? Most boilers have a low-water cutoff that stops the burner if the water level is too low. If you don't know the proper way to add water, your serviceman should be able to tell you over the phone.

21

REPAIRS AND MAINTENANCE YOU CAN DO YOURSELF

You can't blame appliances for all the money spent each year on repairs and services about the house. Each time you call in a plumber to fix a leaky faucet or clear a clogged-up drain, a carpenter to replace a broken pane of window glass or fix a sticking door or an electrician to replace a fuse or broken lamp socket, it takes a big bite out of the family budget. You can't eliminate the need for home repairs, but you can learn to handle many of them yourself and save a bundle of money each year. You don't have to invest a lot of money in tools to make most of the basic home repairs. You can handle a majority of them with only the following: a claw hammer, four or five screwdrivers of different sizes, a putty knife, a pair of slip-joint pliers, an 8-inch adjustable wrench, a ½-inch wood chisel and a push-pull or electric drill for making holes. And you should have a force cup, also known as a "plumber's friend," for clearing clogged drains. That's about all the equipment you'll need at the beginning. As you find the need for more specialized tools, you can always buy or borrow them.

PLUMBING

Even if you don't intend to make any plumbing repairs you should know how to turn off the water inside the house in case of emergency. If a pipe should spring a leak and you don't know how to turn the water off, the house can become quite a mess before the plumber arrives.

There will be a shut-off valve in the main water supply pipe at a point near where the pipe enters the house. This may be in the basement or utility room or even under the kitchen sink. When you close this valve, you shut off water to the entire house—both hot and cold water. Shut off hot water heater when you close main shut-off valve. Generally there are also shut-off valves in the branch lines running to the kitchen, bathrooms, etc. These allow you to shut off water to one area without shutting it off to the entire house. You'll also find shut-off valves in pipes going to certain fixtures such as the bathroom lavatory, toilet flush tank and kitchen sink. These valves are directly under the fixture and easy to reach.

When you make any repairs on the fresh-water system such as fixing a leaky faucet or flush tank, be sure to close off the nearest shut-off valve to the fixture.

PROTECT FIXTURES AND FITTINGS. When you are working around plumbing fixtures or making repairs, be very careful not to damage the finish on the metal fittings or on the fixture itself. Before using a wrench or pliers, put masking tape or a cloth around nuts on fittings so the tool won't scar the thin chrome plating. It's also a good idea to cover the tub, lavatory, toilet, etc., with several layers of newspaper or a cloth, so that if you should drop a hammer or a wrench, it won't crack the porcelain or chip the enamel finish.

Don't use harsh abrasives such as sandpaper, steel wool or even abrasive cleaners on fittings or on fixtures, for these can leave minute scratches which are impossible to remove. This is especially true of fiber glass and acrylic fixtures. And don't allow anyone to use the rim of the tub as a handy shoeshine stand. This thoughtless habit leaves dreadful scratches.

Chipped spots on enamel fixtures can be patched with a liquid porcelain or patching enamel sold at hardware and plumbing supply stores. They do a pretty fair job, but just the same you can easily tell the finish has been patched.

Avoid using strong chemicals and medicine around fixtures, for these can leave permanent stains if accidentally spilt on the fixture.

CHECK FRESH WATER SUPPLY FOR PURITY. If you get your fresh water from a private well—either a deep well or a shallow one— have the water tested once a year for purity. Your local department of health may do this for you or tell you who does it in your area. The cost is around $10. Don't assume that just because the water has been pure it will continue to remain so. Water tables change, especially if there is a lot of building going on in an area and installation of new septic systems. If you should find that your water is contaminated, notify your department of health at once. They can make tests that may locate the cause of the contamination—a broken or defective underground sewer line or septic system, etc.—and have it corrected. And if the cause cannot be corrected, your local or state department of health can recommend the type of purification system to install so that the water will be potable. In the meantime, switch to bottled water for drinking and cooking.

CLOGGED FIXTURE DRAINS. Get after these as soon as you notice them acting a bit sluggish, for the longer you put off clearing them, the more effort it will take.

You'll seldom if ever be bothered with clogged-up drains if you keep hair, bits of soap and greasy cosmetics from going down bathroom lavatory and tub drains. A good way to keep hair out is with a little lint trap that you can get at most hardware stores. The way to keep the kitchen-sink drain happy is to keep grease and food particles from going down it. After washing greasy dishes and pans, boil a kettle of water on the range and pour it down the drain. This will flush out any grease that may have accumulated in the line. If you have a sink garbage disposer unit, you don't have to worry about grease and food particles going down the drain.

HOW TO USE THE PLUMBER'S FRIEND. This rubber force cup with a wood handle is about the best weapon so far invented for dealing with most clogged drains. For the cup to be effective, there must be 4 or 5 inches of water in the fixture. If there is an overflow outlet in the fixture, plug it with a wad of wet cloth.

Place the cup over the drain opening. If you have a pop-up plug drain, the plug should be removed so the drain opening will be exposed. If you can't lift the plug out, get under the lavatory and disconnect it from the drain handle. You can then lift it out.

With the cup over the drain opening, press down on the handle with both hands—hard. Pull the handle up and push down again. This action creates a downward pressure and then a suction, and this is what's needed to clear the drain. Repeat this process a dozen times or so until the drain is clear.

SINK, LAVATORY AND TUB DRAINS. If the plumber's friend won't do the trick, more drastic action is needed. What you use here is a drain auger, which you can generally rent or borrow from a local hardware store. The tool consists of a flexible steel cable with an auger hook at one end and a handle at the other. You insert the hook end into the line and push the cable until the hook strikes the obstruction. Then you turn the handle. The hook will either break up the obstruction or catch into it so it can be pulled out.

The best spot to get the auger into the drain line of a lavatory or kitchen sink is at the trap located directly under the fixture. Most traps have a clean-out plug which you can remove with a wrench. If there is no plug or if the plug opening is too small, remove the entire trap. Some are held in place by friction and all you have to do is pull them off. Others have large nuts that you must loosen. Have a large pail under the trap before you remove the plug or the trap to catch the water in the trap and adjoining lines.

You seldom easily reach bathtub traps because they are set in the wall or floor. Here you must insert the auger through the drain opening. If the strainer in the drain make this impossible, use a chemical drain cleaner.

TOILET BOWLS. About the only thing that can stop up a toilet bowl is a bulky object—a toy, toilet article, wash cloth, etc. Try not to store any of these articles near the bowl where they might get knocked into it and then flushed into the drain. You can often remove the obstruction by first bailing out some of the water from the bowl and then, wearing rubber gloves, reaching into the trap and pulling out the object. A plumber's friend can also be used to clear the obstruction, and if this doesn't work, use the auger.

Some people use chemical drain cleaners on stopped-up drains. We don't care for them because they are not always effective and are dangerous to handle and to have around the house.

LEAKY FAUCETS. These are generally pretty easy to fix. The illustration shows the basic elements of a stem faucet—the kind used on most household plumbing fixtures. They may not all look ex-

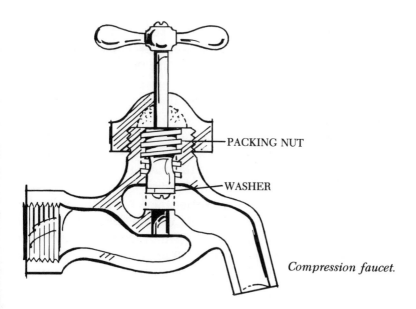

PACKING NUT

WASHER

Compression faucet.

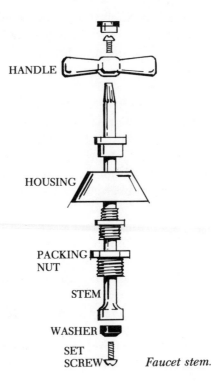

HANDLE

HOUSING

PACKING NUT

STEM

WASHER

SET SCREW

Faucet stem.

actly like the faucet illustrated. Some will be covered with a metal housing, and bathtub and shower faucets are set into the walls with only the handle and housing exposed. But the basic elements of these faucets are all the same.

If water drips out of the spout after the faucet has been turned off, it means the washer is worn and must be replaced. You can get a package of assorted faucet washers at a hardware store. You'll need a screwdriver and an adjustable wrench or slip-joint pliers for this job. And be sure to turn off the water to the faucet before you take it apart.

Basically all you have to do to replace the washer is to loosen the packing nut under the faucet handle with the wrench or pliers. Turn the handle in the direction to open the faucet and the stem will unscrew out of the faucet body. Remove the washer by first removing the little set screw that holds it in place, then replace the washer with a new one of the same size. Put the stem back into the body of the faucet, turn the handle as if to close the faucet, and when the stem is all the way down, replace the packing nut and tighten it.

If the packing nut is covered with a housing, this must be removed before you can loosen the nut. And before you can remove the housing you may have to remove the faucet handle, which is held in place by a small screw at the top or on the side. The housing may be held in place by a lock nut or set screw. Eventually you'll clear away all the parts so you can get at the packing nut.

Tub and shower faucets set into the wall present a problem, because after you've removed the handle and housing you'll find the packing nut set so far into the wall that you can't loosen it with an ordinary wrench, or even with pliers. What you need here is a box wrench with a slight offset, and you may be able to borrow

It may be necessary to chip away some of the tile around a tub or shower faucet to reach the packing nut.

one from your local service station. If not, buy one at any hardware store. Sometimes you may even have to chip out a little of the tile or plaster to make a large enough opening to get to the nut with a box wrench.

When water leaks around the stem of a faucet right below the handle it means that the packing inside the packing nut is worn. First, try tightening the packing nut with a wrench. If this doesn't do the trick, or if the nut must be tightened so much that the faucet is hard to operate, you'll have to replace the packing. Most faucets use a graphite-impregnated string for packing, and you can get this at any hardware store.

Turn off the water to the faucet, remove the faucet handle, loosen the packing nut and slip it off the stem. Dig out the old packing with a screwdriver or knife and install new packing. The string should be wrapped around the stem in the same direction as the packing nut is turned to tighten. Slip the nut back into place and tighten.

Single-lever faucets are a special problem. You may have one of

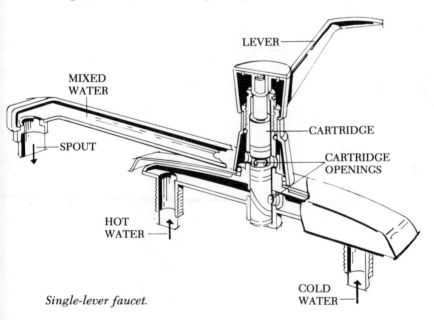

Single-lever faucet.

these on the kitchen sink or lavatory if it is a new-style unit. Single-lever faucets don't work the same way as the stem faucet. If they should leak—and they seldom do—you need a replacement kit to fix them. And you'll need a kit that matches the brand and model of your particular unit. The best place to get these is from a local retailer handing that particular brand of plumbing fixture. Directions for installation are supplied with the kit.

BANGING IN THE WATER PIPES. Loud noises in water pipes made when a faucet is closed or an automatic washer changes cycles are called "water hammer." Water hammer occurs when the flowing water is brought to a sudden stop. Each time the pipe bangs it also vibrates, and in time the vibration can cause leaks in the pipe joints. You can usually stop water hammer at fixtures by closing the faucets slowly so that the flow of water is brought to a gradual stop. And sometimes you can eliminate it by adding more supports

Installing additional pipe supports helps prevent banging in water pipes.

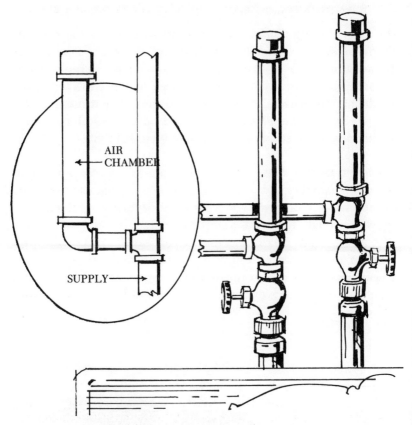

Vertical lengths of pipe with cap at top can be installed at various points in system to eliminate noise caused by water hammer.

to horizontal runs of pipe in the basement or crawl space so they can't vibrate. If these measures don't do the trick, better call in your plumber. He can add some vertical lengths of pipes to the system which act as shock absorbers and usually correct the trouble.

SWEATING FLUSH TANKS. If the air in the bathroom is warm and moist—and it often is—moisture will collect on the outside surfaces of flush tanks and drip onto the floor. The moisture is a result of condensation when the warm moist air strikes the cold tank. An easy and inexpensive way to keep the water from dripping onto the floor is to use one of the special metal trays designed for this very job. They are sold at hardware and department stores and cost from $3 to $5. The trays can be easily attached under the tank. Some trays have a little plastic hose so the water in them runs into the toilet bowl, while others have a detachable cup or sponge so they may be emptied easily by hand.

SWEATING WATER PIPES. Cold-water pipes also sweat in warm moist weather. The way to handle this is to cover them with insulation. You can get insulation made for this purpose at a hardware store. It's easy to apply.

TOILET FLUSH TANKS. Flush-tank mechanisms act up a good deal, but, happily, they are not difficult to repair—once you understand how they work and what needs to be done when they get out of whack.

You can get replacement parts for the flush mechanism at any hardware store. Some of these are of better design than the origi-

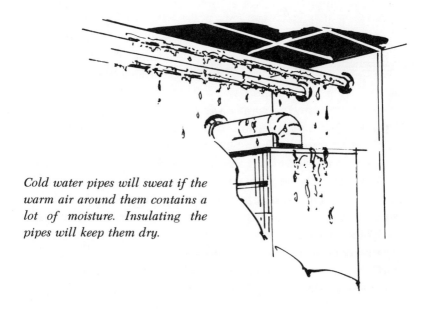

Cold water pipes will sweat if the warm air around them contains a lot of moisture. Insulating the pipes will keep them dry.

nal parts. You can also buy one of the several improved-type flush mechanisms that you can install yourself in place of the existing unit. These improved units are far less likely to get out of adjustment than the common kind of mechanism and are also a good deal quieter.

You'll need to turn off the water supply to the tank to make certain repairs and adjustments. You can do this by closing the shut-off valve directly under the tank or one in the line that supplies cold water to the bathroom. It's also possible to close off the supply to the tank to make adjustments by lifting the float up and tying it up with a piece of string while you work.

The illustration shows the workings of a typical flush tank. The handle on the outside is connected by levers and rods to a ball washer that fits over the large opening at the bottom of the tank. When the toilet is flushed, the washer is raised and allows water to flow into the bowl. As the water level in the tank drops, the ball float, made of copper, glass or plastic and connected by a rod to the supply valve, begins to drop and opens the supply valve so the tank will be refilled. At the same time, the ball washer drops back over the opening to close off the flow to the bowl. Water continues to flow into the tank until the float is raised to the shut-off level and closes the supply valve—called a "ball-cock." There is a large overflow pipe in the tank that runs to the bowl so that the tank can't overflow. A small tube from the supply valve runs to the top of this tube so the bowl will fill with water after it has been flushed.

The most common flush-tank problem is water continuously flowing into the bowl. This happens if, for one reason or another, the ball washer is not making a tight fit over the opening at the bottom of the tank. It may be that the metal rods connected to the washer are bent out of alignment so the washer won't fall easily into place. If you can't bend these rods so they work smoothly, replace them. It may be that the washer itself is worn or is out of shape, and this means you need a new washer. They screw right onto the rods. Also check the metal seat on the opening to make

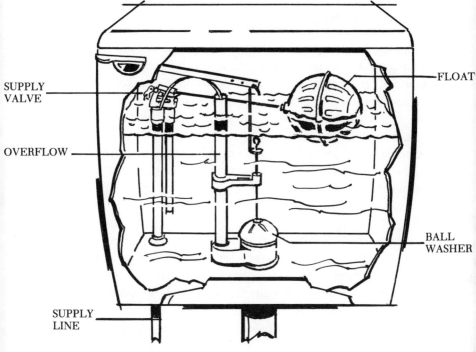

SUPPLY VALVE

OVERFLOW

FLOAT

BALL WASHER

SUPPLY LINE

Major elements of flush tank mechanism.

sure it's not coated with rust or dirt. These can prevent a tight fit between washer and seat.

If the tank fills up correctly after flushing but water continues to flow into the tank and down the overflow pipe into the bowl, the problem is in the float or in the supply valve—the ballcock. Lift up the float to see if this will shut off the flow of water. If it does, unscrew the float from the rod and see if there is water inside it. Install a new float if the old one is leaking. If the float seems okay, try bending the rod that's connected to the float downward in the middle about ½ inch.

If lifting up the float by hand does not turn off the flow of water into the tank, the trouble is in the ballcock—probably a worn washer. The washers are attached to the plunger that fits inside the ballcock, and you can remove this by first removing one or two thumbscrews on the side of the ballcock.

ELECTRICAL REPAIRS

The layout of the house electrical system is discussed in detail in Chapter 1. You should know how to cut off all electric power in case of emergency, where the fuse box or circuit-breaker panel is, and how to reset a circuit breaker or replace a fuse.

If you have any doubts or questions about the main switch, circuit breaker or fuse box in your home, get them cleared up immediately so you'll be able to deal with any emergency. The man who comes to read your electric meter should be able to show you what you need to know about the system or you can ask an electrician.

OVERLOADED CIRCUITS AND SHORT CIRCUITS. A circuit breaker or fuse will blow if you overload it by plugging in more equipment than the particular circuit was designed to handle. Lights, radios, TVs, clocks, etc. don't take much power, so they seldom overload circuits. But appliances that produce heat—toasters, coffee makers, waffle irons, portable room heaters, etc.—do draw a lot of electricity, and if the circuit is already carrying close to its capacity it will blow when one of these items is plugged in.

You must remove the overload before resetting the circuit breaker or replacing the fuse.

If lights dim when you plug in certain appliances or if heating appliances do not get as hot as they should, it usually means that the circuit is overloaded but not quite enough for it to blow. But you should take notice of these warnings and remove some of the load. It doesn't do the appliances any good to run them on an overloaded circuit.

Circuits will blow if there is a short circuit. The most common reason for a short circuit is worn appliance and extension cords. If the insulation is worn away, the two wires can touch, and that produces a short circuit. Loose connections in appliance plugs are another common cause. Sometimes a short circuit is caused by a faulty appliance.

When you have a short circuit, unplug everything on the circuit. Inspect the cords and plugs of each item to see if you can locate the trouble, and when you find it, fix it or have the equipment repaired.

ELECTRIC WALL PLUGS. It's hard to get along these days without knowing how to replace or install a wall plug on a lamp, extension or appliance cord.

The most convenient plug to use on lightweight lamp cords is the snap-on plug. These are designed to take the plastic-coated lamp cord used on so many small electric items about the house. All you have to do to install this sort of plug is to make a clean cut at the end of the cord so that there is no bare wire extending beyond the insulation. Open the clamp on the plug, push the end of the cord into the plug as far as it will go and then push the clamp down. That's all there is to it.

Some cords—especially appliance cords—don't fit the snap-on plug, so you must use the type of plug in which the wires are connected to terminal screws inside the plug. Here's how to handle this job. Separate the two wires in the cord for a distance of about 2 inches. Slip the cord through the plug and tie a knot in the wires as shown in the illustration. This is called an "underwriters' knot." Its purpose is to keep the wires from coming loose from the plug if someone yanks the cord to disconnect the plug from the wall outlet.

Remove about ½ inch of the insulation from the ends of the

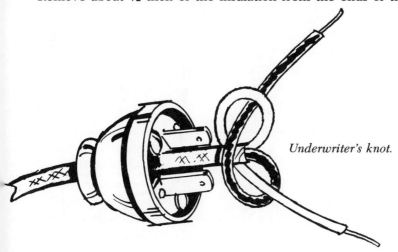

Underwriter's knot.

wire. Try not to cut any of the individual strands of wire. Twist the ends of each wire so all the strands are tightly together. Pull the cord to set the knot into the recess made for it in the plug. Attach the wires to the terminal screws. Each wire should be wrapped around the screw in the same direction that the screw is turned to tighten.

You'll be able to tell if you've done a good job if there are no exposed wires other than around the screws. Replace the little insulation cover over the plug.

REPLACING LAMP SOCKETS AND CORDS. Lamp sockets don't last forever. The switch inside the socket will eventually fail, and when this happens the socket must be replaced. And lamp cords don't last forever either. When they become worn they should be replaced. Never splice or patch a lamp cord.

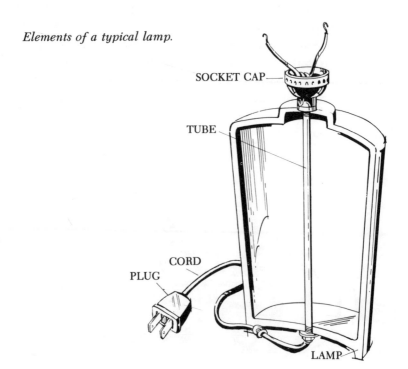

Elements of a typical lamp.

SOCKET CAP

TUBE

CORD

PLUG

LAMP

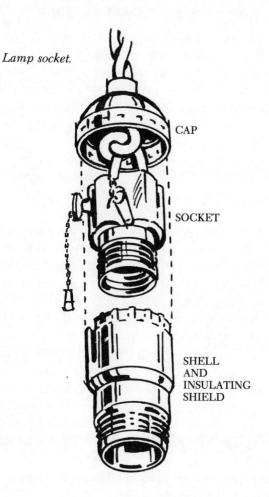

Lamp socket.

CAP

SOCKET

SHELL
AND
INSULATING
SHIELD

The illustration shows the basic elements of the typical lamp socket. This one has a pull chain, but you'll find the exact same set-up in sockets with a key or pull-bar switch. You can get a new socket at any hardware store.

The wires enter the socket through the cap. The cap has a little set screw and is the part of the socket that is fastened to the lamp, usually to a threaded tube that runs up through the lamp and which contains the wires. You don't always have to replace the cap or even remove it to replace the socket. The lamp cord is connected to the two terminal screws on the socket. The socket is covered with an insulating sleeve and an outer shell.

Always disconnect the lamp plug from the wall outlet before you take it apart. If you are working on a ceiling or wall lamp fixture, shut off the electricity to that fixture by removing the fuse, opening the circuit breaker or pulling the main house switch.

All you have to do to take the old socket apart is to remove the lampshade and the bulb and then take a screwdriver and press hard on the spot on the outer shell where it says "Press." You can then remove the outer shell and insulating shell.

If the lamp cord is in good condition you just disconnect it from the socket by loosening the terminal screws. Install the new socket, being sure to wrap the wires around the terminal screws in the same direction that the screws are turned to tighten. Replace the insulating shell and then the outer shell.

The trick to replacing a worn lamp cord is to avoid taking the lamp apart unless you have to. One way to do this is to use a piece of string to pull the new cord up through the lamp to the socket. Disconnect the wires of the old cord from the socket and tie them to a long piece of string. Pull the cord out through the bottom of the lamp until the end of the string appears. Disconnect the string from the old cord and tie it to the new cord. Now gently pull the opposite end of the string until the end of the new cord comes up through the socket cap. Now all you have to do is to split the wires, tie an underwriters' knot so they can't be pulled back through the cap and connect them to the socket.

If the string trick doesn't work—and sometimes it won't—you'll have to take the lamp apart so the new cord can be installed. Lamps are not difficult to take apart but they are not so easy to put back together unless you know which part goes where. Set the lamp on its side and lay the parts in a line just as you take them off. In this way you'll be sure that they are put back in the right order. If you just make a pile of parts, you'll spend hours trying to figure out how they go back together.

You'll also need a plug for the other end of the cord; this can be the snap-on type.

DOORS

DOORS THAT STICK. The reason that a door sticks is usually that some of the screws in the hinges have become loose. Open the door and check each screw with a large screwdriver and tighten any that are loose. If the hole in the wood has become enlarged so the screw can't be tightened but just keeps turning, take the screw out. Cut a wood plug to fit the screw hole, coat it with wood glue and hammer it into place. When you set the screw back into the plug, it should hold.

Another common reason for sticking is that the door was not correctly hung or the door frame, for one of several reasons, has moved just a bit so the door no longer fits properly. You can generally handle this by inserting thin pieces of cardboard, called "shims," under one leaf of a hinge. If the door sticks at the bottom outside corner and the floor or threshold, put a shim under the bottom hinge leaf that is attached to the door jamb. Put a block of wood or a book under the outside bottom edge of the opened door to hold the door upright. Loosen the screws that hold the hinge leaf and insert the cardboard shim. If the sticking occurs at the top corner of the door, place the shim under the top hinge leaf attached to the door jamb. You may need several thin shims to get the required result.

Outside doors often stick in wet or damp weather because the wood has absorbed moisture and has expanded. It's not a good idea to try to free these doors by sanding or planing wood off the edges, because if you do, when the wood shrinks back to its normal size there will be cracks between the door and the frame. Wait until the wood in the door dries out and then keep the wood from absorbing moisture again by coating all the edges—especially top and bottom edge—with paint or a wood preservative.

DOORS THAT WON'T LATCH. When a door is closed, a spring latch slips into a hole in a metal plate—called a strike plate—fastened to the side of the door frame or jamb. If the door frame has moved a bit or if the door or frame has shrunk, the latch won't engage properly in the hole and the door won't stay latched or won't latch at all.

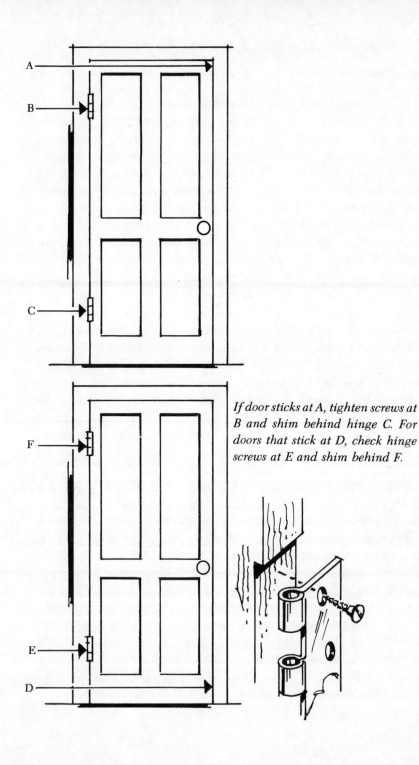

If door sticks at A, tighten screws at B and shim behind hinge C. For doors that stick at D, check hinge screws at E and shim behind F.

Rub a piece of chalk or crayon on the edge of the latch and shut the door. Open the door, and the marks on the strike plate will show you in which direction the plate must be moved so the latch will engage in the latch hole. You can make adjustments in the plate by first taking it off—it is held in place with a couple of small wood screws—and then enlarging the recess in the frame into which the plate fits with a wood chisel. You can also make minor adjustments by enlarging the hole in the plate with a metal file.

If the latch doesn't reach the strike plate because the door or frame has shrunk, move the plate nearer to the latch. You do this by taking the plate off and inserting a couple of pieces of cardboard into the recess.

WINDOWS

STUCK WINDOWS. Wood double-hung windows often become hard or impossible to open or close because of paint in the wrong places or because of swelling of the wood caused by dampness.

If a sash is just balky—hard to open or close—lubricating the tracks often does the trick. A good lubricant for this is the non-staining type that is sold at most hardware stores, but rubbing a piece of candle along the track can also ease it up. Once the track has been lubricated, move the sash up and down a few times to spread the lubricant about.

When a sash won't budge, don't try to force it open by pushing with all your might on the top rail. You might force the top rail lose from the rest of the sash. Also don't try to pry it open by forcing a screwdriver or chisel between the window sill and the bottom of the sash, because this can leave deep dents in the wood and scar the paint.

Try to determine what is causing the window to stick. If there are thick accumulations of paint along the tracks, this is probably the reason for the problem. Try to cut through the paint seal with a putty knife. Force the blade—it may take a light tap with a hammer—into the seam between the sash and stop molding, which is the strip of wood trim that holds the sash in the frame. Once the blade is in the seam, give it a slight twist to pry the

*Ease a sticking sash by driving a putty knife between sash and molding
and twisting the knife slightly to pry the molding away from the sash.*

molding just a hair away from the sash. Do this along the entire
length of the sash, on both sides. Once the sash can be moved,
lubricate the tracks.

If you can't free a sash by cutting through the paint along the
edges, remove the sash from the frame. You can then sand off any
paint or shave off a bit of the wood if the sash is sticking because
it has absorbed moisture.

To remove the sash, take off the piece of stop molding on each
side. These strips are held in place with small nails or screws. If
there are nails, use a chisel and pry the strips from the frame. If
you do this carefully, you won't damage the strips and they can be
replaced. Once the strips are off, the sash can be pulled out of the
frame. Disconnect it from the sash cord or sash chain. Sand off any
accumulations of paint along the edges. If there is no paint, then
the sash is probably sticking because the wood has absorbed moisture and has swelled. Plane or sand off just enough wood from

the edge so that the sash can be moved in the frame. Don't take off more wood than is absolutely necessary, because if you do, once the wood has shrunk back to normal size, the sash will fit too loosely in the frame. Coat the exposed wood with linseed oil or a wood preservative. This will keep the wood from absorbing moisture.

By the way, if you want to take out the upper sash, you must first remove the lower one and then take off the two strips of wood, called parting strips, that separate the upper from the lower sash. These are held in place with small nails or screws. You can't take either sash out of the frame from the outside—you must do the job from the inside.

REPLACING WINDOW SASH CORDS. In older houses you find windows with sash cords, and when these break they must be replaced.

You'll have to pull the sash out of the frame to replace a broken cord. How to remove a sash is explained in the section dealing with sticking windows. Briefly, you must remove the stop molding on the sides of the frame that hold the sash in place. If you must remove the upper sash, the lower sash must be removed first and then the parting strips that separate the lower from the upper sash. Once these strips are out of the way, the upper sash can be pulled out.

After you've gotten the sash out, remove the broken piece of cord from the side. Note how the sash cord was attached, because this is the way you'll have to attach the new cord.

Now you've got to get the sash weight out. This is inside the window frame in something called a "pocket." There will be a cover to this pocket at the bottom of the frame. It's usually held in place with one or two screws. Remove the screws and pry off the cover. You can then reach into the pocket and pull out the sash weight. Feed the new cord over the pulley at the top of the frame and work it down through the frame until you can pull the end out through the pocket. Tie this end to the sash weight, replace the weight in the pocket, and then replace the pocket cover.

Now you fasten the cord to the sash. Hold the sash to the frame

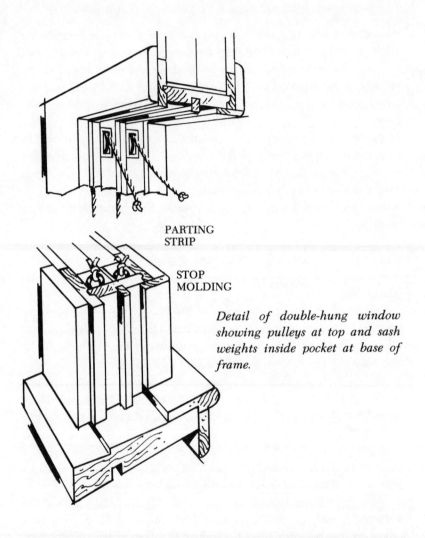

PARTING
STRIP

STOP
MOLDING

Detail of double-hung window showing pulleys at top and sash weights inside pocket at base of frame.

in the "up" position. Pull the cord so the sash weight is just off the bottom of the pocket. Measure the cord and cut it, leaving enough to attach it to the sash—usually with a knot. Put the sash back into the frame and check the operation. When the sash is closed, the sash weight should not strike the bottom of the pocket, and when the sash is all the way open the weight should not strike the pulley at the top.

By the way, sash chains are not any more difficult to install than the cords and last almost indefinitely. And if you don't want to bother with either, you can buy little window latches that can be installed in a matter of minutes and will hold the sash open in the desired position. You can get them at your hardware store.

REPLACING BROKEN WINDOW GLASS. You will find this job a good deal easier if you remove the sash from the frame and put it on a table or workbench. It is especially worth the time it takes to remove the sash if you have one to repair on the second floor, because trying to do the job while you are standing near the top of a high ladder can be risky.

You can get new window glass cut to size at most hardware stores. The glass should be cut ⅛ inch smaller in width and in height than the actual opening in the sash to take care of any irregularities along the edges of the glass or the opening. You'll also need a box of glazier's points, some putty or glazing compound and a small amount of linseed oil or exterior paint.

The best way to remove the old pieces of broken glass is to put on a pair of heavy work gloves and gently "rock" the pieces up and down until the putty around the glass is broken and you can pull the pieces out. Next, remove all the old putty around the opening with a putty knife, chisel or screwdriver. If you can't pry or chisel the putty off, use a little heat to soften it. A soldering iron or propane torch is good for this job. Along with the putty you should remove all the glazier's points. There are the little triangular pieces of metal that hold the glass in place. Pull them out of the wood with pliers.

Use steel wool to clean the recess in the sash where the glass is to fit and then coat the wood with either linseed oil or a thin coat of exterior paint. This helps make a good seal between wood and putty and keeps the wood from absorbing the oils out of the putty.

Measure the opening in the sash and order the glass cut to size.

Apply a thin coat of putty to the shoulders of the opening that the glass will fit against. The purpose of this "bed" is to make a tight seal between glass and sash and to cushion the glass against

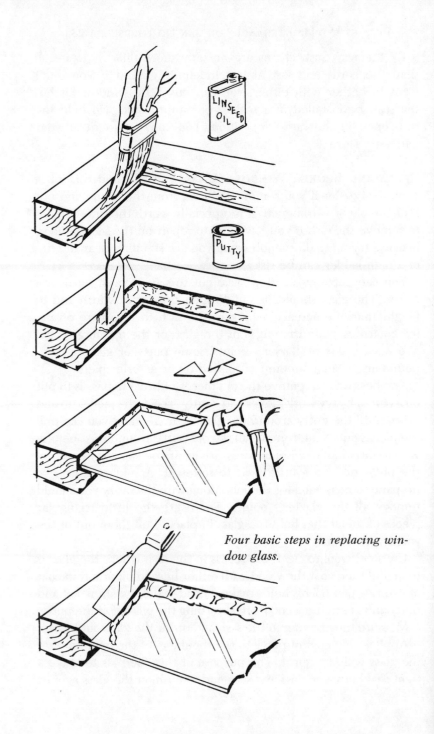

Four basic steps in replacing window glass.

uneven stress. Press the glass into place so that it makes contact with the bed along the entire length of all four sides.

Put in the glazier's points. It is these, and not the putty, that hold the glass in place. On the average pane of glass you need about two points on each side or one every 4 to 6 inches. You can drive the points into place with a screwdriver. Set them into the wood far enough so they are firm but with enough exposed to secure the glass.

Take a quantity of putty, roll in into a long strip about ¼ inch thick and place it in the groove along the edge of the glass. Press it firmly in place with the putty knife. You want to smooth off the putty so it forms a triangular-shaped seal between the edges of the glass and the sash. Inspect the putty on adjoining panes of glass so you get a better idea of what you are trying to achieve. It takes a bit of practice before you can get a perfectly smooth and well-formed seal.

After the putty is in place, wait a week or so and then give it a coat of paint. This will prolong its life.

REPLACING GLASS IN METAL WINDOWS. The glass in metal windows is held in place by either metal clips or a metal strip. You can loosen or remove the clips or strip with a screwdriver. The important point about replacing glass in a metal window is to make sure that there is a bed of putty or glazing compound between the glass and the metal at all points. If you allow the glass to come into direct contact with the metal, it may crack when the metal expands or contracts because of temperature changes.

BATHTUB CAULKING

The crack between a recessed bathtub and the surrounding wall should be filled with caulking. If it isn't, water will get into the crack and eventually damage the wall. It may even seep down to stain the ceiling of the room below. And an open crack around the tub looks ugly and collects dirt. You may also need to caulk around kitchen sinks and bathroom lavatories if they are built in and set in a counter or cabinet.

Most tubs are caulked when they are installed, but the caulking does not last forever. After a few years it dries out and cracks. Bits of it may even come loose and fall out.

You can buy tub caulking at most hardware stores. One type comes in a plastic tube with a special nozzle so you can spread the compound almost as easily as you can spread toothpaste. This caulking is available in several colors to match wall tile and colored tubs as well as in white. Another form of tub caulking, called "tile grout," comes as a paste in a container and you smear it into the crack with a putty knife.

Before applying either kind of caulking, clean out the crack. Remove all loose pieces of the old caulking as well as any of it that has become discolored from mildew. Wash the crack and the area around it with a detergent to remove soap and grease. Wipe the area with a clean damp cloth and allow it to dry thoroughly.

The caulking should be forced into the crack so that it gets way down into the crack and doesn't just sit on the surface. And the surface of the caulking should be smoothed out so it can't catch dirt. No matter what kind of caulking you use, the finger is the best tool for giving it the finishing touches.

REPLACING WALL TILE

It's an easy job to reset a piece of ceramic or plastic wall tile on a kitchen or bathroom wall. And if the tile is damaged or is missing, you can usually get one to match the rest of the tile at most stores that sell wall and floor covering.

You use a special adhesive-type tile cement to replace tile. You can get this at most paint and hardware stores. A thin even coat of the cement is applied to the back of the tile and the tile is then pushed into place. If it is a piece of tile that has fallen out of the wall, scrape off the loose mortar or adhesive from the back of the tile before you apply the tile cement.

Give the adhesive time to dry hard, and then apply grout around the edges of the tile. Use the ready-mixed paste grout. Just rub it into the joints around the tile with your finger and wipe off the excess with a damp cloth or sponge.

Ceramic tile can be reset with a prepared tile cement.

Apply grout around tile with finger.

The ready-mixed grout can also be used to replace missing grout between other tiles.

REPAIRING WALLS AND CEILINGS

Interior walls and ceilings in most houses are made either of plaster on lath or gypsum wallboard (also known as sheetrock, or plasterboard), and as we all know they are subject to cracks and holes. Fortunately they are not difficult to repair, and the materials you'll need to fix them are available at paint and hardware stores.

Certain of the products used to repair walls and ceilings, however, contain asbestos fibers, and dust containing these fibers can be a health hazard. Ask for a brand that does not contain asbestos fibers.

Hairline cracks and small holes made by picture hooks, nails, screws, etc. can be filled with spackle. Spackle comes as a ready-to-use paste. Force the paste into the crack or hole with a finger or putty knife.

Large cracks in plaster are usually caused by shrinkage or movement of the framework to which the lath and plaster are applied. To make a permanent patch, first undercut or dig out the crack so the inside is wider than the outside. A beer-can opener is a good tool for this job. Brush away all loose material from inside the crack and wet down the sides with water just before applying the patch. Patching plaster is best for large cracks, and it must be mixed with water just before use. Force the patching plaster into the crack with a putty knife 3 or 4 inches wide. For cracks over ¼ inch wide, it's easier if the patch is applied in two layers. The first coat should come to within ⅛ inch of the surface. When it is hard, apply a second coat and smooth it out so it's flush with the adjoining surface.

It's a good idea to reinforce the patch to prevent the crack from recurring. There are several good wall and ceiling repair kits that include reinforcing tape along with patching compound and an applicator. The paper tape used to cover the joints between sec-

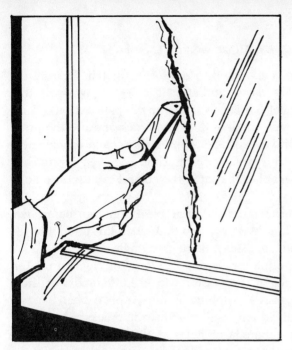

A beer can opener is a handy tool for undercutting cracks in plaster before patching.

Force patching plaster into the crack with a broad putty knife.

tions of wallboard is also good to reinforce a patch. First fill the crack with patching plaster and after it is dry, apply a very thin coat of spackle about 3 inches wide over the patched area. Take a piece of paper tape the length of the crack and use the putty knife to "bed" it into the spackle. Apply a thin coat of spackle over the tape and allow it to dry. Apply a second and even a third coat, feathering the edges of each coat so they blend in with the adjoining surface.

For cracks at corners, use the same treatment, but before you apply the tape, fold it lengthwise so that when it is fitted into the corner it will produce a sharp 90-degree angle.

On large holes in plaster, remove all loose or cracked plaster. Undercut the edges of the plaster with a knife, and wet them down before applying the patching plaster. Apply the patch in two coats just as explained for dealing with wide cracks.

Another way to handle large holes in plaster is to take a piece of gypsum wallboard and cut it to the size of the hole. Set it in the hole and nail it into the lath. It will serve as a base for the patching plaster and will eliminate the need for two coats.

There are several ways to patch large holes in walls or ceilings made of gypsum wallboard. One method is to take a saw and cut out a rectangular section of the wallboard to include the hole and expose about ¾ inch of the wood framework on both sides of the opening. Cut a patch out of wallboard to fit the opening and nail it along the sides to the exposed wood framework. Fill the seams around the patch with spackle and tape.

Another approach is to cut the hole out so that you have a perfect rectangular opening. Cut a piece of wallboard so that it is about 2 inches larger than the hole on all four sides. Place the patch on a worktable with the exposed side down. With a sharp knife cut the gypsum to the exact size of the opening, but do not cut through the heavy paper covering on the underside. Peel off the edges of the gypsum. What you should end up with is a patch that will just fit the opening and with a paper flap along all four sides that you can use to cement the patch to the surface of the surrounding wall. Coat the edges of the gypsum portion of the patch with spackle and apply a wide strip of it to the wall around the opening. Slip the patch into place and bed the paper flaps into the spackle around the sides.

HOW TO HANG THINGS ON WALLS

If you have ever tried to hang or fasten anything to a wall other than a relatively lightweight picture or mirror, you have probably found that it can be a pretty frustrating experience. You may have discovered that the screws usually included with things like shelf brackets, drapery hardware, wall cabinets and bathroom wall fixtures don't hold on most walls and the nails are even more useless.

Even if you're successful in getting whatever it is up, there's apt to be a slightly uneasy feeling—will it stay up? And sometimes it doesn't.

The reason is that you're probably not using the right kind of hanger or fastener for the kind of wall you're dealing with. But if you first determine the kind of wall and then use the proper hanger, your project can proceed in an orderly fashion with an excellent chance of success.

WHAT'S THE WALL MADE OF? Walls in most houses are so-called hollow walls. They can be lath and plaster, gypsum wallboard, plywood, hardboard or some similar surface applied over a vertical wooden framework. They are called hollow walls because, other than the supporting framework, there is nothing but air space or sometimes fibrous insulation between one side of the wall and the other. The wooden framework is made of wood studs usually about 1½ inches wide and 3½ inches deep, as explained in Chapter 1. Depending on the covering, hollow walls run from about ¼ inch thick for certain grades of plywood and hardboard to about ¾ inch thick with lath and plaster.

If you want to know what kind of wall you have, you can find out by driving a slender 3-inch nail into the spot where you plan to hang or fasten something. If the nail goes in easily and you can pull it out easily, it's a hollow wall. If the nail starts to go in easily and then you have to hammer quite hard, you have a hollow wall and have hit one of the wood studs. You're in luck in this case because ordinary screws will do the job, if they are long enough to get a good grip into the wood stud. If the nail goes in for perhaps ¾ inch and absolutely won't go farther, you have solid masonry behind the plaster. That's a situation we'll discuss later on. However, since the majority of walls today are hollow and you might not want to drive a nail into the wall to find out, let's proceed on the assumption that you're dealing with a hollow wall.

HANGING PICTURES AND MIRRORS ON HOLLOW WALLS. Hanging lightweight objects such as pictures and small mirrors presents no great problem most of the time. If you haven't been hanging pictures or mirrors lately, you may not know about a new type of hanger that is excellent. This is a metal hook designed to take not one, but two or three special needlepoint nails. The nails go into the wall at a downward angle, which gives maximum holding power. By using two or three nails in one hanger, the load on each nail is reduced, permitting the use of such slim nails. They make only a pinpoint hole in the wall and can be removed and reused by turning the head with the fingers or a pair of pliers.

A somewhat less desirable hook is the familiar one with a single nail. The heavier the load, the larger the nail, which, of course, can make a rather sizable hole in the wall. These hooks are quite adequate, however, for light- and medium-weight frames.

Pictures and mirrors weighing more than 35 pounds really require two hangers. It is best not to hang them on picture wire, for the pull on the wire can force the sides of the frame out of alignment. The correct method is to install two screw eyes, one on each side of the frame, then slip these over two hangers set into a corresponding position on the wall. The screw eyes should be placed an inch or more below the point where the side pieces join the top of the frame, with the eyes toward the top at approximately a 45-degree angle.

Adhesive-backed picture hooks are also available. These are good for light picture frames, posters and unframed prints. You may find, however, that in time the backing dries out and the hook falls off the wall. Their great advantage is that they make no holes, which can be important for renters whose leases prohibit any sort of hole in the walls.

HANGING HEAVY OBJECTS. Heavy pictures, large mirrors, shelf brackets, cabinets, bathroom wall fixtures, drapery hardware and so forth are somewhat more complicated to hang. Unless the object can be placed so that it is fastened through the wall surface into the studding, you will have to use a plastic expansion anchor, a molly or a toggle bolt. All these fasteners are designed to expand or open up on the back of the wall so that the fastener can't be pulled out. If it does let go, a good-sized chunk of the wall is usually pulled out with it.

• Plastic expansion anchors are good for medium-weight articles such as drapery hardware, small shelf brackets, bathroom soap dishes and lighting fixtures. They consist of a plastic sleeve and a wood screw. The sleeve is inserted into a hole drilled into the wall. The hole should be small enough so that a light tap with a hammer is required to drive the sleeve into place. The screw is run through the hole in the fixture and then threaded into the sleeve. As the screw goes into the sleeve, the end of the sleeve spreads out to grip

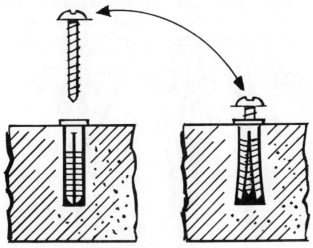

Plastic expansion anchor.

the rear surface of the wall. These little anchors are inexpensive, come in a wide range of sizes and are not difficult to install. Just be sure you use one that is long enough to pass through the wall surface and spread out. If the sleeve is too short, the anchor doesn't work.

• The universal molly is stronger than the plastic expansion anchor and can be used for just about every hanging job from drapery hardware to heavy shelf brackets. Mollies look more complicated than they are. The entire unit is slipped into the hole—another one of those holes that should be exact—until the metal flange under the head of the screw comes in contact with the wall surface. The screw is then tightened with a screwdriver. As the screw is tightened, it splits the metal sleeve and pulls it up against the rear of the wall. The screw is removed, put through the fixture, threaded back into the sleeve, then tightened to pull the object tight against the wall.

Mollies come in a wide range of sizes and are especially useful when a fixture must be removed from time to time for cleaning, because the sleeve remains in the wall. If you ever want to get rid of it the best method is to drive it right through the wall so it falls into the wall cavity.

When using mollies it is sometimes hard to know how much to turn the screw so that the ends of the sleeve will split and be pulled

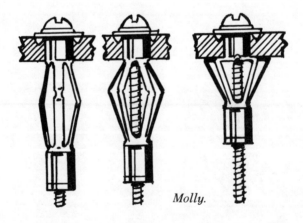

Molly.

up against the rear of the wall. Two indications determine if the molly is set: when the screw begins to turn very hard and when the flange under the screw head begins to turn with the screw.

• Toggle bolts are pretty formidable gadgets and are the strongest of all hollow-wall fasteners. Use them for really heavy things such as large cabinets and brackets that have to hold a lot of books. Also use toggle bolts when you can't get a plastic anchor or molly to hold.

One type of bolt has a wing assembly that screws onto the end. The wings are spring-loaded and are folded back so they can be pushed through the hole in the wall. When the wings reach the wall cavity, they spread out so that as the bolt is tightened, they are pulled up against the rear of the wall. The other type of bolt —much more primitive—has a toggle on the end that pivots. It folds back along the bolt so it can be pushed through the hole and then flips down when it hits the cavity so it can't be pulled back out.

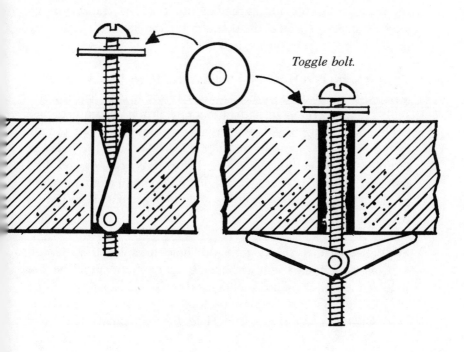

Toggle bolt.

Before hanging a cabinet or something similar, the wings of the toggle must be unscrewed so that the bolt can be threaded through the hole in the cabinet. Now screw the wings back onto the end of the bolt and position them so they can be put through the hole in the wall. Once they get on the other side of the wall surface, tighten up the bolt until the cabinet is securely held against the wall. This is not so easy as it sounds if you are trying to hang a cabinet or bookcase. You'll need two people—one to hold the fixture in place and the other to try to get the business end of the bolt through the hole in the wall.

Toggle bolts come in a wide range of sizes and are not expensive. This is fortunate, because if you should happen to remove the bolt once the unit is in place, the toggle part falls down into the wall cavity and you need a whole new unit to put the fixture back up. There are some kitchen and bathroom walls in old houses and apartment buildings that must contain thousands of toggles.

You may find that the bolts on the larger units are too long for some walls. To be safe, before you try to hang something, take off the wings or toggle and slip the bolt into the hole. If it doesn't go all the way to the head of the bolt, shorten the bolt with a hacksaw or get a unit with a shorter bolt.

WHICH SIZE AND HOW MANY FASTENERS TO USE. With many articles, such as drapery hardware, bathroom wall fixtures and shelf brackets, the size and number of fasteners required are pretty much determined by the size and number of holes already in the fixture. If there are no predrilled holes, use the heaviest fastener that is feasible. Don't place heavy-duty fasteners too close together, though, because you might end up pulling out a hunk of the wall. Heavy cabinets, built-ins and the like should have fasteners about 16 inches apart.

DRILLING HOLES. You've got to drill holes for any of these fasteners; you can't make them with a nail or a kitchen knife. The size hole you need for plastic anchors and mollies is usually given on the package, but many hardware stores sell them loose, so ask the clerk what size hole is required. Holes for toggle bolts don't have to be exact, but they must be slightly larger in diameter than the diameter of the toggle so it can be slipped through.

You can make holes in plaster, gypsum wallboard, plywood, etc. with a hand drill or an electric drill. An ordinary wood bit is all right, but after it has made a few holes in plaster it will get pretty dull.

SPECIAL SITUATIONS. Even the professional sometimes goes wrong estimating the load-carrying ability of a given section of wall. The best thing to do when you have a very heavy piece, such as a kitchen cabinet that is going to be filled with china, and you have some doubts about the strength of the wall—⅜-inch-thick gypsum wallboard, for instance, is not all that strong—is to use furring strips. These are thin strips of wood 2 or 3 inches wide applied horizontally across a section of the wall and fastened to the wall studding with long wood screws—about 3 inches long. The cabinet or whatever can then be screwed into the furring strips.

This, of course, brings up a new problem—locating the position of the studding. There is a theory that if you pound on a wall with your hand or fist, you'll get a solid sound when you are over a stud and a hollow sound elsewhere. This theory works on some but not all walls. A method that can't miss is to drill a line of small holes through the wall until the drill bit starts to turn out sawdust, which means you've hit a stud. As mentioned earlier, studding is usually spaced about 14½ inches apart. (If you want to be technical, it is spaced 16 inches from center to center, and since the width of each stud is 1½ inches, the actual distance between two pieces figures out to be 14½ inches.) Once you've found the middle of one stud, you can measure off 16 inches and be close to the middle of the adjoining one.

This is a good time to mention that when wood paneling is applied over an existing wall, furring strips are usually required. Some types of paneling, however, can be applied with special mastics or adhesives if the wall surface meets requirements.

Plaster is sometimes applied over metal lath, and this can be a great nuisance if you need large holes for toggle bolts. A wood bit won't do much on metal lath except get dull. You should either use a metal bit or cut through the plaster with a wood bit and then go after the lath with one of those little pistol-grip hacksaws.

In older houses and some apartments you may find plaster applied over wood lath. There is just a fraction of an inch spacing between the laths, so chances are that if you drill a hole or drive a nail into these walls, you'll hit lath. Some of this lath is the toughest wood you'll ever run into. It's a first cousin to hardened steel. You'll need a good sharp wood bit in your drill to get through it. If you try to drive a nail for a heavy picture hook into it, the nail won't go in, but the blows of your hammer will push the lath back and probably crack the plaster. Save yourself a patching job by first drilling a small pilot hole through the lath and then drive the nail into it.

A lot of plaster—especially the new stuff they slap on these days —is often so soft that it won't grip the sides of a plastic anchor or a molly and the unit will just spin around as you try to tighten the screw. The more it spins, the larger the hole becomes. Best thing here is to use a toggle bolt. If one isn't handy or you just don't want to, pack the hole with plastic wood or wood putty. Set the anchor or molly into this and let the filler dry until hard. The anchor or molly should then stay put.

SOLID MASONRY. You need a special masonry anchor to fasten things to a solid masonry wall—poured concrete, concrete block, brick, stone, or plaster applied over solid masonry. You can use masonry anchors made of plastic, lead or fiber for lightweight objects, but for heavy loads you need a steel expansion anchor designed to take a lag screw.

Don't try to drill a hole in solid masonry with a wood or even a metal bit. What you need here is either a carbide-tipped bit in an electric drill or a star drill. A star drill is a simple tool you strike on the head with a heavy hammer. Each time you strike the head you rotate the drill one-quarter of a turn and eventually you'll make a hole. Life is easier if you pay a couple of dollars for a carbide-tipped bit and use it in the electric drill.

By the way, the mortar joints between block, brick and stone are easy to drill into, but the mortar joint is the weakest spot. If you have something heavy to hang, put the holes into the solid masonry and not into the joints.

Part Four
REAL ESTATE BUYING GUIDE

Caveat emptor—*"Let the purchaser beware"—should always be a part of your thinking when you buy any kind of real estate—a new house, a used house, a condominium or a plot of land.*

It's true that in the past few years a good many laws, federal and state, have been passed to help protect you when you buy real estate, but it's still up to you to inspect property before buying, assess any conditions that are readily apparent on inspection and ask questions about anything you don't understand. If you don't, and you get a bum deal, it's nobody's fault but your own.

There are specialists, of course, who can help you avoid making a serious mistake—house-inspection services, architects, your own attorney and so on— but in the final analysis, it's up to you to ask the pertinent questions. It is your responsibility to make certain that what you get is exactly what you believe you are getting and not something less.

In these chapters you'll find some of the more important questions to ask in buying various forms of real estate. Don't be shy about asking these questions, because after all it's your money.

22

HOUSE SPECIALISTS YOU SHOULD KNOW ABOUT

How CAN you find out the true condition of a house before you buy it? How can you find out if it is overpriced compared with similar houses in the area? If you are going to sell your house, what can you do to make it more attractive to a potential buyer? Or, if you want to put on an addition, what's the least expensive way to get what you want? Can you be sure that you have enough fire insurance on your house to cover the cost of replacement should it be damaged by fire? What kind of plants and shrubbery can you grow on your property that will be attractive in all seasons and yet require minimum upkeep?

Maybe you know the answers, but most of us really don't. Too often we make important decisions relating to the house and grounds on a kind of hit-or-miss basis, or rely on the limited knowledge of friends, on quasi-experts, or on people who will stand to profit by the advice they give us. There are professionals, however, who can give us informed and objective answers to these and similar questions and often save us money in the bargain.

Like a doctor or lawyer, these specialists have nothing to sell but their talents and experience. Here are the ones you should know about—what they can do for you, what their qualifications are, how much they charge for their services and where you can find them.

ARCHITECT

The architect is qualified not only to design and draw plans for a house or remodeling, but also to advise you on the selection of a building site, the most suitable materials to use and the best contractor for the job. In recommending a contractor, his opinion is based on not only the amount of the contractor's bid but his reputation for quality workmanship and reliability. The architect will specify the manner in which the work is to be done and will supervise the job to make sure that the contractor does it in strict accordance with the plans and specifications. Many architects who specialize in residential work will also do small jobs—giving an objective opinion on a set of plans you may have and perhaps suggesting minor changes, advising you on how you might enlarge a house to contain an expanding family, or showing you how you could make the exterior of your house more attractive.

Because of his extensive training in design and building techniques and his familiarity with the most up-to-date building materials, the architect can often come up with not only an attractive solution to a problem but often the least expensive one as well. In fact, it is not unusual for the savings gained by the use of his talents to be enough to cover his fee.

An individual must be registered in the state where he practices before he can call himself an "architect." He must have a degree from a college with an accredited school of architecture, pass a rigid state examination and work under a registered architect for a required number of years. If, after he is registered by the state, he joins the American Institute of Architects, a professional organization, he may use the initials "A.I.A." after his name. Not all registered architects are members of the A.I.A.

Architects will work either on a percentage basis or at an hourly rate. When an architect handles a large project such as designing and supervising the construction of a new house or an extensive remodeling, his fee is based on the total cost of the project. On new construction this will be around 12 to 15 percent of the total construction cost. On remodeling, usually more complicated and time-consuming than new work, the percentage will range from 15 to 25 percent. Working at an hourly rate, the architect may charge $20 or so. This is a very good arrangement if you need only a limited amount of help, such as ideas and rough sketches on how to expand an existing house, minor changes in stock plans to suit individual requirements or the architect's opinions on a house or a piece of land you are interested in buying.

Before an architect goes to work for you, tell him what your budget is for the entire project, including his fee. Ask him exactly what he charges and whether his charges are on an hourly rate or on a percentage basis.

Not all architects do residential work. Some specialize only in commercial and industrial jobs. In the residential field, the better-known and larger firms will probably charge a somewhat higher fee than the smaller outfits—especially those run by young architects who are just beginning their own practice.

Architects are listed in the Yellow Pages. You will find that by and large they are a very considerate group, and if you call one who isn't interested in your project or who is too expensive for your budget, he'll very likely suggest names of some colleagues. You can also get names of residential architects from local bankers, real estate brokers and general contractors, or write to the American Institute of Architects, 1785 Massachusetts Avenue, Washington, D.C. 20036 and ask for the address of the chapter nearest you. The local chapter can give you a list of architects in your area.

HOUSE INSPECTOR

If you are about to buy a house, especially a used one, you'd be wise to have a house inspector look it over before you sign a contract to buy. You would also be wise to consult a house inspector before you buy a condominium.

The house inspector—who may work as an individual or with a "home inspection service," an "architectural and structural inspection service," or some similarly named company—will check out the house and report everything he finds wrong with it. He'll note if there is poor soil drainage around the house, if there are signs of termites or decay. He'll check out the sewage system, plumbing system, electrical wiring and all the other mechanical items. He will report on the condition and age of the roof, exterior paint, windows, interior walls and ceilings, woodwork, bathroom and kitchen fixtures—even check to see if there are light fixtures in the closets. He'll find out if the house is adequately insulated and if the fireplace smokes. Each time he finds something questionable, he'll indicate how serious he considers the matter to be and what he believes will be necessary to correct it.

The house inspector is not primarily concerned with the market value of the house—just what is wrong with it. He does not give an estimate on what it will cost to correct the flaws he has found, and naturally he does not do repair or improvement work himself. If, after going over his report, you are still interested in the house, give the report to a general contractor and let him give you an estimate on what it will cost to put the house in proper shape. You might wish to use the report and the estimate when you discuss price with the seller or his broker. For example, if it's going to cost around $400 to get rid of termites, the seller may agree to deduct this amount from his asking price. Or if the heating system is shot, he may similarly deduct the cost of repair or replacement.

It's smart to have a house inspector check out a condominium before you buy. It requires this sort of expert to check out the condition of all the common property—structures, street and sidewalk paving, underground sewer lines, even the swimming pool. If any of these items are of poor quality, they will soon require expensive repairs or replacements, and these costs will have to be paid for by the owners of the condominium units.

At this writing, house inspectors do not require a license. Many of them are engineers or have had previous experience as real estate appraisers or as general contractors. Before you hire one, ask him to show you a sample of the report he makes so you can see how detailed it is. Also ask him for the names of other homeowners in your area he's worked for and check a few of these out.

The charge for a complete inspection will vary depending on the firm and the value of the house. One inspection service on the West Coast provides a very detailed report for a house selling for under $25,000 for around $50 and charges $65 for houses selling from $25,000 to $100,000. You may pay somewhat more than this in your area, but it should not be a great deal more.

You'll find house-inspection services listed under "Real Estate Appraisers" in the Yellow Pages. You can also get names from local banks and real estate brokers.

REAL ESTATE APPRAISERS

The real estate appraiser is the expert who can give you an unbiased opinion on the current market value of property—either a house or a piece of land. Briefly stated, market value is the highest price that a buyer willing, but not compelled, to buy would pay and the lowest that a seller willing, but not compelled, to sell would accept.

If you are interested in buying a particular house, an independent appraisal will tell you if the seller is asking more than the house is worth. And if he is, your appraiser's report can be useful ammunition in getting the seller to come down on his price. The report will also give you important information on neighborhood and property-tax trends, which may influence your decision on buying that particular house or any other house in the general area. The appraiser will also give you a good indication of the condition of the house, but not as detailed as one made by a house inspector.

If you are considering making some major improvements to your house—adding a wing, for example—it might be smart to call in an appraiser to find out if you'll be able to get your money out if and when you sell.

If you are not certain whether you have too little or too much fire insurance, an appraisal will tell you the amount you should have to cover the cost of replacement. If you believe that your property is being overassessed for property taxes, an appraisal will help you in your dealings with the local board of real estate tax assessors. If you are ever faced with condemnation of your property under the laws of eminent domain by a state or private agency, and you are not satisfied with the amount of compensation you are offered, an independent appraisal of your property will help in your appeal. And if you are going to put your house on the market, an appraisal will help you decide how much to ask for it.

The true worth of any appraisal depends on the experience and qualifications of the appraiser. If he has had the necessary experience he may be "certified" by one of the professional organizations such as the American Institute of Appraisers or the Society of Real Estate Appraisers if he meets their requirements and can pass their examinations. Before you hire an appraiser, ask him for his qualifications. If he has done work for a unit of government—town, county, state or federal—(FHA or VA, for example)—this is usually a good indication of his ability. Also ask him if he is an expert court witness, for this means that his judgment as to the value of a piece of property will be taken into account by a court of law.

Appraisers charge a flat fee for their services, and for the average house the fee will range from $100 to $150 or so.

You'll find appraisers listed in the Yellow Pages under "Real Estate Appraisers." Your local bank, real estate broker or home-insurance agent can also give you the names of qualified residential appraisers in your area.

LANDSCAPE ARCHITECT

Don't confuse the landscape architect with a nurseryman. A nurseryman, regardless of experience and knowledge of horticulture, is basically in the business of selling trees, shrubs and plants, installing them and caring for them. A landscape architect, like the registered architect, sells nothing but his creative talents. He is a specialist qualified to assess the best way to site a house on a lot to make the most of both house and grounds. He can design a swimming pool to harmonize with the house and grounds, draw up a master landscape plan to be executed either by you or a nurseryman. He can design a terrace, patio or deck, plan a low-maintenance landscape project, suggest the best kind of fencing and help you select plantings suited to your budget, your grounds and the time you wish to spend taking care of them.

In about 26 states, those calling themselves "landscape architects" must be registered. This means that the individual has completed a course in landscape architecture at an accredited college, passed examinations and practiced landscape architecture for a certain number of years.

In those states not requiring registration of landscape architects, you should feel free to ask for qualifications and for the names of people for whom the architect has done work.

Most landscape architects will work on an hourly basis—usually around $25 per hour—or give you a flat rate on work that will take considerable time.

Landscape architects are listed in the Yellow Pages. You can get names from local registered architects and nurserymen. You can also get a list of those in your area from the American Society of Landscape Architects, 1750 Old Meadow Road, McLean, Virginia 22101.

REAL ESTATE BROKER

Unless you want to undertake the chore yourself, this is obviously the expert to use when you want to sell a house or parcel of land, find a tenant or buy a house or piece of land.

If you want to sell your house, the broker will help you decide on a fair market price and often suggest inexpensive ways to make it more attractive to a buyer—cleaning the junk out of the closets, tidying up the yard, giving the front door a coat of paint and so forth. And he'll also discourage you from making expensive improvements that won't add value to your house or make it any easier to sell.

The broker will often advertise your property—at his expense. If he is a member of the local multiple-listing service, he will notify other member brokers so that your house will get the widest possible exposure. He will show your house to prospective buyers, do the selling, negotiate price with the buyer and handle all the financial negotiations, subject, of course, to your approval.

If you want to rent your house, the broker will find you a suitable tenant and check out his references, and if you plan to be away, he can act as your manager—collect the rent, see that your property is maintained and arrange to have repairs made when necessary.

And if you are looking for a house or property to buy, the broker will show you what is available, negotiate price with the seller and help you to arrange financing, and it won't cost you a nickle.

A real estate broker must be licensed by the state where he does business and is subject to rather strict state regulations. Before he can get a license, the broker must pass an examination given by the state. If a broker is a member of the National Association of Real Estate Boards, he may call himself a "realtor."

The real estate broker is paid a commission based on the sales price of the property. This commission is paid by the seller—the broker's client. The amount of commission will vary according to local conditions, but 6 percent is about average. If a broker sells your house for $40,000, his commission would be $2,400. The commission is usually paid to the broker at the time the buyer takes title to the property.

This same arrangement holds true when a broker is used to find a tenant. The landlord pays his commission, and this is usually around 10 percent or sometimes equal to a month's rent. The exception to this rule is in an area where there is a shortage of rental property, in which case it will be the tenant who pays the commission. When a broker acts as manager for property, his commission may run as much as 25 percent of each month's rent, depending on how much time it takes him to handle the property.

When you commission a broker to sell property for you, you should have a contract with him in writing. The contract should specify the amount of his commission, the length of time the contract is in force and whether the broker has an "exclusive listing" or the "exclusive right to sell." There is a difference, and it's an important difference. If the broker has an exclusive listing (sometimes called "exclusive agency"), he will get a portion of his commission if the property is sold by some other broker, but *not* if you sell the house yourself without his assistance. But if he has the exclusive right to sell, he has a legal claim to his full commission even if you find the buyer and make the sale on your own.

You won't have any trouble finding aggressive brokers who specialize in residential property. They will run ads in local newspapers listing property for sale, and you'll see their names on "For Sale" signs in front of property.

23

THE NEW HOUSE YOU CAN AFFORD

HIGH LAND and construction costs have put the typical new single-family house beyond the reach of many, especially young families who don't own a house they can sell, or don't have enough equity in a house to make a down payment on a new one. But there is a type of house that many can afford, and this is the so-called "no-frill" house. These basic houses are being offered by builders throughout the country and at a realistic price—under $30,000 plus land.

If your heart is set on a new house but the going rate has been too steep, then you should look into the no-frill house. It can be a good starter house for a young family. It can be a good house to add to, and it can be a good house for a retirement couple.

The concept of the no-frill house is not exactly new. It's much the same kind of house as those that sold like hotcakes after World War II and that were the dream houses for thousands of families. Simple they were, but they beat living in an apartment and paying rent or living with the in-laws.

This very basic house is making a comeback because builders around the country have learned, the hard way, that fewer and fewer families can afford the kind of house they had been building for the past decade or so—the big-time boom-time house for the big-time bank account. By 1974 the typical house had grown to an average size of 1,560 square feet. It was packed with special features to attract affluent buyers—three-way masonry fireplaces, terraces and decks, outdoor lighting, saunas and just about every amenity you could think of. It had four bedrooms, a two-car garage, two baths and probably a powder room, a separate dining room and a huge family room plus a living room with fireplace. It sat in the middle of a ½-acre or 1-acre lot loaded with plants and a lawn made of sod that cost around 30 cents a square foot. And each year the house cost more to buy and more and more to maintain. By 1974 the cost of the average single-family house was over $41,000—about $15,000 more than most people could afford.

A more basic house with fewer frills is a much more realistic house for this age of spiraling building costs, high real estate taxes and the ever-increasing cost of home energy whether it is electricity, gas or oil. A well-designed basic house can supply a family with all the necessities for a comfortable home. The luxuries can come later when you have the money or time to handle them.

Here are some of the ways that a builder can reduce the cost of a house. And remember, each hundred dollars he shaves off the price means that more people can afford to buy that house. We've pointed out the advantages and disadvantages of each one to the buyer. These can help you decide which you may be able to do without if you go out to buy a basic house.

• Smaller lots. Land is expensive, so a builder can cut the price of his house if he can get more houses on a parcel of land by reducing the size of each lot. Some communities allow houses to be built with a "zero lot line," which means there will be no side yard between adjoining houses. Smaller lots reduce real estate taxes and mean less lawn and less landscaping to maintain. But they may also mean you'll have to install fencing to get privacy for outdoor living areas such as terraces and decks.

• No landscaping. It can cost a builder $500 or more to landscape even a small lot—sod for a lawn plus some foundation planting and a couple of little trees. These are chores many owners can do themselves and get exactly what they want. But the builder should install paved walks and driveway.

• Smaller house. Each square foot of enclosed space costs around $25. This means that a house with 1,200 square feet of living space will cost around $2,500 less than a house with 1,300 square feet. Another advantage to a smaller house is that it will cost less to heat in winter and to cool in summer. And it will naturally cost less to maintain—real estate taxes, painting, etc.

It does, however, take a lot more skill to design a comfortable small house than a comfortable big one, so check the floor plan carefully. There should be good separation between the living areas—living room and kitchen—and the bedrooms and bathroom. There should be a good traffic pattern so you can get from one room to another without having to go right across another room. And all rooms should be large enough to serve your purposes. It is very possible to have a very comfortable and well-designed house with under 1,200 square feet of living space. And this is a three-bedroom house, too.

• Two stories rather than one story. Two-story houses cost less to build than one-story houses of equal living area because there is less roof, less outside wall area and less foundations. And a two-story house takes only half the land required by a one-story house of equal area. The saving on land can be very important if the house is set on a small lot.

There is good separation of areas in a two-story house because the living areas are on the first floor while the bedrooms and bath are on the second. And the bedrooms get a lot of privacy.

A two-story house is less costly to heat than a one-story house of equal area not only because it is compact but because it has less roof and wall areas that allow heat to escape.

Many people don't care for a two-story house because of the stairs. Stairs can be a problem for the very young and very old, but they are good exercise for anyone else in good health.

• No basement. A full basement adds about $2,000 to the cost of a house, and a half basement adds around $1,200. A basement, of course, is one of those items you can't conveniently add after a house has been built. You can have a perfectly comfortable house without a basement, built over crawl space or on a slab.

If a basement is dry—and not all of them are—it makes a good place for storage, for a workshop or hobby area or for a recreation room. But if you don't need all these, you can get along fine without a basement. There must, however, be adequate storage space in the house proper, and there must be a spot for the laundry and heating equipment plus room for odds and ends.

- No family room. A separate family room increases the cost of the average house by around $3,500. This is a room that can be added at some future time and at a reasonable cost if the house has been designed with this addition in mind. The house should be placed on the lot so there will be room for the addition where it would be logical to have it—off the kitchen or living room but not off a bedroom.

- No garage or carport. An attached one-car garage costs around $2,500 and a carport runs about $1,700. You can get along without a garage or carport, and either one can be added at some future date. But if you do not have one or the other, you will need some type of outside storage area for items that are not normally put indoors—garden tools, lawn furniture, bicycles, etc.

- No fireplace. Figure that a brick or stone fireplace will add around $1,500 or more to the price of a house. A metal prefab fireplace with a metal chimney adds around $750 to $1,000. Either type of fireplace can be added after the house is completed, but a brick fireplace is going to cost a lot—maybe as much as $2,000. A prefab can be added at not much more cost than it takes to put one in when the house is built. And a prefab fireplace can be put almost anywhere in the house that you want it, but if you add a masonry fireplace it will have to be set on an outside wall.

- Fewer bathrooms. A second bathroom adds around $1,000 to the cost of the house, while a lavatory with two fixtures adds around $600—plus the cost of the space required at $25 or so per square foot. Adding either a bathroom or lavatory can be very expensive unless the house was planned for this sort of addition. This means that there is space partitioned off and the plumbing lines have been brought in so they can be easily connected to the fixtures.

• No central air conditioning. This increases the cost of the average house by about $1,400. It is not much more expensive than this to add air conditioning later on if the house is heated by forced warm air and the heating system was designed so it can be used for air conditioning. The importance of air conditioning depends on where you live. In the very warm climates it has become pretty essential, but in the moderate climates it is still something of a luxury. Keep in mind that central air conditioning is going to add to operating costs.

• No appliances. When the builder provides the major kitchen appliances—range, built-in oven, refrigerator, dishwasher, etc.— it adds another $1,200 to the price of the house. And a built-in oven costs around $200 more than a free-standing range. You always pay through the nose when you have appliances included in the price of a house because you'll be paying for them for the entire length of the mortgage—25 or 30 years, in some cases. And the life of most of these appliances is only around 14 years. That means you'll be paying on them even after you've replaced them. You'll save a good deal of money if you install appliances you may already own or buy them for cash. If you are not quite ready for a dishwasher, see that the builder provides space for it in a cabinet alongside the sink.

• Unpainted interior. Doing this job yourself can cut the cost of a house by $900. Interior painting is one chore that most people can do and do pretty well if they are not rushed and take the time to do it properly.

• Unfinished interior areas. A builder can reduce the price by $1,000 or more by leaving certain areas unfinished—the second and third bedrooms, the family room, a second bath and so forth. These areas are then completed by the owner. This may involve installing some partitions for closets, covering ceilings and walls with gypsum wallboard, putting down the finish flooring and installing doors and interior trim. It takes a certain amount of skill plus a lot of time to do this sort of work but it's a good way to save on the cost of a house. Some families have done all the inside work themselves. It's important that the builder install the rough wiring and plumbing, for most communities insist that this work be done by licensed mechanics.

LOOK FOR QUALITY
CONSTRUCTION

The way some builders cut the cost of their houses is to cut down on the quality of materials and workmanship. This is one kind of cost cutting you should not accept under any circumstances. The fact that the house may be smaller than the more conventional house, that it may lack certain amenities and may even have some areas unfinished, does not mean that it cannot be a quality-built house. And that's the only kind of house you should buy regardless of the price tag.

One of your best guarantees that a house will be well built is the character of the builder. If he is a good builder, you'll end up with a good house whether it costs $20,000 or $200,000. If he's a bum operator looking for a fast buck you can expect almost anything but you'll probably end up with a lemon.

Look for a local builder or developer who has a good track record over the years in your area. Take the time to visit some of the houses or areas he has developed. The long-established firms are usually the best—they have weathered bad times as well as boom times in the building field. It's a good sign if the builder is a member of the National Association of Home Builders and if the houses he builds qualify for insurance under the Home Owners Warranty Corporation. This is a subsidiary of the National Association of Home Builders. It provides the home buyer with a written warranty, backed by insurance, to cover defects in a new house caused by faulty materials and workmanship. It also provides a means of handling disagreements over defects between builder and owner. You can get additional information on this type of insurance program by writing to Home Owners Warranty Corporation, National Housing Center, 15th and M Sts., N.W., Washington, D.C. 20005

Good local builders and developers are usually members of local civic groups such as the Chamber of Commerce, Lions, Rotary, etc.

You can find out if a particular builder has a poor reputation by checking with the local Better Business Bureau, your state Real Estate Commission, Office of Consumer Protection or Attorney

General. These people can tell you if they have received complaints about a particular builder or developer.

PRODUCTS AND MATERIALS. Another way to check the quality of a house is by the kind of products and materials used to build it. Even if the house has not been built yet, a builder should be able to tell you exactly what kind of products and materials will be used in it. If he can't, find a builder who can.

Most good builders use a large number of brand-name building products and materials. They do this not only because they have found, from experience, that these products give good results but also because they help sell a house. When a buyer sees a house full of products that he or she is familiar with, he feels a good deal more confident about the quality of the house than he would in one put together with stuff he never heard of. You should expect to find a great many brand-name products even in a low-cost house.

While you should expect to find good-quality products and materials, do not expect to get the top-of-the-line or deluxe models. What you should expect are standard units which cost a great deal less than the deluxe models but perform just as well.

Here is a listing of the more important specific items to investigate.

• Roofing. Most houses have roofs covered with asphalt shingles. You want a roof with a warranty from the manufacturer for at least 20 years. And the shingles should be certified by the Underwriters' Laboratory as fire- and wind-resistant.

• Gutters. Some houses have a roof design that eliminates the need of gutters, but if the house is to have gutters, they should be of aluminum or vinyl. Wood and galvanized-steel gutters won't last unless they are well maintained.

• Windows. Except in the very warm areas, wood windows are better than aluminum windows. Either type should come with factory-installed weatherstripping to reduce heat loss in winter and heat gain in summer and also to keep out street noise and dirt.

If you live in an area where central heat is needed, all windows should come with a storm sash or storm panel or be made of insulating glass.

Wood windows should be factory-treated with a wood preservative so the wood won't decay and to keep it from absorbing moisture which will make the sash difficult to open or close in damp
humid weather.

Aluminum windows should have a baked enamel finish or at
least be anodized to prevent them from pitting. If aluminum windows are used as the primary window, there should be a thermal
barrier between the primary window and the storm sash.

• Doors. Outside doors should be either panel or solid-core—
never hollow. If there are glass panels in the door these should be
made of safety glass and not ordinary window glass. All hardware
should be solid brass or aluminum—never brass-plated steel. Sliding glass doors should be made with insulating glass. They should
come with weatherstripping and a keyed lock.

• Insulation. Every house should be thoroughly insulated to cut
the cost of heating in winter and cooling in summer. There should
be insulation at the top of the house—in the attic floor or on the
underside of the roof, in the outside walls, and on the underside
of floors above unheated crawl space. If the house is built on a
concrete slab, the edges of the slab should be insulated. Check
with your state energy agency to find out what the minimum
requirements are for insulation in your area and be sure you get
this amount.

• Interior walls and ceilings. If these are made of gypsum board,
the thickness of the panels should be ½ inch and not ⅜ inch.
Bathroom walls should be insulated to make them sound-resistant.
And insulation should be installed around a recessed tub to reduce
the racket when it is being filled with water.

• Flooring. The kind of finish flooring you get depends pretty
much on how much you are willing to pay for it. But there are a
couple of points to keep in mind. First, if your house has a concrete
slab floor, you'll need to cover it with some form of resilient or soft
floor covering, because concrete can be very hard on the feet,
especially for anyone working in the kitchen. Secondly, many
houses are built with a floor made of a single thickness of plywood
which is covered with wall-to-wall carpeting. This is fine if you
want the carpeting or wish to cover the plywood over with some
other type of floor covering, but you've got to cover it with some-

thing because the plywood alone is not suitable for a finish floor —too many splinters.

• Bathroom Fixtures. Cast-iron bathtubs are a little better than those made of steel but are also more expensive. Lavatory sinks are usually made of vitreous china, cast iron or stainless steel. All three are good. Toilets are made of china. Be sure that the toilet bowl is oval-shaped and not round. A round bowl is difficult to keep clean.

Colored fixtures always cost a good deal more than white units and don't work one bit better.

In the last few years plastic bathroom fixtures, especially tubs and shower stalls, have become quite common. Some firms offer a complete bathroom molded out of plastic. This includes the fixtures, walls, ceiling and floor. Plastic units can be excellent if made by a recognized firm.

• Plumbing. Insist that all the fresh-water lines—both hot and cold—be made of copper. Plastic pipe has been used in place of copper but at this writing there is some question as to whether the water that has come through plastic pipe may not be a health hazard. Plastic pipe is fine, however, for the entire house drainage system.

If there are any plumbing units that are to be added to the house at some future time it's important that the builder "rough in" the plumbing lines during construction. This means bringing the fresh and waste lines to the points where they will be connected to the fixtures. For example, if you plan to install an automatic dishwasher at some time, you'd want supply and drain lines brought to the area where the unit is to be installed. The same would be true if you had an unfinished area where you planned to install a second bathroom. Have the builder bring in all lines and cap them. If this is done the fixtures can be installed with a minimum amount of effort and cost to you.

• Electric Wiring. You should have at least 150-amp electric service to the house. If you plan on electric heat and air conditioning you'll need 200-amp service.

There should be at least one outlet in each room that is controlled by a wall switch. This means you can turn the light on in each room from the door. There should be three-way switches to lights over stairs, to the garage and other areas where it might be desirable to be able to turn the lights on and off from two different points.

The wiring as well as the outlets should be installed in all areas that are left unfinished but are to be completed at some future date.

During the past few years aluminum has been used in place of copper for wiring. There have been some problems with aluminum wiring because of failures at connections which have resulted in fires. If the house is to have aluminum wiring, check with your building inspector to be sure that your local electrical code guarantees a perfectly safe wiring system.

The electric and telephone lines to the house should be underground. There is no excuse these days to have these lines running overhead from a utility pole to the house.

• Sewage. If the house is to have a septic system, check with the local building department to be sure that a percolation test of the soil on the lot has been made and the results of the tests indicate that an approved septic system can be installed. If the sewer lines in the development are to be connected into a city sewer system, check with the same agency to be sure that the lines have been installed so they meet local requirements or that the developer has posted a performance bond so that you and the other property owners won't have to pay to have unsatisfactory work redone.

• Lot. You may not get a landscaped lot, but it should be graded so that there are no low spots and the land should slope away from the house for a distance of about 8 feet. The builder should install walks and drives of blacktop or poured concrete.

24

WHAT TO LOOK FOR WHEN YOU BUY A USED HOUSE

THERE ARE a lot of good reasons why a used house may be a better buy than a new one. You can generally get more house for your money with a used house, and many of them are better built than the new houses going up these days. When you buy a used house you'll be buying into an established neighborhood, and this means you can see in advance what sort of neighbors you'll have, how well the neighborhood is maintained and the quality of essential services—fire and police, schools, mass transportation, convenience to shopping areas, etc.

But buying a used house is also somewhat like buying a used car —you want to check it out carefully before you sign on the dotted line. You want to find out what, if anything, is wrong with the house and how much it will cost to make the necessary repairs. And, of course, you want to make certain that the asking price is in line with comparable houses in the same general area.

You seldom find a used house in perfect condition. There are almost sure to be some flaws. Some of the flaws may be of a minor nature and not unexpected in any house that has been lived in for a period of time. But there may be other flaws of a more serious nature that will have to be corrected almost immediately, sometimes at considerable expense. Each time you visit a house, try to learn exactly what, if anything, is seriously wrong with it and then, if you are still interested, what it will cost to correct the condition. Only when you know the cost of making essential repairs and add these costs to the asking price will you really be able to decide whether or not the house is a suitable one for you.

ASK QUESTIONS

You can find out many things about a house if you ask the right questions and insist on getting straight answers from the seller or his broker.

Remember, however, that the seller or his representative are not required by law to go around pointing out the flaws in the house. But if you ask a direct question, they must give you an honest answer. If they don't, and you buy the house and find out that they did not tell the truth, you can sue for fraud. Of course, if they do not know the answer they can say so, but if they do know the answer and tell you they don't or lie about it, they are guilty of fraud.

So what you have to do is to ask a lot of direct questions and insist on getting direct answers. Don't let the broker or the seller change the subject so your question never gets answered. If they say they don't know the answer to a particular question, ask them to try to find it. Don't accept vague answers such as "It looks fine to me" or "No one ever mentioned any problem here" and so forth.

It can take a lot of time, or money, to make a complete inspection of a house, so the more you can find out by asking questions, the easier it will be for you to decide whether a particular house is worth investigating further or should be crossed off your list.

Here are a list of questions to ask the seller or his broker. They deal with major problems—the ones that can cost you a lot of money. And while it may take someone a little time to dig up some of the answers, you should expect a direct answer to each question.

• What kind of water supply? Is there city water, or does the water supply come from a private well? If it comes from a well, ask if it is a deep or shallow well. Shallow wells often go dry and are easily polluted. If water is from a deep well, ask the rate of flow. It should be at least 6 gallons a minute, and this information will be given on the well driller's log. Have water analyzed for purity before you buy. A new deep well can cost $1,000 or more.

• Is there a septic system? Ask if there is a city sewer line or if the house has a septic system. Find out if the septic system conforms to existing building codes, for if it does not you may have to make some expensive improvements. Ask also when the tank was last pumped out. If it has not been pumped out in the past four or five years the drain field may be clogged and you may have to spend $1,000 or more to get the system back into operation.

• How old is the roof? Most roofing materials last from 15 to 25 years and then they'll have to be replaced. A new roof can cost $2,000 or more.

• When was the house last painted? House paint lasts from 6 to 8 years. If the old paint is allowed to weather too long, it may become so thin that two coats will be needed. The cost of painting the average-size house will be around $1,500.

• What is the capacity of the electric service? If the service is under 100 amps, you won't be able to use many heavy-duty electric appliances such as clothes dryer, range, hot-water heater, air conditioners, etc. The cost to increase a 60-amp service to 150 amps will be around $350. Also ask if house is wired with aluminum rather than copper wire. There has been some difficulty with some installations of aluminum wiring and to replace it may cost $1,000 or more.

• Is the basement dry? A basement that floods at certain times can be a serious drawback to any house. It can cost several thousand dollars to waterproof a basement, and even then the results may not be perfect.

• Is the house fully insulated? There should be at least 6 inches of mineral wool or insulation with a value of R-19 in the attic floor or underside of the roof. The underside of any floor above unheated space should have 4 inches of mineral wool or insulation with an R-16 value. All outside walls should be insulated with 3½ inches of mineral wool. It can cost $2,000 or so to fully insulate an existing house, and if the house is not insulated, it will be terribly expensive to heat in winter and cool in summer.

• Are there storm windows? Except for those made of insulating glass, all windows should have a storm sash unless the house is in a very warm climate. Good-quality combination aluminum storm windows cost about $35 each, installed on the average-size window.

• How much does it cost to heat the house? Ask to see the last season's heating bills. Compare the cost with the cost of heating other houses you've inspected. Keep in mind that the prices for heating energy keep going up.

• How old is the boiler or furnace? If it is over 25 years old, it may be not only very inefficient and waste fuel but it may be in need of expensive repairs. A new heating system can cost $1,500 or more.

• Do the fireplaces work properly? Some flues may be blocked so the fireplace can't be used at all. Other fireplaces may not draw properly and fill the room with smoke. It can cost several hundred dollars to correct a smoking fireplace.

• Has there been any sign of termites? It can cost around $400 to have a termite-control firm come in to rid the house of termites. It may cost several times this amount to repair the damage they have done.

• How old is the hot-water heater? If it is 10 years old or older it is about finished and should be replaced at once. The cost of a new one installed will be around $150. Also ask the capacity of the tank. If it is under 40 gallons it probably won't provide enough hot water for the average family of four.

• Are all fresh-water pipes copper or brass? In many older houses, galvanized iron pipes are found. These will eventually leak or become clogged with rust. The cost of replacing all the fresh-water lines in a house can be several thousand dollars.

• Do all the major appliances in the kitchen come with the house? Many sellers will remove these items unless it is specified in the agreement for sale that they are to be included in the price of the house.

• Is the area zoned exclusively for single-family houses? If it is not, existing houses can be converted into multi-family or commercial use, which will change the character of the neighborhood.

• Have any major improvements been made since the house was last appraised for real estate taxes? If there have been substantial improvements, the real estate taxes may soon be considerably higher than at present.

MAKE YOUR OWN INSPECTION

If, after you get the answers to all these questions, you still find the house of interest, then it is worth taking the time to make a more detailed inspection. Of course, if you have reached the point where you are about to make a firm offer, it would be wise to have the house checked over by a professional house inspector (Chapter 22). He will go over it carefully and give you a detailed report on everything that he finds right and everything he finds wrong. The charge for this service will be from $50 to $150, depending on the value of the house. You can then give this report to a local general contractor, who can give you an estimate of the cost of making the needed repairs. Needless to say, knowing exactly what is wrong with a house and what it will cost to make the repairs will put you in a good position when you negotiate price with the seller.

Obviously there is no point in spending the money to call in a house inspector on every house you visit. You'll save money and time if you make preliminary inspections yourself.

You need very little equipment to inspect a house. Have a flashlight, a penknife, a pair of field glasses and a marble or small rubber ball. Wear old clothes and have a pad and pencil handy. You'll probably do a faster and more thorough job if you don't have the seller or his broker tagging along and perhaps distracting you from some critical area. Let 'em sit.

ROOF. Inspect the roof through your field glasses, if possible, from the south side, because this is the side of the roof that wears out the fastest. Most houses have roofs of asphalt shingles, and these will last from 15 to 25 years depending on the quality of the shingles used. You can tell when asphalt shingles are on their last legs because the mineral granules on the surface of the shingles will have worn off in many spots, exposing the black felt base. If the roof has a lumpy or wavy look, it can mean that there is a layer of wood shingles under the asphalt, and this is going to add a lot to the cost of reroofing.

Wood shingles last around 20 years. The signs of age will be shingles that have curled up at the edges or at the end, or many shingles may have pulled loose or be missing.

Some flat roofs as well as pitched roofs on garages and other outbuildings are sometimes covered with roll roofing. This consists of wide strips of asphalt or tar paper sealed at the edges with tar or asphalt cement. This kind of roofing is only good for five or ten years. Flat roofs may also be covered with a more durable built-up roofing. This consists of several layers of roofing felt cemented together and given a surface coating of minerals. Look for bubbles in the roofing or areas where the mineral granules have worn off. Built-up roofs are relatively inexpensive to renew for it generally is not necessary to remove the old material—just apply a few new layers of roofing felt over the old.

On some houses you may find roofs made of slate or tile. These are very durable but are expensive to repair if they have been neglected. A few houses have pitched or flat roofs covered with metal. Copper, over the years, will have taken on a soft, green patina, and will last almost indefinitely. Tin (called terne) will also last indefinitely if it is kept painted, as will galvanized iron, but inspect such roofs carefully for rust spots.

Take a close look at the metal flashing used to make a watertight joint where different roof planes join to form a valley, and also where the chimney comes through the roof and where the roof and dormers meet. Copper flashing is best, but aluminum is also good. Galvanized iron isn't so good because unless it is painted, the metal eventually rusts. Note if flashing, especially around the chimney and dormers, has pulled loose.

GUTTERS AND DOWNSPOUTS. Gutters must be well supported so they do not sag. Look for stains on the house siding below the gutters, which can indicate a leaky or poorly hung gutter. Also check the outlet of the downspout to see if it is connected to a line to carry the water away from the house or if it simply allows the water to flow right along the foundation wall. This can create a water problem in the basement and also attract termites, which like damp ground.

Gutters and downspouts made of aluminum, copper or vinyl last almost indefinitely and don't require any protective finish. Wood gutters will rot unless they are coated on the inside with a wood preservative or asphalt roofing cement. Galvanized iron gutters will rust on the inside unless they, too, are coated with asphalt roofing cement. It costs around $1.50 a foot to replace gutters.

CHIMNEY CAP. Check that portion of the chimney above the roof. It should be at least 2 feet above the highest point on the roof. If it is not, you may be troubled with a smoking fireplace. Using field glasses, check to see if there are cracks in the masonry or spots where the mortar has cracked or fallen out and whether the top of the chimney has a solid cap of concrete or stone.

OUTSIDE WALLS. If the house has painted wood siding, inspect it carefully to see if there are any areas where the paint has blistered or begun to peel. This can indicate moisture inside the wall, which will have to be corrected. It can also indicate a poor bond between the old paint and the present surface. If this is the case, the entire house should be scraped down to the bare wood before repainting. This can cost $1,000 or more. Also look to see if there are many spots where the paint has worn away so the wood is exposed. This means that when you repaint you'll need two coats instead of one, which will add substantially to the cost of repainting. Prod the wood siding close to the ground or shrubs and plants with your penknife. If the wood is soft and the point goes in easily, it can mean decay or termites.

Examine masonry walls of brick or stone for vertical cracks, for these can indicate that the foundations are settling, and this can be a major flaw and an expensive one to correct. Also prod the mortar between the bricks or stones with a knife to see if it is soft and crumbles easily. If it does, it will all have to be replaced eventually. A white discoloration on the face of brick, called efflorescence, generally means that water is getting inside the walls.

WINDOWS AND DOORS. Check the frames around windows and doors with your knife for signs of softness which indicate decay. Look and see if the joint between the frame and the siding is tightly packed with caulking. Check window panes for cracked, loose or missing putty. If the putty or glazing compound around the panes is in poor condition, it will have to be replaced. It can cost around $20 per window to have this done if you can't handle the job yourself.

TERMITES. These little insects can do serious damage to the house woodwork. Look for signs of little earthen tunnels about ¼ inch wide that the termite workers build to get from their underground nest to the woodwork. You may find them on the inside or outside of foundation and basement walls, along posts and piers of wood or masonry, along water pipes, etc. If you can face it, also look for them under crawl space, porches, wood stoops, steps, etc. Also prod with your penknife any wood close to the ground. If the point goes in easily, the wood may be infested either by termites or decay.

Termites always work inside the wood. They don't leave any visable signs on the outside. A piece of wood can appear to be perfectly sound from the outside but it may be hollow inside from termite damage.

BASEMENT. Look for signs of flooding—water stains along the base of the walls, rust at the base of metal equipment, etc. If there is a sump pump, this means that water does enter the basement, or has in the past.

A basement that does become wet at certain times of the year is no great drawback if the sump pump can prevent water accumulating to a depth where it can damage some of the equipment usually located down there, such as the heating plant, hot-water heater, washer and dryer, etc. But don't plan to use such a basement for a family or recreation room, because you'll first have to have it waterproofed, and this can be a very expensive chore.

Inspect the exposed water pipes to see if they are made of copper or galvanized iron. Galvanized-iron pipes may shortly need to be replaced and at considerable expense. Copper pipes have a reddish color, galvanized-iron have a silver tone. You can double-check with a magnet, for it will be attracted to galvanized iron but not to copper.

Look for rust stains on the side of hot-water heaters, for these indicate that the tank leaks or has leaked and has been patched up to keep it going for a few more months.

Check the furnace or boiler. If there are four or five doors of varying size at the front this means that the unit was once a coal-fired plant that has been converted over to gas or oil. This may be a very inefficient and costly system to operate.

Turn the thermostat up so that the plant goes into operation. Listen to how much noise it makes and see how long it takes before heat comes into the rooms. A forced-warm-air furnace should produce heat in a matter of a few minutes. A boiler should take about 20 minutes before the radiators become warm.

The electric service panel is usually located in the basement. If it consists of a new-looking circuit-breaker panel rated at 100 amps or more, the chances are the wiring in the house is more or less up-to-date. But if there is a hodgepodge of boxes with old-fashioned plug fuses and wires going in every which way, it means an antique system. You can easily spend $500 just making a few modest improvements in an out-of-date wiring system.

ATTIC. This should be vented at each end by operable windows or louvers. Look for water stains on the underside of the roof boards or on the attic floor. These indicate that at one time or another the roof has leaked, and it still may be leaking. If the insulation between the attic joists is exposed, measure the thickness. It should be at least 6 inches thick. If there is no insulation, it will have to be added if you want to keep the house moderately cool in summer and save fuel costs in winter.

HOUSE INTERIOR. Jump on floors and stairs to see if they vibrate to any great degree. This can be due to inadequate construction or insufficient bracing. Put your marble or ball on the center of the floor in each room. If the marble or ball rolls toward one wall at a fast clip it means the floor is very uneven and may indicate a serious flaw in overall construction of the house.

Don't be too concerned over small cracks or holes in plaster walls and ceilings, for these can be easily repaired. But do be concerned if the plaster is bulging in spots or "gives" when you press your hand against it. Also inspect areas that have been stained by water. These may indicate leaks in the plumbing or heating system that will be costly to repair.

If floors are covered with carpeting, pull a corner to see if there is a finish wood floor under the carpeting or only a rough plywood subfloor. If there is plywood and you don't want carpeting, you'll have to install some other form of finish floor over the plywood—hardwood, vinyl, linoleum, etc.

Check windows in each room to see that they operate properly. Ask if there is a storm sash for each window or if they are made with double-pane glass. Also inspect the wall directly under windows for signs of water stains. These stains indicate leaky window frames.

There should certainly be more than one electrical wall outlet for each room. If you find a lot of extension cords or electric cables mounted on the surface of baseboards, the wiring in the house is obviously inadequate and you'll certainly want to add more electric outlets at a cost of around $35 each.

FIREPLACE. You want to make sure that if there is a fireplace it works and works properly. Dirty-looking stains on the chimney breast or mantel often indicate that the fireplace smokes at certain times. The absence of ashes in the pit or soot in the chimney indicates it may not work at all. Use your flashlight to look up the chimney flue to see if it is lined with tile and is moderately free of heavy accumulations of soot. Also see if you see daylight showing at the top when the damper is open wide. If you can, it means that the flue is not blocked up either to conserve heat or by loose masonry falling down from above.

BATHROOMS AND PLUMBING. Examine plumbing fixtures for cracks, spots where the enamel or porcelain has chipped, rough spots and general serviceability. It will cost over $100 to replace a lavatory with a new one of very modest size and design.

Check the water pressure by turning on the cold-water faucet in the kitchen and then turning on the faucet in the bathroom. If you get just a trickle of water through the bathroom faucet it means that the water pressure in the house is low or the pipes are coated on the inside with rust or mineral deposits.

KITCHEN. Look this over carefully to be certain that it will be adequate for your present needs. It can easily cost $5,000 to redo a modest-size kitchen, and without using the most expensive cabinets and appliances. If cabinets and counters are relatively solid, they can be refurbished with paint and new tops at relatively little cost. But if they are in poor shape, they'll have to be replaced almost immediately at considerable cost. Also check the condition of kitchen appliances that are included in the selling price of the house. Ranges, for example, may look fine on the outside but can be so coated with grease on the inside as to make them suitable only for the junk yard.

HEATING SYSTEM. There should be a radiator or warm-air register in every room. Look for stains on the floor near radiators, especially where the pipes join the radiators, for these indicate leaks in the system.

IS THE PRICE FAIR?

If you have been looking at a lot of other used houses in a particular area, you may be able to judge for yourself if the asking price for a particular house is fair and in line with the prices of other houses of comparable size, age and condition. Many real estate brokers, in spite of the fact that they represent the seller, may indicate in one way or another that they feel the asking price on a particular house is way too high. Be alert for any such indications on the part of the broker. However, if you want to learn the true worth of a house—the "market value"—then you should call in a licensed real estate appraiser, as explained in Chapter 22. After he has inspected the property he'll give you a figure that represents the actual market value of the property. He'll base this figure not only on the size, style and condition of the house but also on the neighborhood and on other factors that he knows determine the "true market value."

Once you know the market value, you can judge for yourself whether or not the asking price is reasonable or far higher than the actual market value of the house.

25
WHAT YOU SHOULD KNOW BEFORE YOU BUY A CONDOMINIUM

FIFTEEN YEARS AGO very few people in this country had ever heard of a condominium and even fewer people had ever lived in one, although the practice had been popular in other parts of the world for some time. Today, because of high building costs and increasing land prices, the real estate pages of newspapers throughout the nation are filled with advertisements extolling the virtues of condominium living, describing in glowing terms condominiums of all types, shapes, sizes and designs. Many of these are the so-called resort condominiums—vacation apartments built around natural or man-made recreational facilities. Others are high-rise buildings in the heart of cities. But the large majority of condominiums are of the suburban type—garden apartments, town houses and cluster houses that are designed for year-round living and within commuting distances of places of work. Whatever the type, the emphasis is always on "carefree living."

Do condominiums live up to these promises, and what are those of us who buy one getting into? What are we getting for our money? Is the living really carefree, and most important, what should we know before we buy? There is quite a lot to know, and potential buyers should be sure they know it before they sign on any dotted line, because while a good condominium can be a happy home, a bad one can be a disaster—financially and otherwise.

First let's discuss some of the advantages and disadvantages of condominium ownership.

ADVANTAGES

If you get into a well-designed and well-built condominium, you'll live in pleasant quarters and surroundings that can be considerably better in quality and design than you might otherwise be able to afford, since a condominium living unit can sell for 10 to 30 percent less than a single-family house with comparable living space. And in a condominium of this type the developer usually leaves open space to provide attractive vistas of trees, lawns, gardens and sometimes water. Some also have play areas and other recreational facilities.

You can get a mortgage loan to help finance the purchase of your unit, which means you can deduct the interest you pay on the loan from your income tax. You can also deduct real estate taxes. You are entitled to sell your unit—perhaps at a profit—and you may rent your unit. You will have close neighbors and will probably be very much involved in the community and community living.

Your life is "carefree" to the extent that you don't have to mow the lawn, feed the trees and shrubs, rake leaves, shovel snow or otherwise be concerned with the maintenance of the grounds or with the exterior maintenance of the buildings. Maintenance of recreational facilities is not your problem, either (except financially, which we will get to later). You are, however, totally responsible for the upkeep of the interior of your living quarters.

Condominiums make an excellent "starter" house for a young family that has had enough of renting and wants to build up equity in a home but is not quite ready to take on a single-family house. And they are great as a retirement home.

DISADVANTAGES

You will not have the same degree of freedom as you would have if you owned a single-family house. Every condominium has certain restrictions as to what owners can and cannot do, and many of these may keep you from doing things you want to do. For example, while you may decorate the inside of your individual living unit as you wish, you may not do anything that changes the appearance of the building from the outside. In some condominiums this can apply even to window draperies, except those approved by the management. You have to get permission from the management before you can have a flower or vegetable garden, and it's almost certain that you can't build a backyard jungle gym or other kind of play structure for your children.

You pay a monthly maintenance charge for the upkeep and maintenance of the grounds and recreational facilities. The amount you pay is determined by the management, and you have to pay it whether you like the way the condominium is maintained or not.

You may not like living in a closely knit community, and you may not like close neighbors.

ORGANIZATION OF CONDOMINIUMS

Each condominium, regardless of size, must conform to the statutes of the state in which it is located. Basically these statutes allow the developer to sell individual living units that are an integral part of an overall design or plan. The units may be all in one building, such as a high-rise, or in many, but each includes an undivided share of all common property. This means the land, buildings, walks, roads and recreational facilities. The statutes provide that the developer form an owners' association that will, in time, take over control and management of the condominium from the developer. The owners then elect a board of directors that has the legal authority to manage the condominium.

The board enforces the bylaws and restrictions and collects the monthly maintenance charge from each owner.

PROTECTION FOR THE BUYER

Statutes in each state require that the developer prepare and submit to the proper state regulatory agency—the real estate commission and/or attorney general—certain forms that cover all aspects of the proposed condominium. Once approved, these documents must, by law, be made available to every prospective buyer. The documents include:

- Declaration or master deed. This commits the land to condominium use and gives a description of the development—the number and size of units, the amount of common land and property, recreational facilities, etc.
- Bylaws and regulations. These set forth how the owners' association and board of directors are to be established. They detail the functions of the board of directors and the restrictions on the owners' use of property and facilities.
- Unit deed. This is the deed giving the buyer title to the particular unit. It describes the location and size of the unit purchased.
- Sales agreement. This, in a way, is the most important paper of all, for once you have signed it, you have made a legal contract to buy. It should not only include the selling price and the amount of down payment required but specify the exact location and size of the unit. It should also list all charges due when the buyer takes title—closing costs, title insurance, mortgage fee and so forth.

It is up to the buyer to get all this material from the developer and evaluate it—especially the fine print—to see what he is (or is not) getting for his money. For example, buyers of condominiums in Florida found (many too late) that the statutes in that state allowed the developer (if he so chooses) to keep title to the land for 99 years. This means that each unit owner must pay rent to the developer for the use of the land. Another ploy developers use in many states with poor condominium statutes is to retain ownership of recreational facilities—swimming pools, for example—and rent these to the owners' association under a recreational lease.

The condominium statutes in some states are better than those in others, but no state is perfect in providing all the protection a buyer—wary or not—requires. The U.S. Department of Housing and Urban Development probably has the best regulations governing a condominium, but unless the developer has arranged to have FHA-insured mortgage loans for his units, he does not have to abide by this particular set of regulations and will go along with the state statutes, which may not be so strict.

It is absolutely essential that you consult an attorney—one familiar with condominium law in the state where you are buying—before you sign any sales agreement or even give a check as a binder. Give your attorney all the documents the developer must supply you with before you make a purchase, and give him time to study them carefully. Go over this material with him so you know exactly what you are and are not getting and whether you are financially protected in the event the development fails.

For example, some of the better developers will guarantee to buy back your unit within a specified time if you want to get out or if the unit is not completed in the time stated in the sales agreement. (Not all will do this, however, as many people have learned to their dismay.) You will take a loss on the buy-back arrangement, but it will be small compared to what some buyers have lost on a bum condominium.

Your attorney should also make a credit check on the developer, for while a well-financed developer does not necessarily mean everything is going to be just dandy, a developer with a shaky financial picture is one you should certainly avoid.

HOW TO JUDGE A CONDOMINIUM

The best way to find out about the quality of a condominium that's already occupied is by talking to some of the unit owners. They can fill you in on the quality of construction, the good and the bad features of the developer and any number of other interesting and vital facts. You can also see whether they are the kind of people you would like as close neighbors and whether condominium living is right for you and your family.

Evaluating a condominium that is just getting started is something else again. First, inspect the location. If the neighborhood is stable and well established or is beginning to grow into a pleasant residential area, you are on pretty solid ground. If it seems to be deteriorating or if there are indications that commercial or industrial buildings may be in process, be careful. It is always a good idea to check with the local planning and zoning board to make certain that the condominium is being built in an area zoned exclusively for residential use. Resale value can be good in a stable or improving residential area, but obviously if the area is going downhill or attractive single-family houses are available in the same price range as the condominium units, you'll have trouble selling at a good price.

Study the master deed and master plan for the entire development. These will tell you how many units are to be built and their size, design and relationship to one another. You'll be able to see how much of the land is open space—the more the better—and what recreational facilities will be included. A good condominium has pleasingly designed buildings, and all living units are arranged so that each family has a fair degree of privacy. Parking facilities should be convenient to each living unit but placed so that when you look out a living-room or bedroom window, you don't see a cluster of cars. And there should be enough parking space to provide all unit owners with an absolute minimum of one and a half spaces. Playgrounds should be close at hand for those who have young children. If there are to be recreational facilities such as swimming pools, find out the ratio of the size or number of pools to the number of units. One dinky little pool per hundred living units means a pretty crowded pool on a hot Saturday afternoon.

Find out, if you can, how rapidly the units are selling. Good sales are usually an indication of a quality condominium—especially if units of different sizes, in different price ranges and in different locations are all selling well. If sales are slow or the developer has recently cut his prices, watch out. Slow sales can mean trouble in more ways than one, for if a developer can't sell his units, he may begin to rent those that are completed. This changes the character of the entire project from a community of homeowners into one primarily of renters. Slow sales also means that it may be years— if ever—before the development reaches the point of actually becoming a condominium.

HOW TO JUDGE QUALITY OF CONSTRUCTION

It's most essential that construction be of top quality. Your concern is not only with the structures but with all other elements—walks, driveways, parking areas, recreational facilities, even the underground sewer pipes. If these don't hold up or if they don't meet local building requirements, you and the other owners will have to pay to have them repaired or replaced. Shoddy construction is one of the chief complaints of condominium owners in every state.

Ask the developer how many of the materials used in construction have a warranty from the manufacturer. Look for materials you may be familiar with in the model units or in the sales literature. Find out what steps have been taken to soundproof walls and floors between living units, for inadequate sound control can be a major headache in a multi-family dwelling.

Check with the local building department to find out whether the developer has had any difficulty getting approval for work completed. If the quality of construction is good, the building inspector won't require it to be redone. Also check with the state real estate commission or attorney general's office to find out whether the developer has had complaints on previous developments because of inferior construction—or anything else, for that matter. All this is going to take some time, but if you don't do it, you may be sorrier than you realize.

It's a very smart idea to call in a professional house inspection service and pay them the $50 to $100 it may cost for them to make a careful check on all aspects of the construction.

COMMON QUESTIONS

There are many questions to ask about condominiums. Here are the answers to the most common ones.

WHEN DO THE OWNERS ASSUME MANAGEMENT? This is stated in the bylaws. It may be after a certain period of time, after a certain number of units have been sold, or both. Most families who live in condominiums agree that the sooner the owners take over management, the better. The developer's primary interest is to sell his units and make a profit; the owner's interest is to see that it is a pleasant place to live. These interests are not always compatible.

WHAT ABOUT MAINTENANCE CHARGES? Each unit owner must pay a monthly maintenance charge based on the cost of his unit. The more expensive units pay a higher share than those in the lower price range. The sales literature will list estimated maintenance charges for each unit, but these charges are often underestimated. A realistic maintenance charge on a suburban condominium is in the $60 range. Charges in expensive resort areas are several times that amount.

The maintenance charge does not cover everything, of course. It does cover fire and liability insurance on the structures and on all common areas and facilities. The charge also covers repair and maintenance of the exterior of buildings as well as maintenance of all other common property. It does not include the real estate tax you must pay, but it sometimes covers utilities such as gas, electricity and heat. It does not include fire and theft insurance on the contents of your unit or liability insurance if someone is injured on your premises. You have to take out a separate policy to protect yourself in these areas not covered by the policy for the entire condominium. Several insurance firms now have a special policy for condominium owners that covers them in all areas not covered by the condominium insurance.

WILL MAINTENANCE CHARGES GO UP? Yes—as long as we have inflation. They may go up as much as 10 percent a year just to cover increases in materials and labor. Also, when the owners take over management, charges may go up as much as one-third or more if the developer has skimped on maintenance while he was in charge. And if the quality of construction is poor, maintenance charges will go up—for a time at least—to cover the cost of repairs to common property. Maintenance charges will also go up as recreational facilities are completed and put into use or if the owners' association votes to add facilities.

CAN YOU SELL YOUR UNIT? The bylaws may require that you give the owners' association first refusal at the same price offered to you by a bona fide buyer. If the association is not interested you are free to sell. There are no restrictions on sales if you have an FHA-insured mortgage.

CAN YOU RENT YOUR UNIT? Usually, yes—but make sure that you get tenants who will abide by all the regulations of the association. If they don't, you will be held liable and can be sued for damages by the association. Many resort condominiums have rental pools so that the owners can—and sometimes must—make their units available for rental for a certain portion of each year. Often the owner is charged a fee by the management for handling this matter. Make sure there's a competent agent available. While renting can help defray some of the cost of owning a resort condominium, recent changes in tax laws have eliminated some of the deductions that were previously allowed. So don't buy a resort or vacation condominium just to find a happy tax shelter.

26

PACKAGED HOUSES CAN BE A GOOD BUY

IF YOU are planning to build a house on your own lot—a year-round house or vacation house—you'd be wise to consider a packaged house. These houses, which arrive in parts ready to fit together, can provide you with a better house for less money, in less time and with fewer headaches than a comparable conventionally built house.

The packaged house you buy from a manufacturer or his local dealer can cost less than a custom house—by 5 percent or more —for a variety of reasons. As this is a manufactured house, to one degree or another, there will be savings in costly on-site labor. These can be considerable if you are building in an area where labor is scarce, expensive or not too efficient. Other savings are achieved by the manufacturer's care to reduce waste to a minimum (waste on lumber with conventional on-site construction can run as high as 20 percent) and by the lower cost of materials to a manufacturer who buys them in volume. There is also less of the costly handling of materials by many people that occurs in the conventionally built house.

A packaged house takes far less time to erect than a convention-

Manufactured houses can be custom tailored to fit individual site requirements.

ally built house—many of them can be erected in a day or two and completed in less than 30 days. It usually takes several months to complete a "stick built" house of equal size, and until the structure is enclosed, bad weather can stop construction and pilferage can drain off hundreds of dollars worth of building materials.

You will also find, in many cases, far better designs in a packaged house than those built from stock plans supplied by a local builder. Many manufacturers turn to outstanding architects to design their product, and if you buy one of the more popular models, you'll know it has been "people tested" by families with needs similar to yours.

When you buy a packaged house you know in advance exactly what materials are to be used in it, and if you visit a model or completed house, you'll know the quality of workmanship that you can expect in your house. Chances are you will find better-quality materials and workmanship in the packaged house than you will get in a conventionally built house in the same price range.

And finally, you can know in advance what your house is going to cost and not be in for the unpleasant surprise that is often the rule when you build from scratch, especially in a remote area where you may be putting up a vacation house.

WHAT COMES IN THE PACKAGE?

This will vary not only among manufacturers but also in the different packages offered by the same manufacturer. Some packages consist of just the basic structure, what is called a "shell"—four outside walls, a floor, roof, outside doors and windows. With others, you get a complete house ready to move into and start enjoying. And between these extremes are countless variations. Some include everything except kitchen cabinets and bathroom fixtures. Others provide everything but wiring and plumbing.

Most houses are offered with many optional features such as decks, carports, additional bathrooms, laundry rooms, more expensive materials for siding and roofing and so on.

What is never included, of course, is the cost of the land and basic site preparation—grading, putting in a road and bringing in electric power. A few manufacturers include an allowance for water and a septic system in their basic price. If these cost less than the allowance, you get a credit. If they cost more, you pay the difference. The same thing holds true with foundations—a few include this in their basic price but most don't. Some manufacturers include the cost of shipping the house to your site—within a certain number of miles from the factory—as part of the basic price, and others figure it as an added charge.

Because of the wide range of what can be included in the package, when you buy one you want to be absolutely certain that you know exactly what you are getting for your money and what the total cost will be to bring the house to the stage of completion you want. The manufacturer or his dealer should be able to furnish you with accurate cost figures on those items that are not included in his package, such as shipping, foundations, septic system, water supply, grading the site and putting in a road. If he can't furnish you with all of these costs, get them from a local contractor. All these costs must be added to the total price of the package to give you a true picture of what your finished house will cost.

PRICES

There is a packaged house for just about every budget. For around $2,500 you can get a 12-by-12-foot basic structure you can put up yourself that could be a starter vacation home. And you can pay as much as $100,000 for a spacious year-round house. The most popular year-round houses are in the $30,000 to $60,000 range; the most popular vacation houses are in the $10,000 to $20,000 range.

DESIGN

You can find almost every design in a packaged house from ultramodern to rustic log, along with Cape Cod, ranch and so forth. There is a wide range of floor plans, of course, and often there will be several plans with different room arrangements for the same house. For a slight additional charge it is commonly possible to have the floor plan modified to suit individual needs.

TYPES OF HOUSES

There are three types of manufactured packaged houses: precut, panelized (also called prefabricated) and modular.

PRECUT. The major elements of the precut house are factory-cut to size and keyed for easy assembly on the site. These packages often consist of boards or logs, with windows, doors and roofing material. This is a very flexible method of construction, so you'll find a wide range of designs and sizes. The simpler precut houses, such as the log cabins, can be erected by the owner with a little help from a strong friend or two, but the more elaborate ones require professionals to put up the major elements.

Since the precut house can be shipped by rail as well as by truck, manufacturers in this field can provide rather extensive distribution.

PANELIZED OR PREFABRICATED. Large panels of the house are factory-built and shipped by truck to the site. The basic house can be erected in a matter of days; the amount of on-site labor required to complete the house depends on the manufacturer. Some ship panels that include everything—exterior siding, insulation, windows and doors, wiring and plumbing as well as floors, interior walls and ceilings. Others just ship a basic panel and all the finishing work must be done on the site. A panelized house usually requires an experienced crew to assemble the panels.

MODULAR. These are manufactured in two or more complete sections that include everything—plumbing, wiring, bathroom fixtures, even the kitchen stove. If all the on-site work has been done in advance, a modular house can be ready to live in a few weeks after it has been delivered to the site.

THE SHELL HOUSE

This is not another type of manufactured house, but a basic package to create just the house enclosure or "shell" consisting of the exterior walls, roof, floor, windows and outside doors. Everything else is extra—interior partitions and doors, wiring, plumbing, bathroom fixtures and kitchen cabinets along with all other interior details. Shell houses are usually precut, but some are panelized. You can buy a shell that you put together yourself, or one that the manufacturer will erect for you, or one for which the manufacturer will supply whatever you want of the materials and labor to finish it off.

If you have a limited budget and can do a lot of the work yourself or if you don't mind roughing it in an unfinished house until you can afford to pay someone to complete it for you, the shell house is a very good arrangement. If you do all the work yourself, you will save about one-third of what a completed house would cost if you paid for all the work.

CAN A PACKAGED HOUSE BE BUILT ANYWHERE?

Not always. Most of them, of course, do meet FHA minimum standards and will conform to most local building codes, but there are some communities with very restrictive codes and these may require some adjustment in the house. This will naturally increase the cost. Most problems with local codes occur in the area of plumbing and wiring, and if these are installed on the site rather than in the factory, there is usually no serious problem. Before you buy, you want written assurance from the maker that the house will conform to all local building regulations.

If you plan to build on land you own in a development, you also want to be certain that the house you buy conforms to the standards set by the development.

WHO MAKES PACKAGED HOUSES?

There are hundreds of companies in this field. Some are very large with factories in several areas so that almost every state can be served. Others serve specific regions, such as the Southwest, Middle West, Northeast, Pacific Coast and so on, and many just operate in one small locale.

Some of the large companies advertise nationally in magazines and you can write them for the names of the dealer nearest to you. Both national and regional manufacturers advertise in local newspapers, so check these. You can also get a listing of many of the companies in this field by writing to the National Association of Building Manufacturers, 1619 Massachusetts Avenue, N.W., Washington, D.C. 20036.

Many manufacturers will ship all over the world, but you are better off to buy as near to the factory as possible. In fact, some manufacturers limit their distribution to a radius of 350 miles or so from the plant. As mentioned previously, precut houses have about the greatest distribution range from the factory, especially those that can be erected by the owner or a local contractor.

As shipping charges can eliminate the saving from factory construction, it's best to buy a package made by a concern that has a plant near to your site or one that has already established good distribution in your area.

WHO PUTS UP THE HOUSE?

This will depend on the manufacturer as well as the type of house involved. Some concerns have their own crews and handle the entire job. Others may work through a local builder or contrac-

tor in the area. And some leave it up to you to find a contractor
or do the job yourself.

When the work is to be done either by the owner or by a local
contractor who has had no previous experience with that particular house—and some employ rather specialized construction techniques—many manufacturers will arrange to have a representative on hand at the time the house is delivered to see that the
package is all complete and to get the job off on the right foot.
Some concerns provide this service as part of the package, while
others charge $50 or $75 a day as long as the man is needed.

Unless you plan to put up the house yourself or know of a good
contractor, it is better to buy a package that will be put up by the
manufacturer than to take on the headaches involved in finding
a contractor or acting as your own.

You can, of course, save around 10 percent on the total cost of
the work involved if you act as your own contractor. But it is not
easy. You not only have to line up the men to do the various jobs
—carpentry, plumbing, wiring, heating, masonry and so forth—
but you also have to coordinate the project so that nothing gets
held up because someone did not complete his part. And you
shouldn't try being your own contractor unless you can be on hand
all the time.

HOW LONG DOES IT TAKE TO PUT UP THE HOUSE?

The package can often be delivered to the site a couple of weeks
after you have signed the contract and placed the order. And it
may take only a few days to erect the house and less than 30 to
complete all phases of the work. But it's best to count on it taking
longer than this or longer than what you have been told because
of factors beyond the manufacturer's control. Most of these factors
have to do with work on the site, which has to be completed before
the house is habitable—getting the well drilled, having the septic
system installed and getting electric power to the house.

FINANCING AND PURCHASING

The best way to finance the house is the way you would an
ordinary house—a mortgage loan through a local bank or lender.

Many manufacturers of packaged houses can arrange financing for you, but this usually entails a higher rate of interest than you'll get through your own bank or lender.

If at all possible, inspect a model or completed unit of the house you intend to buy. If there isn't one in your area, ask the manufacturer to send you photographs of the house if there are none in the catalog. Don't judge a house by an artist's rendering—it can make a house appear larger and more attractive.

Study the plan carefully to see if the house will adapt itself easily to your site. If you have a good view, you want a house that can be placed so that the main living area will face the view and not the neighbor's back yard. The style of the house should harmonize with the terrain and other houses in the immediate area.

If your intention is to start off small and add space in the future, be sure that the plan lends itself to easy and economical expansion. Ask the manufacturer to show you how the house can be expanded and how much it will cost.

Ask the manufacturer or his authorized dealer for a statement itemizing every last element that is included in the basic package as well as all items not included and their cost, whether they are to be supplied by the manufacturer, a local contractor or by you. Go over this statement with the manufacturer so that you will be absolutely certain just what it will cost you to bring the house to the degree of completeness you require.

Before you sign anything, have this statement and the sales contract checked over by your attorney—preferably a local one familiar with packaged houses as well as local real estate regulations.

And finally, arrange your financing before you sign a sales contract.

27
BUYING COUNTRY LAND

IF THERE'S a piece of land in your future and you've started looking around with an eye to building either a vacation house or possibly a country home, there's a lot more to it than just finding an attractive site at the right price.

No matter how beautiful the view, the land itself must be suitable for building. It must be of the type that can handle a septic sewage system—clay and ledge rock, for instance, cannot. Unless there are other sources of fresh water available, you must be able to put in a well that will provide ample pure water for daily needs. Also, you want to be certain that the cost of putting in a road or driveway and bringing in electric power will not become a major financial undertaking.

Equally important, the land must conform to local land restrictions, conservation guidelines, health regulations and building codes.

In more and more rural communities—especially those in attractive recreational areas—you will find town, county and state restrictions designed not only to ensure that growth takes place in a controlled and orderly fashion, but to protect the ecology and natural environment of the area. These restrictions apply to individual landowners as well as to commercial land developers.

You may find, for example, that if the soil is not suitable for an approved septic system, you will not be allowed to put a dwelling on your land. There may even be regulations which will prevent you from occupying an existing dwelling until the sewage system is made to conform to the more rigid standards that have recently been put into effect.

If you buy a large piece of land with the idea of selling off certain parcels—even to relatives or friends—there may be zoning or other restrictions that prevent you from doing this or that govern the size of the parcels you can sell. You may also be required to make certain improvements to the property, such as putting in roads that conform to town or county specifications or installing a central sewage treatment plant before you are allowed to sell off any parcels.

It is also possible that local building codes may prohibit lightly constructed "summer cabins" or mobile homes on the property. In some areas you may be able to occupy your house only in summer and not year-round. This state of affairs can occur when there is a concentration of vacation houses on small plots of land near or on a lake, large pond, reservoir or river, and where the soil can adequately support the septic sewage systems for only a relatively short period of time.

While these various regulations do restrict your freedom to do as you wish with your land, they are primarily designed to protect you. Be very wary of any area where there are no such restrictions. You might end up with a garbage dump, a drag strip or a shopping center as your neighbor and a lake or stream not fit to swim in because of pollution.

It's up to you to find out before you buy land whether the land is suitable for your purposes, whether it will remain so for the foreseeable future and how much it will cost to make it suitable for a dwelling.

SOURCES OF INFORMATION

Reliable sources for the information you will need include various municipal agencies that are involved in matters concerning land. You will find these at the town hall or, if there is no town unit of government, at the county seat.

PLANNING AND ZONING BOARD. This body is primarily concerned with land use. The board can tell you if the land you are considering is in an area set aside for single-family residences, multi-family dwellings, commercial or industrial use. They can also tell you what you can and cannot do with the land—subdivide it, put more than one dwelling on it, raise chickens or whatever. They should also be able to tell you about future plans for the immediate area—a projected highway, public recreational facilities, a large housing development or shopping center.

In most communities you will be able to get a copy of the zoning regulations, including maps, showing which zones are designated residential, commercial, industrial and recreational.

Should you find that there are zoning regulations that will prevent you doing what you want with the land, you may be able to get a variance from the planning and zoning board, or even appeal the decision at the planning and zoning board of appeals. But— and this is a big but—there is absolutely no way of knowing in advance what the final decision will be. There are many instances of experienced commercial land developers who have lost their shirts because they went ahead and began to develop land on the assumption that they would get a variance and who then were turned down.

BUILDING INSPECTOR. You'll find him at the town hall or town office, and he can tell you what type of dwelling you can build on the land. The inspector may require you to submit detailed plans in advance and will not permit you to build unless the plans and specifications conform to local building codes. He may not even grant an approval of occupancy of an existing dwelling unless it conforms to local building codes. If you are considering putting up a manufactured house, the inspector may tell you that the plumbing or wiring included in the particular house does not meet local standards and must be reworked. And he may not give you a permit to build any type of structure on the land until you have submitted the results of a soil percolation test to determine if the soil is adequate for an approved septic sewage system. (We'll have more on percolation tests later on in this section.)

HIGHWAY DEPARTMENT. If the planning and zoning board can't tell you, this is the place to find out if the access road to the property you're considering buying is a town, county, state or private road. If it's a private road this means that the owner or owners have to maintain it, and if it is not maintained it may become impassable at certain times of the year.

COUNTY AGRICULTURAL AGENT AND COOPERATIVE EXTENSION SERVICE. While these services—which operate under the Department of Agriculture and the land-grant state colleges— have no regulatory power over what you can and cannot do with land, they can provide you with valuable information about the area in general, about soil conservation and about water resources. The agency can tell you a good deal about the soil in the area— clay, ledge rock, hardpan, sandy, etc.—and may even be familiar with the type of soil on the particular property you are considering. The town clerk can tell you where to reach the county agent.

PRACTICAL CONSIDERATIONS

Other essential items to check out before buying property include the availability of electric power, telephone, septic sewage system and fresh water.

ELECTRIC POWER. The only source where you can find out exactly how much it will cost to bring in electric power (and how long it will take to bring it in) is the local utility company. Given the distance in feet from the nearest utility pole to your building site, they can give you a rough figure of what it will cost you for them to bring in power. If the land is heavily wooded there will be an additional cost for removing trees or branches to meet the specifications of the local utility.

TELEPHONE. Getting phone lines in is no problem once the poles are up for the electric power, for they are strung on the same poles and there will be only a small charge for any additional wiring required.

SEPTIC SEWAGE SYSTEM. To be certain that the soil is adequate for an approved septic system you must have a percolation test made. This consists of drilling a certain number of holes—usually three—to a depth of 36 inches or so in the area where the system is to be installed, filling the holes with water and measuring the time it takes the soil to absorb the water. Percolation tests must be made in accordance with local health and building department regulations, and these departments can tell you who in the area is qualified to make the tests and in which seasons of the year they can be made. They probably will not, for example, allow tests to be made during prolonged dry periods because the soil would naturally absorb water very rapidly. If the results of the tests—and they can be made in several different sites on the land if necessary —do not conform with local regulations, forget this particular piece of property and look elsewhere. The cost of percolation tests should be around $100.

Some sellers will have percolation tests made before they put a piece of property on the market. If this is the case with the land you are considering buying, check with the local building department to be certain that the tests are completely satisfactory. Do not rely entirely on the word of the seller or his agent.

FRESH-WATER SUPPLY. It is essential to be absolutely certain that you will have an adequate supply of pure water. If there is an existing water supply on the property—well, spring, lake or pond —have the water tested for potability; it may contain coliform or other bacteria. Your local health department, building inspector or county agent can tell you where this can be done. The cost for testing a sample of water will be around $10.

If there is no existing water supply, or if it is polluted, you are going to need a well—a deep well, usually. This can be an expensive item even if you strike a good supply of water at a reasonable depth—under 100 feet. But often you have to go far deeper—200, 300, 400 feet, and at around $6 per foot for drilling added to the cost of a pump, you will spend $2,000 or so just for water. And— incredible as it may sound—it is possible to end up with a dry hole; no water at all.

No one can tell you for certain how deep you may have to go for water, but you can get some idea of what you may be up against by talking with your county agent about the general availability of water in the area, or if you have a neighbor with a deep well, asking how deep he had to go before getting water. You can also call in a local licensed well driller for his opinion or have a local geologist (you can probably get the name of one from your county agent, real estate broker or building inspector) inspect the property and give you his opinion.

ROADS. The cost of building a long driveway from the nearest paved road to a building site can turn a budget-priced piece of land into a very high-ticket item. Ask a local contractor (listed in the Yellow Pages under "Contractors-Excavating") to come over and give you a rough estimate on the job.

BUILDING SITE. The best way to be certain there is a suitable building site on the property is to have an architect inspect the land. Many architects have an hourly rate—around $20 for consultation work—and a local architect might only need an hour or so to make his inspection and give you his report. A geologist can also be helpful, and so can a local building contractor, who can also give you an idea of how much it will cost for basic site preparation work —removing trees and boulders, grading the land and so forth.

SURVEY. If you want positive proof of the exact amount of land involved and the true boundaries, the only reliable way to get this is with a survey map prepared by a licensed surveyor or a civil engineer. A map drawn by the seller or by a broker is not necessarily reliable. If the seller does not have such a survey of the property, you may be able to talk him into having one made or sharing the cost with you. The cost will depend on the amount of land

Improper grading allows water to accumulate around house, causing wet basement.

involved and also the nature of the terrain, which has a lot to do with how much time the job requires. The average daily rate for a survey team is around $200.

TITLE SEARCH. The only way to determine if the title to the property is clear and free from any legal restrictions that might interfere with your use of the land or cause future litigation is to have the title searched. You should have an attorney handle this job, and it's wise to use a local attorney who will be familiar with local and state regulations.

PUTTING ALL THE PIECES TOGETHER

The trick to buying land is not to lose a good parcel if you find one, but to also give yourself enough time to make sure that all the vital questions are answered to your satisfaction and that the land will make a suitable place for a dwelling.

Zoning, building regulations, cost of utility lines and roads can be checked out in a day or so just by going to the right people. Your attorney or real estate broker can do much of this work for you, but be sure to tell them exactly what you wish to learn and what you plan to do with the property. But it will take time to have a percolation test made, to find out if you can get water without going broke, to have a survey made if it seems advisable and to have the title searched. And if you are going to have to finance part of the purchase price, you need time to arrange this matter. The way to gain this time is to have the attorney or broker who draws up the agreement of sale—the contract to buy—specify in the agreement that the final sale is contingent on the following:

- The size of the parcel of land and the boundaries are as the seller indicated.
- The title to the land is clear and free of any restrictions other than those the seller has indicated.
- The results of the percolation test will meet all local and state requirements.
- A well can be sunk that will produce an adequate supply of water at a reasonable depth—the average of existing wells in the area.
- The buyer will be able to get a satisfactory loan to assist in the purchase of the property.

The costs of a title search and a percolation test are relatively small. The survey can be an expensive item, and you should certainly push the seller to assume all costs if it turns out that the property is not nearly so large as he gave you to believe and for this reason you do not wish to purchase the property. The matter of the well is something else again, because as stated previously, it is impossible to know exactly how far you have to drill before you find a satisfactory amount of water. You may be able to talk the seller into paying all or part of the cost if the well turns out to be a dry hole. But don't count on this. You may have to accept the risk and the cost, but even so, it is better to be out a few hundred dollars for drilling a dry hole than to be stuck with an expensive parcel of land that you can't live on and may have difficulty ever selling to anyone else—except a wealthy camel.

INDEX

309

Packaged house *(cont.)*
  erectors of, 298–99
  financing and purchase of,
    299–300
  inspection of model, 300
  locations for, 297–98
  manufacturers of, 298
  modular, 297
  panelized or prefabricated,
    296–97
  precut, 296
  prices of, 296
  shell type, 297
  time required for erection of,
    299
  types of, 296–97
Paint
  "all-purpose," 120
  cautions in use of, 121–22
  epoxy, 124–25
  exterior, 18–19
  for metals, 120, 122, 124,
    127–28
  types of, 120–24
  on wallpaper, 122
Painting, 120–31
  of aluminum, 127
  of bamboo, rattan, or wicker
    furniture, 129–30
  of basement, 125–26
  of bathroom, 124
  of canvas awnings, 130
  of ceiling, 123
  of concrete floors, 126
  of entire room, 122–23
  of fences, 130–31
  of galvanized steel, 128
  goggles for, 126
  of hot surfaces, 126
  of iron and steel, 127–28
  of kitchen, 123–24
  of metal, 120–28
  of pipes, 124–25
  of radiators, 123
  surface preparation in, 122
  of window boxes, 130
  of windows, 123

Painting *(cont.)*
  of wood and wood furniture,
    129
Patching plaster, 238–39
Phone calls, burglaries and,
    65–66, 70
Picture hanging, on hollow walls,
    242
Pipes, 24–28
  draining of, 149
  freezing of, 149
  banging in, 217–18
  sweating of, 219
  see also Plumbing system
Planning board, country land
    and, 303
Plaster
  cracks in, 281
  toggle bolts and, 247–48
Plastic sheeting, for storm
    windows, 161
Playroom, noise control in, 57–
    58
Plumber's friend, 209, 212
Plumbing costs, in remodeling,
    99–101, 107
Plumbing fittings, repairs to, 210
Plumbing fixtures
  clogged, 211–12
  protection of, 210–11
Plumbing system, 23–29
  drain lines for, 26
  freezing of, 149
  home repairs to, 210–21
  in new house, 270
  noise control for, 61
  piping for, 24
  septic tanks and, 26–29
  shut-off valve for, 24
  traps in, 26–28
  in used house, 275, 282
  vents for, 26
  see also Pipes
Plunger, *see* Plumber's friend
Police, notifying, in burglaries,
    70–71
Porch enclosure, cost of, 102
Power equipment, care of, 50